The Super Easy
AIR FRYER
Cookbook
for Beginners

2000+ Days of Wholesome and Satisfying Air Fryer Meals, Snacks, and Treats for Healthier Cooking Without Compromise

Kenneth Gutierrez

Copyright© 2025 By Kenneth Gutierrez

All rights reserved worldwide.

No part of this book may be reproduced or transmitted in any form or by any means, electronic or mechanical, including photo- copying, recording or by any information storage and retrieval system, without written permission from the publisher, except for the inclusion of brief quotations in a review.

Warning-Disclaimer

The purpose of this book is to educate and entertain. The author or publisher does not guarantee that anyone following the techniques, suggestions, tips, ideas, or strategies will become successful. The author and publisher shall have neither liability or responsibility to anyone with respect to any loss or damage caused, or alleged to be caused, directly or indirectly by the information contained in this book.

Table of Contents

INTRODUCTION 1

Chapter 1 Breakfasts 3

Chapter 2 Family Favorites 14

Chapter 3 Fast and Easy Everyday Favorites 20

Chapter 4 Poultry 26

Chapter 5 Beef, Pork, and Lamb 38

Chapter 6 Fish and Seafood 50

Chapter 7 Snacks and Appetizers 61

Chapter 8 Vegetables and Sides 72

Chapter 9 Vegetarian Mains 82

Chapter 10 Desserts 88

Appendix 1 Basic Kitchen Conversions & Equivalents 94

Appendix 2 Index 95

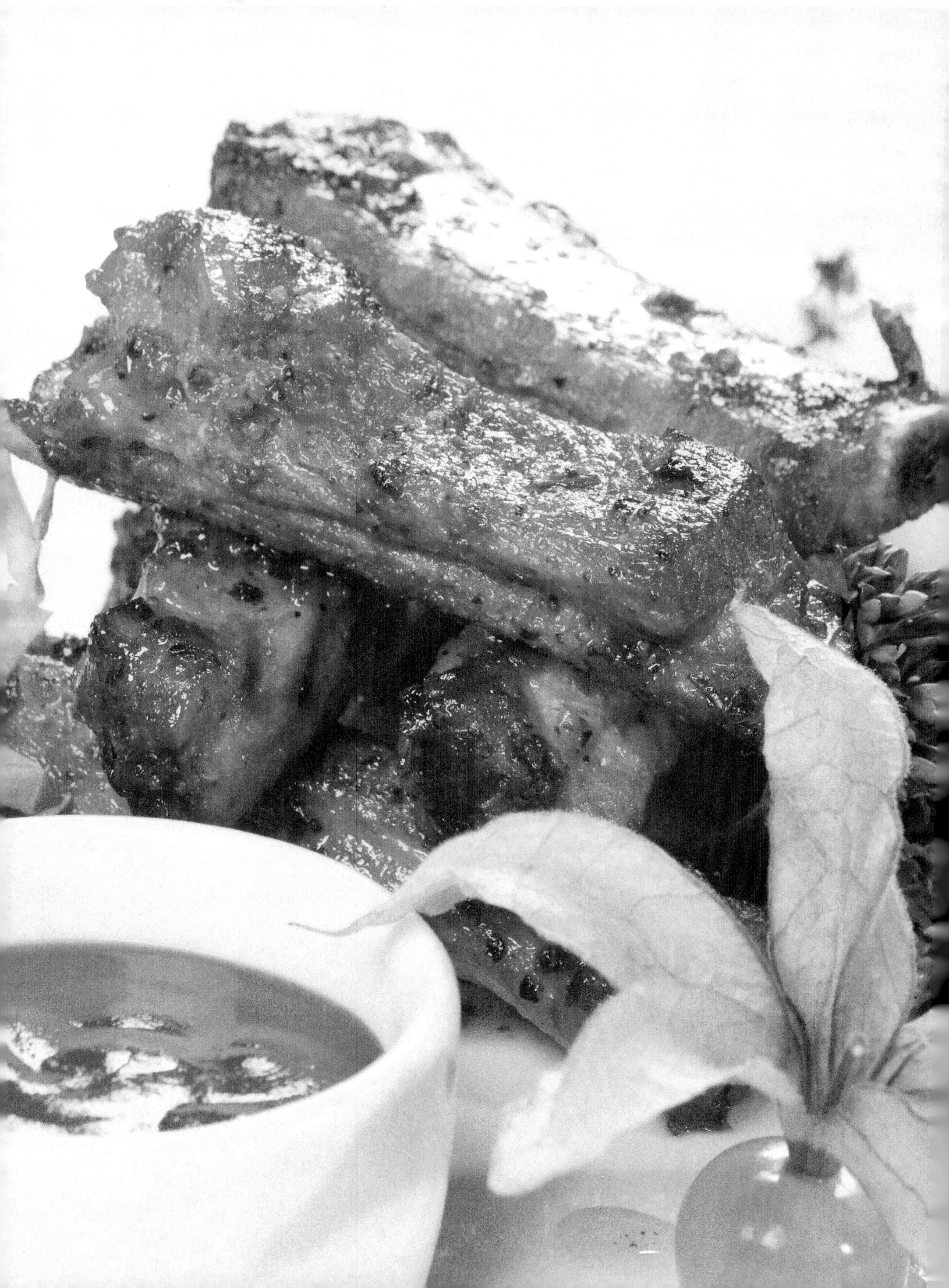

INTRODUCTION

If you're looking to revolutionize your home cooking with healthier, flavorful meals that don't compromise on taste or convenience, The Super Easy Air Fryer Cookbook for Beginners is your perfect kitchen companion. With over 2,000 days' worth of recipes, this book is thoughtfully designed to help you master your air fryer while creating satisfying meals, snacks, and treats for every occasion.

Why This Cookbook is Perfect for Beginners ?

Whether you've just unpacked your first air fryer or are looking to expand your culinary skills, this cookbook ensures a smooth learning curve with its beginner-friendly approach. The recipes are clearly organized with detailed instructions, making it easy to prepare dishes that look and taste as if they came from a professional chef. From simple everyday meals to creative treats for special occasions, the recipes cater to every palate and skill level.

The introduction covers everything you need to know about using an air fryer, including tips on preheating, cleaning, and choosing the right temperature settings. You'll also learn how to adjust cooking times for different types of foods, ensuring that you achieve the perfect crispness every time.

What You'll Find Inside ?

This cookbook is packed with a wide variety of recipes, ranging from nutritious breakfasts to decadent desserts. Here's what makes this collection unique:

1. A Variety of Recipe Categories:

➢ **Breakfasts:** Start your day right with wholesome air-fried classics like crispy hash browns, fluffy French toast sticks, and protein-packed breakfast burritos.

➢ **Lunches and Dinners:** From golden chicken wings to perfectly roasted vegetables, the main course options are both delicious and quick to prepare.

➢ **Snacks and Appetizers:** Indulge in guilt-free snacking with options like zucchini fries, crispy chickpeas, and stuffed mushrooms.

➢ **Desserts:** Sweeten your day with air-fried churros, molten lava cakes, or classic apple crisps.

➢ **Vegetarian and Vegan Options:** A dedicated section for plant-based eaters features recipes such as cauliflower steaks, falafel bites, and vegan chocolate brownies.

2. Recipes for Every Occasion: Whether you're hosting a casual family dinner, preparing snacks for a party, or planning weekly meal prep, this cookbook has you covered. The recipes are tailored for busy schedules, with options that take as little as 10 minutes to prepare.

Key Features of the Cookbook

1. Healthier Cooking, No Compromise: The air fryer is a game-changer for anyone seeking a healthier lifestyle without sacrificing taste. By using minimal oil, this cookbook allows you to create crispy, flavorful dishes that are lower in fat compared to traditional frying methods. Every recipe includes nutritional information, so you can keep track of calories, fat, and other key metrics.

2. Easy-to-Follow Instructions: Each recipe is broken down into simple steps, making it accessible for beginners and seasoned cooks alike. Handy tips and tricks are sprinkled throughout, helping you avoid common pitfalls and achieve restaurant-quality results.

3. Time-Saving Techniques: Most recipes are designed to be quick and efficient, taking advantage of the air fryer's speed and versatility. This makes it an ideal resource for busy families, students, or anyone who wants to enjoy home-cooked meals without spending hours in the kitchen.

4. Customizable Recipes: With over 2,000 days' worth of meals, this cookbook encourages creativity and flexibility. Many recipes include suggestions for substitutions and variations, allowing you to tailor dishes to your taste preferences or dietary needs.

Benefits of Using an Air Fryer

If you're new to air frying, this cookbook also highlights the numerous benefits of this innovative cooking method:

Energy Efficiency: Air fryers cook food faster than traditional ovens, saving time and electricity.

Versatility: Beyond frying, you can bake, roast, grill, and even dehydrate with an air fryer.

Ease of Cleanup: Most air fryer components are dishwasher-safe, making cleanup a breeze.

Who This Cookbook is For ?

➢ **Beginners:** Those who are new to air frying and want a comprehensive guide to get started.

➢ **Health-Conscious Cooks:** Anyone looking to reduce oil and fat in their meals without compromising on flavor.

➢ **Busy Families:** Parents and caregivers who need quick, nutritious meals to feed their loved ones.

➢ **Food Enthusiasts:** Experienced cooks who want to expand their repertoire with creative air fryer recipes.

Final Thoughts

The Super Easy Air Fryer Cookbook for Beginners isn't just a collection of recipes—it's a guide to transforming the way you cook. By embracing the versatility and convenience of the air fryer, you can create meals that are both healthier and satisfying. With this book, you'll gain the confidence to explore new culinary possibilities, one crispy bite at a time.

Whether you're cooking for yourself, your family, or a crowd, this cookbook will quickly become a staple in your kitchen. Say goodbye to greasy frying pans and hello to delicious, air-fried perfection!

Chapter 1
Breakfasts

Savory Egg and Mushroom Cups

Prep time: 5 minutes | Cook time: 15 minutes | Serves 6

Olive oil cooking spray
6 large eggs
1 garlic clove, minced
½ teaspoon salt
½ teaspoon black pepper
Pinch red pepper flakes
8 ounces (227 g) baby bella mushrooms, sliced
1 cup fresh baby spinach
2 scallions, white parts and green parts, diced

1. Preheat the air fryer to 320°F (160°C). Lightly coat the inside of six silicone muffin cups or a six-cup muffin tin with olive oil cooking spray. 2. In a large bowl, beat the eggs, garlic, salt, pepper, and red pepper flakes for 1 to 2 minutes, or until well combined. 3. Fold in the mushrooms, spinach, and scallions. 4. Divide the mixture evenly among the muffin cups. 5. Place into the air fryer and bake for 12 to 15 minutes, or until the eggs are set. 6. Remove and allow to cool for 5 minutes before serving.

Pizza Eggs

Prep time: 5 minutes | Cook time: 10 minutes | Serves 2

1 cup shredded Mozzarella cheese
7 slices pepperoni, chopped
1 large egg, whisked
¼ teaspoon dried oregano
¼ teaspoon dried parsley
¼ teaspoon garlic powder
¼ teaspoon salt

1. Place Mozzarella in a single layer on the bottom of an ungreased round nonstick baking dish. Scatter pepperoni over cheese, then pour egg evenly around baking dish. 2. Sprinkle with remaining ingredients and place into air fryer basket. Adjust the temperature to 330°F (166°C) and bake for 10 minutes. When cheese is brown and egg is set, dish will be done. 3. Let cool in dish 5 minutes before serving.

Sweet Potato and Veggie Hash

Prep time: 15 minutes | Cook time: 18 minutes | Serves 6

2 medium sweet potatoes, peeled and cut into 1-inch cubes
½ green bell pepper, diced
½ red onion, diced
4 ounces (113 g) baby bella mushrooms, diced
2 tablespoons olive oil
1 garlic clove, minced
½ teaspoon salt
½ teaspoon black pepper
½ tablespoon chopped fresh rosemary

1. Preheat the air fryer to 380°F (193°C). 2. In a large bowl, toss all ingredients together until the vegetables are well coated and seasonings distributed. 3. Pour the vegetables into the air fryer basket, making sure they are in a single even layer. (If using a smaller air fryer, you may need to do this in two batches.) 4. Roast for 9 minutes, then toss or flip the vegetables. Roast for 9 minutes more. 5. Transfer to a serving bowl or individual plates and enjoy.

Breakfast Sandwiches

Prep time: 15 minutes | Cook time: 20 minutes | Serves 5

Biscuits:
6 large egg whites
2 cups blanched almond flour, plus more if needed
1½ teaspoons baking powder
½ teaspoon fine sea salt
¼ cup (½ stick) very cold unsalted butter (or lard for dairy-free), cut into ¼-inch pieces

Eggs:
5 large eggs
½ teaspoon fine sea salt
¼ teaspoon ground black pepper
5 (1 ounce / 28 g) slices Cheddar cheese (omit for dairy-free)
10 thin slices ham

1. Spray the air fryer basket with avocado oil. Preheat the air fryer to 350°F (177°C). Grease two pie pans or two baking pans that will fit inside your air fryer. 2. Make the biscuits: In a medium-sized bowl, whip the egg whites with a hand mixer until very stiff. Set aside. 3. In a separate medium-sized bowl, stir together the almond flour, baking powder, and salt until well combined. Cut in the butter. Gently fold the flour mixture into the egg whites with a rubber spatula. If the dough is too wet to form into mounds, add a few tablespoons of almond flour until the dough holds together well. 4. Using a large spoon, divide the dough into 5 equal portions and drop them about 1 inch apart on one of the greased pie pans. (If you're using a smaller air fryer, work in batches if necessary.) Place the pan in the air fryer and bake for 11 to 14 minutes, until the biscuits are golden brown. Remove from the air fryer and set aside to cool. 5. Make the eggs: Set the air fryer to 375°F (191°C). Crack the eggs into the remaining greased pie pan and sprinkle with the salt and pepper. Place the eggs in the air fryer to bake for 5 minutes, or until they are cooked to your liking. 6. Open the air fryer and top each egg yolk with a slice of cheese (if using). Bake for another minute, or until the cheese is melted. 7. Once the biscuits are cool, slice them in half lengthwise. Place 1 cooked egg topped with cheese and 2 slices of ham in each biscuit. 8. Store leftover biscuits, eggs, and ham in separate airtight containers in the fridge for up to 3 days. Reheat the biscuits and eggs on a baking sheet in a preheated 350°F (177°C) air fryer for 5 minutes, or until warmed through.

Ranch Parmesan Rice

Prep time: 10 minutes | Cook time: 30 minutes | Serves 2

1 tablespoon olive oil
1 clove garlic, minced
1 tablespoon unsalted butter
1 onion, diced
¾ cup Arborio rice
2 cups chicken stock, boiling
½ cup Parmesan cheese, grated

1. Preheat the air fryer to 390°F (199°C). 2. Grease a round baking tin with olive oil and stir in the garlic, butter, and onion. 3. Transfer the tin to the air fryer and bake for 4 minutes. Add the rice and bake for 4 more minutes. 4. Turn the air fryer to 320°F (160°C) and pour in the chicken stock. Cover and bake for 22 minutes. 5. Scatter with cheese and serve.

Spinach and Feta Egg Bake

Prep time: 7 minutes | Cook time: 23 to 25 minutes | Serves 2

Avocado oil spray
⅓ cup diced red onion
1 cup frozen chopped spinach, thawed and drained
4 large eggs
¼ cup heavy (whipping) cream
Sea salt and freshly ground black pepper, to taste
¼ teaspoon cayenne pepper
½ cup crumbled feta cheese
¼ cup shredded Parmesan cheese

1. Spray a deep pan with oil. Put the onion in the pan, and place the pan in the air fryer basket. Set the air fryer to 350°F (177°C) and bake for 7 minutes. 2. Sprinkle the spinach over the onion. 3. In a medium bowl, beat the eggs, heavy cream, salt, black pepper, and cayenne. Pour this mixture over the vegetables. 4. Top with the feta and Parmesan cheese. Bake for 16 to 18 minutes, until the eggs are set and lightly brown.

Strawberry Toast

Prep time: 10 minutes | Cook time: 8 minutes | Makes 4 toasts

4 slices bread, ½-inch thick
Butter-flavored cooking spray
1 cup sliced strawberries
1 teaspoon sugar

1. Spray one side of each bread slice with butter-flavored cooking spray. Lay slices sprayed side down. 2. Divide the strawberries among the bread slices. 3. Sprinkle evenly with the sugar and place in the air fryer basket in a single layer. 4. Air fry at 390°F (199°C) for 8 minutes. The bottom should look brown and crisp and the top should look glazed.

Whole Wheat Blueberry Muffins

Prep time: 10 minutes | Cook time: 15 minutes | Serves 6

Olive oil cooking spray
½ cup unsweetened applesauce
¼ cup raw honey
½ cup nonfat plain Greek yogurt
1 teaspoon vanilla extract
1 large egg
1½ cups plus 1 tablespoon whole wheat flour, divided
½ teaspoon baking soda
½ teaspoon baking powder
½ teaspoon salt
½ cup blueberries, fresh or frozen

1. Preheat the air fryer to 360°F (182°C). Lightly coat the inside of six silicone muffin cups or a six-cup muffin tin with olive oil cooking spray. 2. In a large bowl, combine the applesauce, honey, yogurt, vanilla, and egg and mix until smooth. 3. Sift in 1½ cups of the flour, the baking soda, baking powder, and salt into the wet mixture, then stir until just combined. 4. In a small bowl, toss the blueberries with the remaining 1 tablespoon flour, then fold the mixture into the muffin batter. 5. Divide the mixture evenly among the prepared muffin cups and place into the basket of the air fryer. Bake for 12 to 15 minutes, or until golden brown on top and a toothpick inserted into the middle of one of the muffins comes out clean. 6. Allow to cool for 5 minutes before serving.

Savory Egg Muffins

Prep time: 10 minutes | Cook time: 11 to 13 minutes | Serves 4

4 eggs
Salt and pepper, to taste
Olive oil
4 English muffins, split
1 cup shredded Colby Jack cheese
4 slices ham or Canadian bacon

1. Preheat the air fryer to 390°F (199°C). 2. Beat together eggs and add salt and pepper to taste. Spray a baking pan lightly with oil and add eggs. Bake for 2 minutes, stir, and continue cooking for 3 or 4 minutes, stirring every minute, until eggs are scrambled to your preference. Remove pan from air fryer. 3. Place bottom halves of English muffins in air fryer basket. Take half of the shredded cheese and divide it among the muffins. Top each with a slice of ham and one-quarter of the eggs. Sprinkle remaining cheese on top of the eggs. Use a fork to press the cheese into the egg a little so it doesn't slip off before it melts. 4. Air fry at 360°F (182°C) for 1 minute. Add English muffin tops and cook for 2 to 4 minutes to heat through and toast the muffins.

Breakfast Pizza

Prep time: 5 minutes | Cook time: 8 minutes | Serves 1

- 2 large eggs
- ¼ cup unsweetened, unflavored almond milk (or unflavored hemp milk for nut-free)
- ¼ teaspoon fine sea salt
- ⅛ teaspoon ground black pepper
- ¼ cup diced onions
- ¼ cup shredded Parmesan cheese (omit for dairy-free)
- 6 pepperoni slices (omit for vegetarian)
- ¼ teaspoon dried oregano leaves
- ¼ cup pizza sauce, warmed, for serving

1. Preheat the air fryer to 350ºF (177ºC). Grease a cake pan. 2. In a small bowl, use a fork to whisk together the eggs, almond milk, salt, and pepper. Add the onions and stir to mix. Pour the mixture into the greased pan. Top with the cheese (if using), pepperoni slices (if using), and oregano. 3. Place the pan in the air fryer and bake for 8 minutes, or until the eggs are cooked to your liking. 4. Loosen the eggs from the sides of the pan with a spatula and place them on a serving plate. Drizzle the pizza sauce on top. Best served fresh.

Mini Cinnamon Biscuits with Double Coating

Prep time: 15 minutes | Cook time: 13 minutes | Makes 8 biscuits

- 2 cups blanched almond flour
- ½ cup Swerve confectioners'-style sweetener or equivalent amount of liquid or powdered sweetener
- 1 teaspoon baking powder
- ½ teaspoon fine sea salt

Glaze:
- ½ cup Swerve confectioners'-style sweetener or equivalent amount of powdered sweetener
- ¼ cup plus 2 tablespoons (¾ stick) very cold unsalted butter
- ¼ cup unsweetened, unflavored almond milk
- 1 large egg
- 1 teaspoon vanilla extract
- 3 teaspoons ground cinnamon
- ¼ cup heavy cream or unsweetened, unflavored almond milk

1. Preheat the air fryer to 350ºF (177ºC). Line a pie pan that fits into your air fryer with parchment paper. 2. In a medium-sized bowl, mix together the almond flour, sweetener (if powdered; do not add liquid sweetener), baking powder, and salt. Cut the butter into ½-inch squares, then use a hand mixer to work the butter into the dry ingredients. When you are done, the mixture should still have chunks of butter. 3. In a small bowl, whisk together the almond milk, egg, and vanilla extract (if using liquid sweetener, add it as well) until blended. Using a fork, stir the wet ingredients into the dry ingredients until large clumps form. Add the cinnamon and use your hands to swirl it into the dough. 4. Form the dough into sixteen 1-inch balls and place them on the prepared pan, spacing them about ½ inch apart. (If you're using a smaller air fryer, work in batches if necessary.) Bake in the air fryer until golden, 10 to 13 minutes. Remove from the air fryer and let cool on the pan for at least 5 minutes. 5. While the biscuits bake, make the glaze: Place the powdered sweetener in a small bowl and slowly stir in the heavy cream with a fork. 6. When the biscuits have cooled somewhat, dip the tops into the glaze, allow it to dry a bit, and then dip again for a thick glaze. 7. Serve warm or at room temperature. Store unglazed biscuits in an airtight container in the refrigerator for up to 3 days or in the freezer for up to a month. Reheat in a preheated 350ºF (177ºC) air fryer for 5 minutes, or until warmed through, and dip in the glaze as instructed above.

Apple Cinnamon Rolls

Prep time: 20 minutes | Cook time: 20 to 24 minutes | Makes 12 rolls

Apple Rolls:
- 2 cups all-purpose flour, plus more for dusting
- 2 tablespoons granulated sugar
- 1 teaspoon salt
- 3 tablespoons butter, at room temperature
- ¾ cup milk, whole or 2%

Icing:
- ½ cup confectioners' sugar
- ½ teaspoon vanilla extract
- ½ cup packed light brown sugar
- 1 teaspoon ground cinnamon
- 1 large Granny Smith apple, peeled and diced
- 1 to 2 tablespoons oil
- 2 to 3 tablespoons milk, whole or 2%

1. In a large bowl, whisk the flour, granulated sugar, and salt until blended. Stir in the butter and milk briefly until a sticky dough forms. 2. In a small bowl, stir together the brown sugar, cinnamon, and apple. 3. Place a piece of parchment paper on a work surface and dust it with flour. Roll the dough on the prepared surface to ¼ inch thickness. 4. Spread the apple mixture over the dough. Roll up the dough jelly roll-style, pinching the ends to seal. Cut the dough into 12 rolls. 5. Preheat the air fryer to 320ºF (160ºC). 6. Line the air fryer basket with parchment paper and spritz it with oil. Place 6 rolls on the prepared parchment. 7. Bake for 5 minutes. Flip the rolls and bake for 5 to 7 minutes more until lightly browned. Repeat with the remaining rolls. Make the Icing 8. In a medium bowl, whisk the confectioners' sugar, vanilla, and milk until blended. 9. Drizzle over the warm rolls.

Banana-Walnut Whole Wheat Bread

Prep time: 10 minutes | Cook time: 23 minutes | Serves 6

- Olive oil cooking spray
- 2 ripe medium bananas
- 1 large egg
- ¼ cup nonfat plain Greek yogurt
- ¼ cup olive oil
- ½ teaspoon vanilla extract
- 2 tablespoons raw honey
- 1 cup whole wheat flour
- ¼ teaspoon salt
- ¼ teaspoon baking soda
- ½ teaspoon ground cinnamon
- ¼ cup chopped walnuts

1. Preheat the air fryer to 360°F(182°C). Lightly coat the inside of a 8-by-4-inch loaf pan with olive oil cooking spray. (Or use two 5 ½-by-3-inch loaf pans.) 2. In a large bowl, mash the bananas with a fork. Add the egg, yogurt, olive oil, vanilla, and honey. Mix until well combined and mostly smooth. 3. Sift the whole wheat flour, salt, baking soda, and cinnamon into the wet mixture, then stir until just combined. Do not overmix. 4. Gently fold in the walnuts. 5. Pour into the prepared loaf pan and spread to distribute evenly. 6. Place the loaf pan in the air fryer basket and bake for 20 to 23 minutes, or until golden brown on top and a toothpick inserted into the center comes out clean. 7. Allow to cool for 5 minutes before serving.

Hash Browns with Mushroom & Tomato Filling

Prep time: 10 minutes | Cook time: 20 minutes | Serves 4

- Olive oil cooking spray
- 1 tablespoon plus 2 teaspoons olive oil, divided
- 4 ounces (113 g) baby bella mushrooms, diced
- 1 scallion, white parts and green parts, diced
- 1 garlic clove, minced
- 2 cups shredded potatoes
- ½ teaspoon salt
- ¼ teaspoon black pepper
- 1 Roma tomato, diced
- ½ cup shredded mozzarella

1. Preheat the air fryer to 380°F(193°C). Lightly coat the inside of a 6-inch cake pan with olive oil cooking spray. 2. In a small skillet, heat 2 teaspoons olive oil over medium heat. Add the mushrooms, scallion, and garlic, and cook for 4 to 5 minutes, or until they have softened and are beginning to show some color. Remove from heat. 3. Meanwhile, in a large bowl, combine the potatoes, salt, pepper, and the remaining tablespoon olive oil. Toss until all potatoes are well coated. 4. Pour half of the potatoes into the bottom of the cake pan. Top with the mushroom mixture, tomato, and mozzarella. Spread the remaining potatoes over the top. 5. Bake in the air fryer for 12 to 15 minutes, or until the top is golden brown. 6. Remove from the air fryer and allow to cool for 5 minutes before slicing and serving.

Spaghetti Squash Fritters

Prep time: 15 minutes | Cook time: 8 minutes | Serves 4

- 2 cups cooked spaghetti squash
- 2 tablespoons unsalted butter, softened
- 1 large egg
- ¼ cup blanched finely ground almond flour
- 2 stalks green onion, sliced
- ½ teaspoon garlic powder
- 1 teaspoon dried parsley

1. Remove excess moisture from the squash using a cheesecloth or kitchen towel. 2. Mix all ingredients in a large bowl. Form into four patties. 3. Cut a piece of parchment to fit your air fryer basket. Place each patty on the parchment and place into the air fryer basket. 4. Adjust the temperature to 400°F (204°C) and set the timer for 8 minutes. 5. Flip the patties halfway through the cooking time. Serve warm.

Pumpkin Donut Holes

Prep time: 15 minutes | Cook time: 14 minutes | Makes 12 donut holes

- 1 cup whole-wheat pastry flour, plus more as needed
- 3 tablespoons packed brown sugar
- ½ teaspoon ground cinnamon
- 1 teaspoon low-sodium baking powder
- ⅓ cup canned no-salt-added pumpkin purée (not pumpkin pie filling)
- 3 tablespoons 2% milk, plus more as needed
- 2 tablespoons unsalted butter, melted
- 1 egg white
- Powdered sugar (optional)

1. In a medium bowl, mix the pastry flour, brown sugar, cinnamon, and baking powder. 2. In a small bowl, beat the pumpkin, milk, butter, and egg white until combined. Add the pumpkin mixture to the dry ingredients and mix until combined. You may need to add more flour or milk to form a soft dough. 3. Divide the dough into 12 pieces. With floured hands, form each piece into a ball. 4. Cut a piece of parchment paper or aluminum foil to fit inside the air fryer basket but about 1 inch smaller in diameter. Poke holes in the paper or foil and place it in the basket. 5. Put 6 donut holes into the basket, leaving some space around each. Air fry at 360°F (182°C) for 5 to 7 minutes, or until the donut holes reach an internal temperature of 200°F (93°C) and are firm and light golden brown. 6. Let cool for 5 minutes. Remove from the basket and roll in powdered sugar, if desired. Repeat with the remaining donut holes and serve.

Turkey Sausage and Egg Pizza

Prep time: 15 minutes | Cook time: 24 minutes | Serves 2

4 large eggs, divided
1 tablespoon water
½ teaspoon garlic powder
½ teaspoon onion powder
½ teaspoon dried oregano
2 tablespoons coconut flour
3 tablespoons grated Parmesan cheese
½ cup shredded provolone cheese
1 link cooked turkey sausage, chopped (about 2 ounces / 57 g)
2 sun-dried tomatoes, finely chopped
2 scallions, thinly sliced

1. Preheat the air fryer to 400°F (204°C). Line a cake pan with parchment paper and lightly coat the paper with olive oil. 2. In a large bowl, whisk 2 of the eggs with the water, garlic powder, onion powder, and dried oregano. Add the coconut flour, breaking up any lumps with your hands as you add it to the bowl. Stir the coconut flour into the egg mixture, mixing until smooth. Stir in the Parmesan cheese. Allow the mixture to rest for a few minutes until thick and dough-like. 3. Transfer the mixture to the prepared pan. Use a spatula to spread it evenly and slightly up the sides of the pan. Air fry until the crust is set but still light in color, about 10 minutes. Top with the cheeses, sausage, and sun-dried tomatoes. 4. Break the remaining 2 eggs into a small bowl, then slide them onto the pizza. Return the pizza to the air fryer. Air fry 10 to 14 minutes until the egg whites are set and the yolks are the desired doneness. Top with the scallions and allow to rest for 5 minutes before serving.

Portobello Eggs Benedict

Prep time: 10 minutes | Cook time: 10 to 14 minutes | Serves 2

1 tablespoon olive oil
2 cloves garlic, minced
¼ teaspoon dried thyme
2 portobello mushrooms, stems removed and gills scraped out
2 Roma tomatoes, halved lengthwise
Salt and freshly ground
black pepper, to taste
2 large eggs
2 tablespoons grated Pecorino Romano cheese
1 tablespoon chopped fresh parsley, for garnish
1 teaspoon truffle oil (optional)

1. Preheat the air fryer to 400°F (204°C). 2. In a small bowl, combine the olive oil, garlic, and thyme. Brush the mixture over the mushrooms and tomatoes until thoroughly coated. Season to taste with salt and freshly ground black pepper. 3. Arrange the vegetables, cut side up, in the air fryer basket. Crack an egg into the center of each mushroom and sprinkle with cheese. Air fry for 10 to 14 minutes until the vegetables are tender and the whites are firm. When cool enough to handle, coarsely chop the tomatoes and place on top of the eggs. Scatter parsley on top and drizzle with truffle oil, if desired, just before serving.

Avocado Toast with Poached Eggs

Prep time: 5 minutes | Cook time: 7 minutes | Serves 4

Olive oil cooking spray
4 large eggs
Salt
Black pepper
4 pieces whole grain bread
1 avocado
Red pepper flakes (optional)

1. Preheat the air fryer to 320°F(160°C). Lightly coat the inside of four small oven-safe ramekins with olive oil cooking spray. 2. Crack one egg into each ramekin, and season with salt and black pepper. 3. Place the ramekins into the air fryer basket. Close and set the timer to 7 minutes. 4. While the eggs are cooking, toast the bread in a toaster. 5. Slice the avocado in half lengthwise, remove the pit, and scoop the flesh into a small bowl. Season with salt, black pepper, and red pepper flakes, if desired. Using a fork, smash the avocado lightly. 6. Spread a quarter of the smashed avocado evenly over each slice of toast. 7. Remove the eggs from the air fryer, and gently spoon one onto each slice of avocado toast before serving.

Three-Berry Dutch Pancake

Prep time: 10 minutes | Cook time: 12 to 16 minutes | Serves 4

2 egg whites
1 egg
½ cup whole-wheat pastry flour
½ cup 2% milk
1 teaspoon pure vanilla extract
1 tablespoon unsalted butter, melted
1 cup sliced fresh strawberries
½ cup fresh blueberries
½ cup fresh raspberries

1. In a medium bowl, use an eggbeater or hand mixer to quickly mix the egg whites, egg, pastry flour, milk, and vanilla until well combined. 2. Use a pastry brush to grease the bottom of a baking pan with the melted butter. Immediately pour in the batter and put the basket back in the fryer. Bake at 330°F (166°C) for 12 to 16 minutes, or until the pancake is puffed and golden brown. 3. Remove the pan from the air fryer; the pancake will fall. Top with the strawberries, blueberries, and raspberries. Serve immediately.

Canadian Bacon Muffin Sandwiches

Prep time: 5 minutes | Cook time: 8 minutes | Serves 4

4 English muffins, split	4 slices cheese
8 slices Canadian bacon	Cooking spray

1. Preheat the air fryer to 370°F (188°C). 2. Make the sandwiches: Top each of 4 muffin halves with 2 slices of Canadian bacon, 1 slice of cheese, and finish with the remaining muffin half. 3. Put the sandwiches in the air fryer basket and spritz the tops with cooking spray. 4. Bake for 4 minutes. Flip the sandwiches and bake for another 4 minutes. 5. Divide the sandwiches among four plates and serve warm.

Mexican Egg-Stuffed Pepper Rings

Prep time: 5 minutes | Cook time: 10 minutes | Serves 4

Olive oil	4 eggs
1 large red, yellow, or orange bell pepper, cut into four ¾-inch rings	Salt and freshly ground black pepper, to taste
	2 teaspoons salsa

1. Preheat the air fryer to 350°F (177°C). Lightly spray a baking pan with olive oil. 2. Place 2 bell pepper rings on the pan. Crack one egg into each bell pepper ring. Season with salt and black pepper. 3. Spoon ½ teaspoon of salsa on top of each egg. 4. Place the pan in the air fryer basket. Air fry until the yolk is slightly runny, 5 to 6 minutes or until the yolk is fully cooked, 8 to 10 minutes. 5. Repeat with the remaining 2 pepper rings. Serve hot.

Bunless Breakfast Turkey Burgers

Prep time: 5 minutes | Cook time: 15 minutes | Serves 4

1 pound (454 g) ground turkey breakfast sausage	¼ cup seeded and chopped green bell pepper
½ teaspoon salt	2 tablespoons mayonnaise
¼ teaspoon ground black pepper	1 medium avocado, peeled, pitted, and sliced

1. In a large bowl, mix sausage with salt, black pepper, bell pepper, and mayonnaise. Form meat into four patties. 2. Place patties into ungreased air fryer basket. Adjust the temperature to 370°F (188°C) and air fry for 15 minutes, turning patties halfway through cooking. Burgers will be done when dark brown and they have an internal temperature of at least 165°F (74°C). 3. Serve burgers topped with avocado slices on four medium plates.

Mediterranean Bagels

Prep time: 10 minutes | Cook time: 10 minutes | Makes 2 bagels

½ cup self-rising flour, plus more for dusting	4 teaspoons everything bagel spice mix
½ cup plain Greek yogurt	Cooking oil spray
1 egg	1 tablespoon butter, melted
1 tablespoon water	

1. In a large bowl, using a wooden spoon, stir together the flour and yogurt until a tacky dough forms. Transfer the dough to a lightly floured work surface and roll the dough into a ball. 2. Cut the dough into 2 pieces and roll each piece into a log. Form each log into a bagel shape, pinching the ends together. 3. In a small bowl, whisk the egg and water. Brush the egg wash on the bagels. 4. Sprinkle 2 teaspoons of the spice mix on each bagel and gently press it into the dough. 5. Insert the crisper plate into the basket and the basket into the unit. Preheat the unit by selecting BAKE, setting the temperature to 330°F (166°C), and setting the time to 3 minutes. Select START/STOP to begin. 6. Once the unit is preheated, spray the crisper plate with cooking spray. Drizzle the bagels with the butter and place them into the basket. 7. Select BAKE, set the temperature to 330°F (166°C), and set the time to 10 minutes. Select START/STOP to begin. 8. When the cooking is complete, the bagels should be lightly golden on the outside. Serve warm.

Classic British Breakfast

Prep time: 5 minutes | Cook time: 25 minutes | Serves 2

1 cup potatoes, sliced and diced	2 eggs
	1 tablespoon olive oil
2 cups beans in tomato sauce	1 sausage
	Salt, to taste

1. Preheat the air fryer to 390°F (199°C) and allow to warm. 2. Break the eggs onto a baking dish and sprinkle with salt. 3. Lay the beans on the dish, next to the eggs. 4. In a bowl, coat the potatoes with the olive oil. Sprinkle with salt. 5. Transfer the bowl of potato slices to the air fryer and bake for 10 minutes. 6. Swap out the bowl of potatoes for the dish containing the eggs and beans. Bake for another 10 minutes. Cover the potatoes with parchment paper. 7. Slice up the sausage and throw the slices on top of the beans and eggs. Bake for another 5 minutes. 8. Serve with the potatoes.

Coconut Brown Rice Porridge with Dates

Prep time: 10 minutes | Cook time: 23 minutes | Serves 1 to 2

1 cup canned coconut milk
½ cup cooked brown rice
¼ cup unsweetened shredded coconut
¼ cup packed dark brown sugar
½ teaspoon kosher salt
¼ teaspoon ground cardamom
4 large Medjool dates, pitted and roughly chopped
Heavy cream, for serving (optional)

1. In a cake pan, stir together the coconut milk, rice, shredded coconut, brown sugar, salt, cardamom, and dates and place in the air fryer. Bake at 375°F (191°C) until reduced and thickened and browned on top, about 23 minutes, stirring halfway through. 2. Remove the pan from the air fryer and divide the porridge among bowls. Drizzle the porridge with cream, if you like, and serve hot.Banana-Walnut Whole Wheat Bread

Savory Onion Omelet

Prep time: 10 minutes | Cook time: 12 minutes | Serves 2

3 eggs
Salt and ground black pepper, to taste
½ teaspoons soy sauce
1 large onion, chopped
2 tablespoons grated Cheddar cheese
Cooking spray

1. Preheat the air fryer to 355°F (179°C). 2. In a bowl, whisk together the eggs, salt, pepper, and soy sauce. 3. Spritz a small pan with cooking spray. Spread the chopped onion across the bottom of the pan, then transfer the pan to the air fryer. 4. Bake in the preheated air fryer for 6 minutes or until the onion is translucent. 5. Add the egg mixture on top of the onions to coat well. Add the cheese on top, then continue baking for another 6 minutes. 6. Allow to cool before serving.

Western Frittata

Prep time: 10 minutes | Cook time: 19 minutes | Serves 1 to 2

½ red or green bell pepper, cut into ½-inch chunks
1 teaspoon olive oil
3 eggs, beaten
¼ cup grated Cheddar cheese
¼ cup diced cooked ham
Salt and freshly ground black pepper, to taste
1 teaspoon butter
1 teaspoon chopped fresh parsley

1. Preheat the air fryer to 400°F (204°C). 2. Toss the peppers with the olive oil and air fry for 6 minutes, shaking the basket once or twice during the cooking process to redistribute the ingredients. 3. While the vegetables are cooking, beat the eggs well in a bowl, stir in the Cheddar cheese and ham, and season with salt and freshly ground black pepper. Add the air-fried peppers to this bowl when they have finished cooking. 4. Place a cake pan into the air fryer basket with the butter using an aluminum sling to lower the pan into the basket. Air fry for 1 minute at 380°F (193°C) to melt the butter. Remove the cake pan and rotate the pan to distribute the butter and grease the pan. Pour the egg mixture into the cake pan and return the pan to the air fryer, using the aluminum sling. 5. Air fry at 380°F (193°C) for 12 minutes, or until the frittata has puffed up and is lightly browned. Let the frittata sit in the air fryer for 5 minutes to cool to an edible temperature and set up. Remove the cake pan from the air fryer, sprinkle with parsley and serve immediately.

Layered Cake

Prep time: 10 minutes | Cook time: 7 minutes | Serves 4

½ cup blanched finely ground almond flour
¼ cup powdered erythritol
½ teaspoon baking powder
2 tablespoons unsalted butter, softened
1 large egg
½ teaspoon unflavored gelatin
½ teaspoon vanilla extract
½ teaspoon ground cinnamon

1. In a large bowl, mix almond flour, erythritol, and baking powder. Add butter, egg, gelatin, vanilla, and cinnamon. Pour into a round baking pan. 2. Place pan into the air fryer basket. 3. Adjust the temperature to 300°F (149°C) and set the timer for 7 minutes. 4. When the cake is completely cooked, a toothpick will come out clean. Cut cake into four and serve.

Hole in One

Prep time: 5 minutes | Cook time: 6 to 7 minutes | Serves 1

1 slice bread
1 teaspoon soft butter
1 egg
Salt and pepper, to taste
1 tablespoon shredded Cheddar cheese
2 teaspoons diced ham

1. Place a baking dish inside air fryer basket and preheat the air fryer to 330°F (166°C). 2. Using a 2½-inch-diameter biscuit cutter, cut a hole in center of bread slice. 3. Spread softened butter on both sides of bread. 4. Lay bread slice in baking dish and crack egg into the hole. Sprinkle egg with salt and pepper to taste. 5. Cook for 5 minutes. 6. Turn toast over and top it with shredded cheese and diced ham. 7. Cook for 1 to 2 more minutes or until yolk is done to your liking.

Fried Cheese Grits

Prep time: 10 minutes | Cook time: 10 to 12 minutes | Serves 4

⅔ cup instant grits	cheese, at room temperature
1 teaspoon salt	1 large egg, beaten
1 teaspoon freshly ground black pepper	1 tablespoon butter, melted
¾ cup whole or 2% milk	1 cup shredded mild Cheddar cheese
3 ounces (85 g) cream	Cooking spray

1. Mix the grits, salt, and black pepper in a large bowl. Add the milk, cream cheese, beaten egg, and melted butter and whisk to combine. Fold in the Cheddar cheese and stir well. 2. Preheat the air fryer to 400ºF (204ºC). Spray a baking pan with cooking spray. 3. Spread the grits mixture into the baking pan and place in the air fryer basket. 4. Air fry for 1o to 12 minutes, or until the grits are cooked and a knife inserted in the center comes out clean. Stir the mixture once halfway through the cooking time. 5. Rest for 5 minutes and serve warm.

French Toast Fingers

Prep time: 10 minutes | Cook time: 9 minutes | Serves 4

Oil, for spraying	cinnamon
6 large eggs	8 slices bread, cut into thirds
1⅓ cups milk	
2 teaspoons vanilla extract	Syrup of choice, for serving
1 teaspoon ground	

1. Preheat the air fryer to 370ºF (188ºC). Line the air fryer basket with parchment and spray lightly with oil. 2. In a shallow bowl, whisk the eggs, milk, vanilla, and cinnamon. 3. Dunk one piece of bread in the egg mixture, making sure to coat both sides. Work quickly so the bread doesn't get soggy. Immediately transfer the bread to the prepared basket. 4. Repeat with the remaining bread, making sure the pieces don't touch each other. You may need to work in batches, depending on the size of your air fryer. 5. Air fry for 5 minutes, flip, and cook for another 3 to 4 minutes, until browned and crispy. 6. Serve immediately with your favorite syrup.

Bacon, Cheese, and Avocado Melt

Prep time: 5 minutes | Cook time: 3 to 5 minutes | Serves 2

1 avocado	2 tablespoons salsa
4 slices cooked bacon, chopped	1 tablespoon heavy cream
	¼ cup shredded Cheddar cheese

1. Preheat the air fryer to 400ºF (204ºC). 2. Slice the avocado in half lengthwise and remove the stone. To ensure the avocado halves do not roll in the basket, slice a thin piece of skin off the base. 3. In a small bowl, combine the bacon, salsa, and cream. Divide the mixture between the avocado halves and top with the cheese. 4. Place the avocado halves in the air fryer basket and air fry for 3 to 5 minutes until the cheese has melted and begins to brown. Serve warm.

Crispy Kale and Potato Bites

Prep time: 10 minutes | Cook time: 18 minutes | Serves 4

1 teaspoon extra virgin olive oil	mashed
1 clove garlic, minced	⅛ cup milk
4 cups kale, rinsed and chopped	Salt and ground black pepper, to taste
2 cups potatoes, boiled and	Cooking spray

1. Preheat the air fryer to 390ºF (199ºC). 2. In a skillet over medium heat, sauté the garlic in the olive oil, until it turns golden brown. Sauté with the kale for an additional 3 minutes and remove from the heat. 3. Mix the mashed potatoes, kale and garlic in a bowl. Pour in the milk and sprinkle with salt and pepper. 4. Shape the mixture into nuggets and spritz with cooking spray. 5. Put in the air fryer basket and air fry for 15 minutes, flip the nuggets halfway through cooking to make sure the nuggets fry evenly. 6. Serve immediately.

Egg in Toast

Prep time: 5 minutes | Cook time: 5 minutes | Serves 1

1 slice bread	1 tablespoon shredded Cheddar cheese
1 teaspoon butter, softened	
1 egg	2 teaspoons diced ham
Salt and pepper, to taste	

1. Preheat the air fryer to 330ºF (166ºC). Place a baking dish in the air fryer basket. 2. On a flat work surface, cut a hole in the center of the bread slice with a 2½-inch-diameter biscuit cutter. 3. Spread the butter evenly on each side of the bread slice and transfer to the baking dish. 4. Crack the egg into the hole and season as desired with salt and pepper. Scatter the shredded cheese and diced ham on top. 5. Bake in the preheated air fryer for 5 minutes until the bread is lightly browned and the egg is cooked to your preference. 6. Remove from the basket and serve hot.

Gluten-Free Granola Cereal

Prep time: 7 minutes | Cook time: 30 minutes | Makes 3½ cups

Oil, for spraying
1½ cups gluten-free rolled oats
½ cup chopped walnuts
½ cup chopped almonds
½ cup pumpkin seeds
¼ cup maple syrup or honey
1 tablespoon toasted sesame oil or vegetable oil
1 teaspoon ground cinnamon
½ teaspoon salt
½ cup dried cranberries

1. Preheat the air fryer to 250°F (121°C). Line the air fryer basket with parchment and spray lightly with oil. (Do not skip the step of lining the basket; the parchment will keep the granola from falling through the holes.) 2. In a large bowl, mix together the oats, walnuts, almonds, pumpkin seeds, maple syrup, sesame oil, cinnamon, and salt. 3. Spread the mixture in an even layer in the prepared basket. 4. Cook for 30 minutes, stirring every 10 minutes. 5. Transfer the granola to a bowl, add the dried cranberries, and toss to combine. 6. Let cool to room temperature before storing in an airtight container.

Cinnamon and Raisin Bagels

Prep time: 30 minutes | Cook time: 10 minutes | Makes 4 bagels

Oil, for spraying
¼ cup raisins
1 cup self-rising flour, plus more for dusting
1 cup plain Greek yogurt
1 teaspoon ground cinnamon
1 large egg

1. Line the air fryer basket with parchment and spray lightly with oil. 2. Place the raisins in a bowl of hot water and let sit for 10 to 15 minutes, until they have plumped. This will make them extra juicy. 3. In a large bowl, mix together the flour, yogurt, and cinnamon with your hands or a large silicone spatula until a ball is formed. It will be quite sticky for a while. 4. Drain the raisins and gently work them into the ball of dough. 5. Place the dough on a lightly floured work surface and divide into 4 equal pieces. Roll each piece into an 8- or 9-inch-long rope and shape it into a circle, pinching the ends together to seal. 6. In a small bowl, whisk the egg. Brush the egg onto the tops of the dough. 7. Place the dough in the prepared basket. 8. Air fry at 350°F (177°C) for 10 minutes. Serve immediately.

Avocado Bacon and Egg Breakfast

Prep time: 15 minutes | Cook time: 20 minutes | Serves 4

6 large eggs
¼ cup heavy whipping cream
1½ cups chopped cauliflower
1 cup shredded medium Cheddar cheese
1 medium avocado, peeled and pitted
8 tablespoons full-fat sour cream
2 scallions, sliced on the bias
12 slices sugar-free bacon, cooked and crumbled

1. In a medium bowl, whisk eggs and cream together. Pour into a round baking dish. 2. Add cauliflower and mix, then top with Cheddar. Place dish into the air fryer basket. 3. Adjust the temperature to 320°F (160°C) and set the timer for 20 minutes. 4. When completely cooked, eggs will be firm and cheese will be browned. Slice into four pieces. 5. Slice avocado and divide evenly among pieces. Top each piece with 2 tablespoons sour cream, sliced scallions, and crumbled bacon.

Butternut Squash and Ricotta Frittata

Prep time: 10 minutes | Cook time: 33 minutes | Serves 2 to 3

1 cup cubed (½-inch) butternut squash (5½ ounces / 156 g)
2 tablespoons olive oil
Kosher salt and freshly ground black pepper, to taste
4 fresh sage leaves, thinly sliced
6 large eggs, lightly beaten
½ cup ricotta cheese
Cayenne pepper

1. In a bowl, toss the squash with the olive oil and season with salt and black pepper until evenly coated. Sprinkle the sage on the bottom of a cake pan and place the squash on top. Place the pan in the air fryer and bake at 400°F (204°C) for 10 minutes. Stir to incorporate the sage, then cook until the squash is tender and lightly caramelized at the edges, about 3 minutes more. 2. Pour the eggs over the squash, dollop the ricotta all over, and sprinkle with cayenne. Bake at 300°F (149°C) until the eggs are set and the frittata is golden brown on top, about 20 minutes. Remove the pan from the air fryer and cut the frittata into wedges to serve.

Green Eggs and Ham

Prep time: 5 minutes | Cook time: 10 minutes | Serves 2

1 large Hass avocado, halved and pitted
2 thin slices ham
2 large eggs
2 tablespoons chopped green onions, plus more for garnish
½ teaspoon fine sea salt
¼ teaspoon ground black pepper
¼ cup shredded Cheddar cheese (omit for dairy-free)

1. Preheat the air fryer to 400°F (204°C). 2. Place a slice of ham into the cavity of each avocado half. Crack an egg on top of the ham, then sprinkle on the green onions, salt, and pepper. 3. Place the avocado halves in the air fryer cut side up and air fry for 10 minutes, or until the egg is cooked to your desired doneness. Top with the cheese (if using) and air fry for 30 seconds more, or until the cheese is melted. Garnish with chopped green onions. 4. Best served fresh. Store extras in an airtight container in the fridge for up to 4 days. Reheat in a preheated 350°F (177°C) air fryer for a few minutes, until warmed through.

Chapter 2
Family Favorites

Phyllo-Wrapped Veggie Triangles

Prep time: 15 minutes | Cook time: 6 to 11 minutes | Serves 6

- 3 tablespoons minced onion
- 2 garlic cloves, minced
- 2 tablespoons grated carrot
- 1 teaspoon olive oil
- 3 tablespoons frozen baby peas, thawed
- 2 tablespoons nonfat cream cheese, at room temperature
- 6 sheets frozen phyllo dough, thawed
- Olive oil spray, for coating the dough

1. Toss the onion, garlic, carrot, and olive oil together in a baking pan, then air fry at 390°F (199°C) for about 2 to 4 minutes, just until the vegetables are tender-crisp. Transfer them to a bowl. 2. Add the peas and cream cheese to the bowl with the vegetables, stirring to combine. Let the mixture cool while preparing the phyllo dough. 3. Lay one phyllo sheet on a clean surface and give it a light spray with olive oil. Place a second sheet on top. Repeat this process with the remaining phyllo sheets, creating 3 stacks of 2 layers each. Slice each stack lengthwise into 4 even strips, making 12 strips in total. 4. Spoon a small amount (around 2 teaspoons) of filling near the bottom edge of each strip. Fold one corner up to enclose the filling in a triangle, then keep folding in triangles, like folding a flag. Use a bit of water to seal the final edge. Repeat for all the strips. 5. Arrange the triangles in the air fryer in two batches and cook for 4 to 7 minutes, or until golden and crispy. Serve hot and enjoy.

Grilled Fish and Veggie Taco Wraps

Prep time: 15 minutes | Cook time: 9 to 12 minutes | Serves 4

- 1 pound (454 g) white fish fillets, such as sole or cod
- 2 teaspoons olive oil
- 3 tablespoons freshly squeezed lemon juice, divided
- 1½ cups chopped red cabbage
- 1 large carrot, grated
- ½ cup low-sodium salsa
- ⅓ cup low-fat Greek yogurt
- 4 soft low-sodium whole-wheat tortillas

1. Lightly coat the fish with olive oil and drizzle 1 tablespoon of lemon juice over the top. Place it in the air fryer basket and cook at 390°F (199°C) for 9 to 12 minutes, or until the fish flakes easily with a fork. 2. While the fish is cooking, combine the remaining 2 tablespoons of lemon juice, red cabbage, carrot, salsa, and yogurt in a medium bowl, mixing until well blended. 3. Once the fish is done, remove it from the air fryer basket and gently break it into large chunks. 4. Serve the fish alongside tortillas and the cabbage mixture, allowing each person to build their own tacos.

Tuna and Veggie Melt Sandwiches

Prep time: 15 minutes | Cook time: 7 to 11 minutes | Serves 4

- 2 low-sodium whole-wheat English muffins, split
- 1 (6 ounces / 170 g) can chunk light low-sodium tuna, drained
- 1 cup shredded carrot
- ⅓ cup chopped mushrooms
- 2 scallions, white and green parts, sliced
- ⅓ cup nonfat Greek yogurt
- 2 tablespoons low-sodium stone ground mustard
- 2 slices low-sodium low-fat Swiss cheese, halved

1. Arrange the English muffin halves in the air fryer basket and cook at 340°F (171°C) for 3 to 4 minutes, or until they turn crisp. Take them out and set aside. 2. In a medium-sized bowl, combine the tuna, carrot, mushrooms, scallions, yogurt, and mustard, mixing thoroughly. Spread one-fourth of the tuna mixture onto each muffin half and top with a half slice of Swiss cheese. 3. Return the topped muffins to the air fryer and cook for 4 to 7 minutes, until the tuna mixture is heated through and the cheese is melted with a slight golden color. Serve immediately while hot.

Steak Tips with Roasted Potatoes

Prep time: 10 minutes | Cook time: 20 minutes | Serves 4

- Oil, for spraying
- 8 ounces (227 g) baby gold potatoes, cut in half
- ½ teaspoon salt
- 1 pound (454 g) steak, cut into ½-inch pieces
- 1 teaspoon Worcestershire sauce
- 1 teaspoon granulated garlic
- ½ teaspoon salt
- ½ teaspoon freshly ground black pepper

1. Place a sheet of parchment paper in the air fryer basket and give it a light spray of oil. 2. Combine the potatoes and salt in a microwave-safe bowl, then add enough water to cover the bottom by about ½ inch. Microwave for around 7 minutes, or until the potatoes are just shy of fully tender. Drain and set aside. 3. In a large mixing bowl, gently toss the steak, microwaved potatoes, Worcestershire sauce, garlic, salt, and black pepper until well combined. Spread this mixture evenly in the prepared air fryer basket. 4. Cook at 400°F (204°C) for 12 to 17 minutes, stirring the ingredients after 5 to 6 minutes to ensure even cooking. Adjust the total cooking time based on the thickness of the steak and your preferred level of doneness.

French-Style Beignets

Prep time: 30 minutes | Cook time: 6 minutes | Makes 9 beignets

Oil, for greasing and spraying	1 cup milk
3 cups all-purpose flour, plus more for dusting	2 tablespoons packed light brown sugar
1½ teaspoons salt	1 tablespoon unsalted butter
1 (2¼ teaspoons) envelope active dry yeast	1 large egg
	1 cup confectioners' sugar

1. Lightly oil a large bowl and set it aside.2. In a small bowl, combine the flour, salt, and yeast, mixing well. Set aside.3. Heat the milk in a glass measuring cup in the microwave in 1-minute intervals until it reaches a boil.4. In a large mixing bowl, whisk together the brown sugar and butter. Gradually pour in the hot milk, whisking until the sugar fully dissolves. Allow the mixture to cool to room temperature.5. Whisk the egg into the cooled milk mixture, then gently fold in the flour mixture until a dough forms.6. Transfer the dough to a lightly floured surface and knead it for 3 to 5 minutes until smooth and elastic.7. Place the kneaded dough into the oiled bowl, cover it with a clean kitchen towel, and let it rise in a warm spot for about 1 hour, or until it doubles in size.8. Roll out the risen dough on a lightly floured surface to about ¼ inch thick. Cut it into 3-inch squares and arrange them on a lightly floured baking sheet. Cover loosely with a kitchen towel and let rise again until doubled in size, about 30 minutes.9. Line the air fryer basket with parchment paper and lightly spray it with oil.10. Place the dough squares in the prepared basket, ensuring they don't overlap. Lightly spray the tops with oil. If needed, work in batches to avoid overcrowding.11. Air fry the dough at 390ºF (199ºC) for 3 minutes. Flip the squares, spray again with oil, and cook for another 3 minutes, or until they are golden and crispy.12. Dust the cooked squares with confectioners' sugar before serving. Enjoy warm!

Mixed Berry Crisp

Prep time: 10 minutes | Cook time: 11 to 16 minutes | Serves 4

½ cup chopped fresh strawberries	⅔ cup whole-wheat pastry flour
½ cup fresh blueberries	3 tablespoons packed brown sugar
⅓ cup frozen raspberries	
1 tablespoon freshly squeezed lemon juice	2 tablespoons unsalted butter, melted
1 tablespoon honey	

1. Combine the strawberries, blueberries, and raspberries in a baking pan. Drizzle the mixture evenly with lemon juice and honey.2. In a small bowl, mix together the pastry flour and brown sugar until well blended.3. Add the butter to the dry mixture and stir until it forms a crumbly texture. Evenly sprinkle the crumbly mixture over the fruit.4. Bake in the air fryer at 380ºF (193ºC) for 11 to 16 minutes, or until the fruit becomes tender and bubbly and the topping turns golden brown. Serve warm for the best flavor.

Crispy Meringue Cookies

Prep time: 15 minutes | Cook time: 1 hour 30 minutes | Makes 20 cookies

Oil, for spraying	1 cup sugar
4 large egg whites	Pinch cream of tartar

1. Preheat the air fryer to 140ºF (60ºC). Line the basket with parchment paper and lightly spray it with oil.2. In a small heatproof bowl, combine the egg whites and sugar. Place a saucepan filled halfway with water over medium heat and bring it to a gentle simmer. Set the bowl over the saucepan, ensuring the bowl's bottom does not touch the water. Whisk the egg white mixture until the sugar completely dissolves.3. Pour the mixture into a large bowl, add the cream of tartar, and use an electric mixer to beat on high speed until glossy and stiff peaks form. Spoon the mixture into a piping bag or a zip-top bag with the corner snipped off.4. Pipe small rounds onto the prepared parchment in the basket, leaving space between each. Depending on your air fryer's size, you may need to cook in batches.5. Air fry for 1 hour and 30 minutes.6. After cooking, turn off the air fryer and leave the meringues inside to cool completely. The remaining heat will help them dry out further, creating the perfect texture.

Bacon-Wrapped Sausages

Prep time: 5 minutes | Cook time: 10 minutes | Serves 4

Oil, for spraying	4 hot dog buns
4 bacon slices	Toppings of choice
4 all-beef hot dogs	

1. Prepare the air fryer basket by lining it with parchment paper and lightly spraying it with oil.2. Wrap each hot dog tightly with a strip of bacon, ensuring the tips are covered to prevent over-crisping. Secure both ends of the bacon with toothpicks to keep it in place during cooking.3. Arrange the bacon-wrapped hot dogs in the prepared basket, making sure they do not overlap.4. Air fry at 380ºF (193ºC) for 8 to 9 minutes, adjusting the time based on your preferred bacon crispiness. For a crispier finish, increase the temperature to 400ºF (204ºC) and cook for 6 to 8 minutes.5. Place the cooked hot dogs into buns and return them to the air fryer for an additional 1 to 2 minutes, just until the buns are warmed through. Add your favorite toppings and serve immediately.

Cinnamon Sugar Churro Bites

Prep time: 5 minutes | Cook time: 6 minutes | Makes 36 bites

Oil, for spraying
1 (17¼ ounces / 489 g) package frozen puffed pastry, thawed
1 cup granulated sugar
1 tablespoon ground cinnamon
½ cup confectioners' sugar
1 tablespoon milk

1. Preheat the air fryer to 400°F (204°C). Line the basket with parchment paper and lightly coat it with oil spray. 2. Roll out the puff pastry onto a clean surface and, using a sharp knife, cut it into 36 small, bite-sized pieces. 3. Arrange the dough pieces in a single layer in the prepared basket, ensuring they don't touch or overlap. 4. Air fry for 3 minutes, flip the pieces, and cook for an additional 3 minutes, or until they are puffed and golden brown. 5. In a small bowl, combine the granulated sugar and cinnamon, mixing thoroughly. 6. In a separate bowl, whisk together the confectioners' sugar and milk to create the icing. 7. Toss the puffed bites in the cinnamon-sugar mixture, coating them evenly. 8. Serve warm with the icing on the side for dipping.

Grilled Steak and Veggie Skewers

Prep time: 15 minutes | Cook time: 5 to 7 minutes | Serves 4

2 tablespoons balsamic vinegar
2 teaspoons olive oil
½ teaspoon dried marjoram
⅛ teaspoon freshly ground black pepper
¾ pound (340 g) round steak, cut into 1-inch pieces
1 red bell pepper, sliced
16 button mushrooms
1 cup cherry tomatoes

1. In a medium bowl, mix the balsamic vinegar, olive oil, marjoram, and black pepper until well combined. 2. Add the steak to the bowl and toss to coat evenly. Allow the steak to marinate at room temperature for 10 minutes. 3. Thread the beef, red bell pepper, mushrooms, and tomatoes alternately onto 8 bamboo or metal skewers, ensuring they fit inside the air fryer basket. 4. Cook the skewers in the air fryer at 390°F (199°C) for 5 to 7 minutes, or until the beef is browned and the internal temperature reaches at least 145°F (63°C) when checked with a meat thermometer. Serve immediately while hot.

Egg & Avocado Breakfast Wrap

Prep time: 10 minutes | Cook time: 3 to 5 minutes | Serves 4

2 hard-boiled egg whites, chopped
1 hard-boiled egg, chopped
1 avocado, peeled, pitted, and chopped
1 red bell pepper, chopped
3 tablespoons low-sodium salsa, plus additional for serving (optional)
1 (1.2 ounces / 34 g) slice low-sodium, low-fat American cheese, torn into pieces
4 low-sodium whole-wheat flour tortillas

1. In a medium bowl, combine the egg whites, whole egg, avocado, red bell pepper, salsa, and cheese, mixing until evenly blended. 2. Lay the tortillas flat on a work surface and divide the filling evenly among them. Fold in the edges of each tortilla and roll tightly to form burritos. Use toothpicks to secure them if needed. 3. Arrange the burritos in the air fryer basket, making sure they do not overlap. Air fry at 390°F (199°C) for 3 to 5 minutes, or until they are golden brown and crispy. Serve warm with extra salsa, if desired.

Fried Pastry Elephant Ears

Prep time: 5 minutes | Cook time: 5 minutes | Serves 8

Oil, for spraying
1 (8 ounces / 227 g) can buttermilk biscuits
3 tablespoons sugar
1 tablespoon ground cinnamon
3 tablespoons unsalted butter, melted
8 scoops vanilla ice cream (optional)

1. Line the air fryer basket with parchment paper and lightly coat it with oil spray. 2. Divide the dough and, using a rolling pin, flatten each biscuit into a circle measuring 6 to 8 inches in diameter. 3. Arrange the dough circles in the prepared basket, ensuring they don't overlap, and generously spray them with oil. If needed, cook in batches based on the size of your air fryer. 4. Air fry the dough at 350°F (177°C) for about 5 minutes, or until they turn lightly golden. 5. In a small bowl, combine the sugar and cinnamon, stirring until evenly mixed. 6. Brush the freshly air-fried elephant ears with melted butter, then sprinkle them generously with the cinnamon-sugar mixture. 7. Serve warm, adding a scoop of ice cream on top if desired.

Stuffed Pork Meatballs

Prep time: 10 minutes | Cook time: 12 minutes | Makes 35 meatballs

Oil, for spraying
1½ pounds (680 g) ground pork
1 cup bread crumbs
½ cup milk
¼ cup minced onion
1 large egg
1 tablespoon dried rosemary
1 tablespoon dried thyme
1 teaspoon salt
1 teaspoon freshly ground black pepper
1 teaspoon finely chopped fresh parsley

1. Line the air fryer basket with parchment paper and lightly coat it with oil spray. 2. In a large mixing bowl, combine the ground pork, bread crumbs, milk, onion, egg, rosemary, thyme, salt, black pepper, and parsley, mixing thoroughly. 3. Scoop about 2 tablespoons of the mixture and shape it into a ball. Repeat this process until all the mixture is used, forming 30 to 35 meatballs. 4. Arrange the meatballs in a single layer in the prepared basket, ensuring there is space between each one. If necessary, cook in batches to avoid overcrowding. 5. Air fry at 390°F (199°C) for 10 to 12 minutes, flipping the meatballs halfway through, until they are golden brown and the internal temperature reaches 160°F (71°C). Serve hot.

Meatball Sub Sandwich

Prep time: 15 minutes | Cook time: 19 minutes | Serves 6

Oil, for spraying
1 pound (454 g) 85% lean ground beef
½ cup Italian bread crumbs
1 tablespoon dried minced onion
1 tablespoon minced garlic
1 large egg
1 teaspoon salt
1 teaspoon freshly ground black pepper
6 hoagie rolls
1 (18 ounces / 510 g) jar marinara sauce
1½ cups shredded Mozzarella cheese

1. Line the air fryer basket with parchment paper and lightly coat it with oil spray. 2. In a large mixing bowl, combine the ground beef, bread crumbs, onion, garlic, egg, salt, and black pepper. Mix well and shape the mixture into 18 meatballs. 3. Arrange the meatballs in a single layer in the prepared air fryer basket. 4. Cook the meatballs in the air fryer at 390°F (199°C) for 15 minutes, or until they are fully cooked. 5. Place three cooked meatballs into each hoagie roll and top with marinara sauce and Mozzarella cheese. 6. Return the assembled rolls to the air fryer and cook for 3 to 4 minutes, or until the cheese is melted and bubbly. If needed, cook in batches depending on the size of your air fryer. Serve immediately while hot.

Asian-Style Spareribs

Prep time: 30 minutes | Cook time: 8 minutes | Serves 4

Oil, for spraying
12 ounces (340 g) boneless pork spareribs, cut into 3-inch-long pieces
1 cup soy sauce
¾ cup sugar
½ cup beef or chicken stock
¼ cup honey
2 tablespoons minced garlic
1 teaspoon ground ginger
2 drops red food coloring (optional)

1. Prepare the air fryer basket by lining it with parchment paper and lightly spraying it with oil. 2. In a large zip-top plastic bag, combine the ribs, soy sauce, sugar, beef stock, honey, garlic, ginger, and food coloring (if desired). Seal the bag and shake thoroughly until the ribs are evenly coated. Refrigerate for at least 30 minutes to marinate. 3. Arrange the marinated ribs in the prepared air fryer basket, ensuring they are in a single layer. 4. Cook in the air fryer at 375°F (191°C) for 8 minutes, or until the ribs are cooked through and the internal temperature reaches 165°F (74°C). Serve warm.

Homemade Beef Jerky

Prep time: 30 minutes | Cook time: 2 hours | Serves 8

Oil, for spraying
1 pound (454 g) round steak, cut into thin, short slices
¼ cup soy sauce
3 tablespoons packed light brown sugar
1 tablespoon minced garlic
1 teaspoon ground ginger
1 tablespoon water

1. Prepare the air fryer basket by lining it with parchment paper and lightly spraying it with oil. 2. In a zip-top plastic bag, combine the steak, soy sauce, brown sugar, garlic, ginger, and water. Seal the bag tightly and shake well to ensure the steak is evenly coated with the marinade. Place the bag in the refrigerator for 30 minutes to marinate. 3. Arrange the marinated steak in a single layer in the prepared air fryer basket, leaving space between pieces. If needed, cook in batches to avoid overcrowding. 4. Air fry at 180°F (82°C) for at least 2 hours, or longer if you prefer your jerky to be tougher. Check periodically for your desired texture. Serve or store once cooled.

Crispy Coconut Chicken Strips

Prep time: 10 minutes | Cook time: 12 minutes | Serves 4

Oil, for spraying
2 large eggs
¼ cup milk
1 tablespoon hot sauce
1½ cups sweetened flaked coconut
¾ cup panko bread crumbs
1 teaspoon salt
½ teaspoon freshly ground black pepper
1 pound (454 g) chicken tenders

1. Line the air fryer basket with parchment paper and lightly coat it with oil spray.2. In a small bowl, whisk together the eggs, milk, and hot sauce until well blended.3. In a shallow dish, combine the coconut, bread crumbs, salt, and black pepper, mixing thoroughly.4. Dip each piece of chicken into the egg mixture, ensuring it is fully coated, then dredge it in the coconut mixture, pressing gently to adhere the coating evenly.5. Arrange the coated chicken pieces in the prepared air fryer basket and generously spray them with oil.6. Cook in the air fryer at 400°F (204°C) for 6 minutes. Flip the chicken, spray again with oil, and continue cooking for an additional 6 minutes, or until the internal temperature reaches 165°F (74°C). Serve hot.

Southern-style Fried Green Tomatoes

Prep time: 15 minutes | Cook time: 6 to 8 minutes | Serves 4

4 medium green tomatoes
⅓ cup all-purpose flour
2 egg whites
¼ cup almond milk
1 cup ground almonds
½ cup panko bread crumbs
2 teaspoons olive oil
1 teaspoon paprika
1 clove garlic, minced

1. Rinse the tomatoes and pat dry. Cut the tomatoes into ½-inch slices, discarding the thinner ends. 2. Put the flour on a plate. In a shallow bowl, beat the egg whites with the almond milk until frothy. And on another plate, combine the almonds, bread crumbs, olive oil, paprika, and garlic and mix well. 3. Dip the tomato slices into the flour, then into the egg white mixture, then into the almond mixture to coat. 4. Place four of the coated tomato slices in the air fryer basket. Air fry at 400°F (204°C) for 6 to 8 minutes or until the tomato coating is crisp and golden brown. Repeat with remaining tomato slices and serve immediately.

Mixed Berry Cheesecake

Prep time: 5 minutes | Cook time: 10 minutes | Serves 4

Oil, for spraying
8 ounces (227 g) cream cheese
6 tablespoons sugar
1 tablespoon sour cream
1 large egg
½ teaspoon vanilla extract
¼ teaspoon lemon juice
½ cup fresh mixed berries

1. Preheat the air fryer to 350°F (177°C). Line the basket with parchment paper and lightly spray it with oil.2. In a blender, combine the cream cheese, sugar, sour cream, egg, vanilla, and lemon juice. Blend until the mixture is completely smooth. Pour the batter into a 4-inch springform pan.3. Place the pan in the prepared air fryer basket.4. Air fry for 8 to 10 minutes, or until the cheesecake is set around the edges but the center still jiggles slightly when the pan is moved.5. Let the cheesecake cool slightly, then refrigerate it in the pan for at least 2 hours to fully set.6. Remove the sides of the springform pan, top the cheesecake with mixed berries, and serve chilled.

Spicy Buffalo Cauliflower Bites

Prep time: 15 minutes | Cook time: 5 minutes | Serves 6

1 large head cauliflower, separated into small florets
1 tablespoon olive oil
½ teaspoon garlic powder
⅓ cup low-sodium hot wing sauce
⅔ cup nonfat Greek yogurt
½ teaspoons Tabasco sauce
1 celery stalk, chopped
1 tablespoon crumbled blue cheese

1. In a large mixing bowl, drizzle the cauliflower florets with olive oil and toss to coat evenly. Sprinkle garlic powder over the florets and toss again to ensure an even coating. Place half of the cauliflower in the air fryer basket, making sure they are in a single layer. Air fry at 380°F (193°C) for 5 to 7 minutes, shaking the basket once during cooking, until the cauliflower is browned.2. Transfer the cooked cauliflower to a serving bowl and toss with half of the wing sauce until well coated. Repeat the process with the remaining cauliflower and wing sauce.3. In a small bowl, combine the yogurt, Tabasco sauce, celery, and blue cheese, stirring until blended. Serve the cauliflower hot with the yogurt dipping sauce on the side.

Chapter 3
Fast and Easy Everyday Favorites

Homemade Potato Chips with Lemon Dip

Prep time: 20 minutes | Cook time: 15 minutes | Serves 2 to 4

2 large russet potatoes, sliced into ⅛-inch slices, rinsed
Lemony Cream Dip:
½ cup sour cream
¼ teaspoon lemon juice
2 scallions, white part only, minced
Sea salt and freshly ground black pepper, to taste
Cooking spray
1 tablespoon olive oil
¼ teaspoon salt
Freshly ground black pepper, to taste

1. Submerge the potato slices in a bowl of water and let them soak for 10 minutes. Drain and pat them dry thoroughly with paper towels.2. Preheat the air fryer to 300°F (149°C).3. Place the potato slices in the preheated air fryer basket, ensuring they are spread out evenly. Lightly spritz the slices with cooking spray. If necessary, work in batches to avoid overcrowding.4. Air fry for 15 minutes, shaking the basket periodically to ensure even cooking, until the chips are crispy and golden brown. In the final minute of cooking, sprinkle the chips with salt and ground black pepper.5. While the chips are frying, mix the ingredients for the dip in a small bowl, stirring until smooth and well combined.6. Serve the freshly made potato chips immediately with the prepared dip on the side. Enjoy while warm and crispy.

Classic Melted Queso

Prep time: 10 minutes | Cook time: 25 minutes | Serves 4

4 ounces (113 g) fresh Mexican chorizo, casings removed
1 medium onion, chopped
3 cloves garlic, minced
1 cup chopped tomato
2 jalapeños, deseeded and diced
2 teaspoons ground cumin
2 cups shredded Oaxaca or Mozzarella cheese
½ cup half-and-half
Celery sticks or tortilla chips, for serving

1. Preheat the air fryer to 400°F (204°C).2. In a baking pan, combine the chorizo, onion, garlic, tomato, jalapeños, and cumin. Mix thoroughly to evenly distribute the ingredients.3. Place the baking pan into the air fryer basket and cook for 15 minutes, stirring halfway through to break up the sausage and ensure even cooking.4. Add the cheese and half-and-half to the cooked mixture, stirring until well combined. Return the pan to the air fryer and cook for an additional 10 minutes, or until the cheese is fully melted and creamy.5. Serve immediately with celery sticks or tortilla chips for dipping. Enjoy warm.

Savory Cheesy Potato Patties

Prep time: 5 minutes | Cook time: 10 minutes | Serves 8

2 pounds (907 g) white potatoes
½ cup finely chopped scallions
½ teaspoon freshly ground black pepper, or more to taste
1 tablespoon fine sea salt
½ teaspoon hot paprika
2 cups shredded Colby cheese
¼ cup canola oil
1 cup crushed crackers

1. Preheat the air fryer to 360°F (182°C).2. Boil the potatoes until they are soft, then drain and dry them. Peel the potatoes and mash thoroughly, ensuring there are no lumps.3. In a large bowl, mix the mashed potatoes with scallions, pepper, salt, paprika, and cheese until evenly combined.4. Shape the mixture into balls using your hands, then flatten them gently into patties with your palm.5. In a shallow dish, mix the canola oil and crushed crackers. Coat each patty in the crumb mixture, ensuring all sides are evenly covered.6. Place the patties in the air fryer basket in a single layer and cook for about 10 minutes. If necessary, work in batches to avoid overcrowding.7. Serve the patties hot for the best flavor and texture.

Lemon Beet Salad

Prep time: 10 minutes | Cook time: 12 to 15 minutes | Serves 4

6 medium red and golden beets, peeled and sliced
1 teaspoon olive oil
¼ teaspoon kosher salt
Vinaigrette:
2 teaspoons olive oil
2 tablespoons chopped
½ cup crumbled feta cheese
8 cups mixed greens
Cooking spray
fresh chives
Juice of 1 lemon

1. Preheat the air fryer to 360°F (182°C).2. In a large bowl, toss the beet pieces with olive oil and kosher salt until evenly coated.3. Lightly spray the air fryer basket with cooking spray, then place the beets in a single layer inside the basket. Air fry for 12 to 15 minutes, shaking the basket halfway through, until the beets are tender.4. While the beets are cooking, prepare the vinaigrette in a separate bowl by whisking together olive oil, lemon juice, and chives until well combined.5. Once the beets are done, transfer them to the bowl with the vinaigrette and toss to coat thoroughly. Let the beets cool for about 5 minutes.6. Arrange the mixed greens on a serving plate, top with the dressed beets, sprinkle with feta cheese, and serve immediately.

Savory Baked Grits

Prep time: 10 minutes | Cook time: 12 minutes | Serves 6

¾ cup hot water
2 (1-ounce / 28-g) packages instant grits
1 large egg, beaten
1 tablespoon butter, melted
2 cloves garlic, minced
½ to 1 teaspoon red pepper flakes
1 cup shredded Cheddar cheese or jalapeño Jack cheese

1. Preheat the air fryer to 400ºF (204ºC). 2. In a baking pan, mix together the water, grits, egg, butter, garlic, and red pepper flakes, stirring until the ingredients are fully combined. Fold in the shredded cheese and mix thoroughly. 3. Place the baking pan into the air fryer basket and cook for 12 minutes, or until the grits are set and a knife inserted near the center comes out clean. 4. Allow the grits to rest for 5 minutes before serving to let them firm up slightly. Serve warm.

Air-Fried Edamame Bites

Prep time: 5 minutes | Cook time: 7 minutes | Serves 6

1½ pounds (680 g) unshelled edamame
2 tablespoons olive oil
1 teaspoon sea salt

1. Preheat the air fryer to 400ºF (204ºC). 2. Add the edamame to a large bowl and drizzle with olive oil. Toss thoroughly to ensure all the pods are evenly coated. 3. Place the edamame into the preheated air fryer basket, spreading them out in a single layer. Cook for 7 minutes, shaking the basket at least three times during the cooking process to promote even heating. 4. Transfer the cooked edamame to a serving plate and sprinkle generously with salt. Toss gently to combine, then let them rest for about 3 minutes to allow the flavors to infuse before serving. Enjoy warm.

Golden Salmon Croquettes

Prep time: 15 minutes | Cook time: 10 minutes | Serves 6

2 egg whites
1 cup almond flour
1 cup panko breadcrumbs
1 pound (454 g) chopped salmon fillet
⅔ cup grated carrots
2 tablespoons minced garlic cloves
½ cup chopped onion
2 tablespoons chopped chives
Cooking spray

1. Preheat the air fryer to 350ºF (177ºC) and lightly spritz the basket with cooking spray. 2. Prepare three bowls: whisk the egg whites in one, place the flour in the second, and fill the third with breadcrumbs. Set them aside. 3. In a large bowl, combine the salmon, carrots, garlic, onion, and chives, mixing thoroughly until evenly combined. 4. Shape the salmon mixture into small balls using your hands. Coat each ball by rolling it first in the flour, then in the egg whites, and finally in the breadcrumbs, ensuring an even coating. 5. Arrange the salmon balls in a single layer in the preheated air fryer basket and spray them lightly with cooking spray. 6. Air fry for 10 minutes, shaking the basket halfway through, until the salmon balls are golden brown and crispy. 7. Serve immediately while warm and enjoy.

Traditional Canadian Poutine

Prep time: 15 minutes | Cook time: 25 minutes | Serves 2

2 russet potatoes, scrubbed and cut into ½-inch sticks
2 teaspoons vegetable oil
2 tablespoons butter
¼ onion, minced
¼ teaspoon dried thyme
1 clove garlic, smashed
3 tablespoons all-purpose flour
1 teaspoon tomato paste
1½ cups beef stock
2 teaspoons Worcestershire sauce
Salt and freshly ground black pepper, to taste
⅔ cup chopped string cheese

1. Bring a pot of water to a boil and blanch the potato sticks for 4 minutes. 2. Preheat the air fryer to 400ºF (204ºC). 3. Drain the blanched potato sticks and rinse them under cold running water to stop the cooking process. Pat them dry thoroughly with paper towels. 4. Place the potato sticks in a large bowl, drizzle with vegetable oil, and toss until evenly coated. 5. Arrange the potato sticks in the preheated air fryer basket in a single layer. Air fry for 25 minutes, shaking the basket at least three times during cooking, until the sticks are golden brown and crispy. 6. While the potatoes cook, prepare the gravy. In a saucepan over medium heat, melt the butter. 7. Add the onion, thyme, and garlic to the melted butter and sauté for about 5 minutes, or until the onion is translucent. 8. Stir in the flour and cook for 2 minutes, then mix in the tomato paste and beef stock. Simmer for another minute, stirring constantly, until the gravy begins to thicken slightly. 9. Add Worcestershire sauce to the gravy and season with salt and ground black pepper. Reduce the heat to low to keep the gravy warm until serving. 10. Once the potato sticks are done, transfer them to a plate and sprinkle with salt and black pepper. Scatter string cheese over the fries and drizzle generously with the warm gravy. Serve immediately while hot and gooey.

Savory Spinach Carrot Balls

Prep time: 10 minutes | Cook time: 10 minutes | Serves 4

2 slices toasted bread
1 carrot, peeled and grated
1 package fresh spinach, blanched and chopped
½ onion, chopped
1 egg, beaten
½ teaspoon garlic powder
1 teaspoon minced garlic
1 teaspoon salt
½ teaspoon black pepper
1 tablespoon nutritional yeast
1 tablespoon flour

1. Preheat the air fryer to 390°F (199°C).2. Place the toasted bread in a food processor and pulse until it forms fine bread crumbs. Transfer the bread crumbs to a shallow dish or bowl.3. In a separate bowl, combine all the remaining ingredients, mixing thoroughly until well blended.4. Shape the mixture into small balls using your hands. Roll each ball in the bread crumbs, ensuring they are evenly coated on all sides.5. Arrange the coated balls in the air fryer basket in a single layer and air fry for 10 minutes, or until golden brown and cooked through.6. Serve immediately while hot and crispy. Enjoy!

Baked Halloumi with Fresh Salsa

Prep time: 15 minutes | Cook time: 6 minutes | Serves 4

Salsa:
1 small shallot, finely diced
3 garlic cloves, minced
2 tablespoons fresh lemon juice
2 tablespoons extra-virgin olive oil
1 teaspoon freshly cracked black pepper
Pinch of kosher salt
½ cup finely diced English cucumber
1 plum tomato, deseeded and finely diced
2 teaspoons chopped fresh parsley
1 teaspoon snipped fresh dill
1 teaspoon snipped fresh oregano

Cheese:
8 ounces (227 g) Halloumi cheese, sliced into ½-inch-thick pieces
1 tablespoon extra-virgin olive oil

1. Preheat the air fryer to 375°F (191°C).2. To make the salsa, combine the shallot, garlic, lemon juice, olive oil, pepper, and salt in a medium bowl. Add the cucumber, tomato, parsley, dill, and oregano, tossing gently until evenly mixed. Set aside.3. For the cheese, place the slices in a medium bowl and drizzle with olive oil, tossing gently to ensure they are evenly coated. Arrange the cheese slices in a single layer in the air fryer basket. Air fry for 6 minutes until the cheese is warm and slightly golden.4. Transfer the cheese slices to four serving plates. Spoon the prepared salsa over the top and serve immediately for the best flavor.

Southern Fried Okra

Prep time: 5 minutes | Cook time: 8 to 10 minutes | Serves 4

1 cup self-rising yellow cornmeal
1 teaspoon Italian-style seasoning
1 teaspoon paprika
1 teaspoon salt
½ teaspoon freshly ground black pepper
2 large eggs, beaten
2 cups okra slices
Cooking spray

1. Preheat the air fryer to 400°F (204°C) and line the basket with parchment paper.2. In a shallow bowl, mix together the cornmeal, Italian-style seasoning, paprika, salt, and pepper until well combined. In a separate shallow bowl, place the beaten eggs.3. Toss the okra in the beaten eggs to coat evenly. Transfer the egg-coated okra to the cornmeal mixture and stir until each piece is fully coated.4. Arrange the coated okra in a single layer on the parchment paper and spritz lightly with oil.5. Air fry for 4 minutes, then shake the basket to ensure even cooking. Spritz with oil again and continue air frying for an additional 4 to 6 minutes, or until the okra is crispy and lightly browned.6. Serve hot and enjoy immediately for the best texture and flavor.

Stuffed Bacon-Wrapped Prunes

Prep time: 5 minutes | Cook time: 7 minutes | Serves 12

24 petite pitted prunes (4½ ounces / 128 g)
¼ cup crumbled blue cheese, divided
8 slices center-cut bacon, cut crosswise into thirds

1. Preheat the air fryer to 400°F (204°C).2. Slice the prunes lengthwise without cutting them completely in half, creating a pocket. Fill the center of each prune with ½ teaspoon of cheese. Wrap each prune with a strip of bacon, securing it with a toothpick.3. Place the bacon-wrapped prunes in a single layer in the air fryer basket, working in batches if necessary to avoid overcrowding. Air fry for about 7 minutes, flipping halfway through, until the bacon is crispy and fully cooked.4. Allow the prunes to cool slightly before serving. Serve warm and enjoy.

Lemon & Garlic Asparagus Spears

Prep time: 5 minutes | Cook time: 10 minutes | Makes 10 spears

10 spears asparagus (about ½ pound / 227 g in total), snap the ends off
1 tablespoon lemon juice
2 teaspoons minced garlic
½ teaspoon salt
¼ teaspoon ground black pepper
Cooking spray

1. Preheat the air fryer to 400°F (204°C) and line the basket with parchment paper.2. Place the asparagus spears in a large bowl. Drizzle with lemon juice, then sprinkle with minced garlic, salt, and ground black pepper. Toss thoroughly to ensure the spears are evenly coated.3. Transfer the seasoned asparagus to the preheated air fryer basket and lightly spritz with cooking spray. Cook for 10 minutes, flipping the spears halfway through, until they are tender and slightly wilted.4. Serve immediately while warm and flavorful.

Hot Cheese Sandwich

Prep time: 5 minutes | Cook time: 8 minutes | Serves 2

2 tablespoons mayonnaise
4 thick slices sourdough bread
4 thick slices Brie cheese
8 slices hot capicola

1. Preheat the air fryer to 350°F (177°C).2. Spread mayonnaise evenly on one side of each slice of bread. Place two slices, mayonnaise-side down, in the air fryer basket.3. Layer the slices of Brie and capicola on top of the bread, then cover with the remaining slices of bread, mayonnaise-side up.4. Air fry for 8 minutes, or until the cheese is melted and the bread is golden brown.5. Serve immediately while warm and enjoy.

Roasted Chickpeas with Orange and Rosemary

Prep time: 5 minutes | Cook time: 10 to 12 minutes | Makes 4 cups

4 cups cooked chickpeas
2 tablespoons vegetable oil
1 teaspoon kosher salt
1 teaspoon cumin
1 teaspoon paprika
Zest of 1 orange
1 tablespoon chopped fresh rosemary

1. Preheat the air fryer to 400°F (204°C).2. Ensure the chickpeas are thoroughly dried before roasting. In a medium bowl, toss the chickpeas with oil, salt, cumin, and paprika until evenly coated.3. Spread the chickpeas in a single layer in the air fryer basket, working in batches if necessary to avoid overcrowding. Air fry for 10 to 12 minutes, shaking the basket halfway through, until the chickpeas are crisp and golden.4. Transfer the warm chickpeas back to the bowl and toss with orange zest and rosemary. Allow them to cool completely to enhance the crunch.5. Serve and enjoy as a flavorful snack.

Quick Cinnamon Sugar Toast

Prep time: 5 minutes | Cook time: 20 minutes | Serves 6

1½ teaspoons cinnamon
1½ teaspoons vanilla extract
½ cup sugar
2 teaspoons ground black pepper
2 tablespoons melted coconut oil
12 slices whole wheat bread

1. Preheat the air fryer to 400°F (204°C).2. In a large bowl, combine all the ingredients except the bread, stirring until evenly mixed.3. Dip each slice of bread into the mixture, ensuring both sides are well coated. Gently shake off any excess before proceeding.4. Arrange the coated bread slices in a single layer in the preheated air fryer, leaving space between each slice. Air fry for 5 minutes, flipping halfway through, until golden brown. If necessary, cook in batches to avoid overcrowding.5. Once cooked, remove the bread slices from the air fryer, slice as desired, and serve immediately. Enjoy warm.

Traditional Potato Latkes

Prep time: 15 minutes | Cook time: 10 minutes | Makes 4 latkes

1 egg
2 tablespoons all-purpose flour
2 medium potatoes, peeled and shredded, rinsed and drained
¼ teaspoon granulated garlic
½ teaspoon salt
Cooking spray

1. Preheat the air fryer to 380°F (193°C) and lightly spritz the basket with cooking spray.2. In a large bowl, whisk together the egg, flour, potatoes, garlic, and salt until the mixture is well combined.3. Divide the mixture into four equal portions and shape each portion into a flat circle. Arrange the latke circles in a single layer in the preheated air fryer basket.4. Lightly spray the tops of the latkes with cooking spray and air fry for 10 minutes, flipping them halfway through, until they are golden brown and crispy.5. Serve immediately while hot for the best texture and flavor. Enjoy!

Fried Green Tomatoes Slices

Prep time: 10 minutes | Cook time: 8 minutes | Makes 12 slices

½ cup all-purpose flour
1 egg
½ cup buttermilk
1 cup cornmeal
1 cup panko

2 green tomatoes, cut into ¼-inch-thick slices, patted dry
½ teaspoon salt
½ teaspoon ground black pepper
Cooking spray

1. Preheat the air fryer to 400°F (204°C) and line the basket with parchment paper. 2. Place the flour in one bowl, whisk together the egg and buttermilk in a second bowl, and mix the cornmeal and panko in a third bowl. 3. Coat each tomato slice by dredging it first in the flour, then dipping it into the egg mixture, and finally pressing it into the cornmeal mixture to ensure an even coating. Shake off any excess. 4. Arrange the coated tomato slices in a single layer in the preheated air fryer. Sprinkle with salt and ground black pepper for seasoning. 5. Lightly spritz the tomato slices with cooking spray and air fry for 8 minutes, flipping halfway through, until they are crispy and golden brown. 6. Serve immediately while hot and enjoy their crunchy texture.

Brown Rice and Pepper Fritters

Prep time: 10 minutes | Cook time: 8 to 10 minutes | Serves 4

1 (10 ounces / 284 g) bag frozen cooked brown rice, thawed
1 egg
3 tablespoons brown rice flour
⅓ cup finely grated carrots

⅓ cup minced red bell pepper
2 tablespoons minced fresh basil
3 tablespoons grated Parmesan cheese
2 teaspoons olive oil

1. Preheat the air fryer to 380°F (193°C). 2. In a small bowl, mix the thawed rice, egg, and flour until well combined. 3. Add the carrots, bell pepper, basil, and Parmesan cheese to the mixture, stirring until evenly incorporated. 4. Shape the mixture into 8 fritters and lightly drizzle them with olive oil. 5. Carefully place the fritters in the air fryer basket, ensuring they do not overlap. Air fry for 8 to 10 minutes, flipping halfway through, until they are golden brown and fully cooked. 6. Serve hot and enjoy immediately for the best flavor and texture.

Homemade Crunchy Croutons

Prep time: 5 minutes | Cook time: 8 minutes | Serves 4

2 slices friendly bread
1 tablespoon olive oil

Hot soup, for serving

1. Preheat the air fryer to 390°F (199°C). 2. Cut the slices of bread into medium-sized chunks, ensuring even pieces for uniform cooking. 3. Lightly brush the air fryer basket with oil to prevent sticking. 4. Arrange the bread chunks in the basket in a single layer and air fry for about 8 minutes, or until they are golden and crisp. Shake the basket halfway through for even browning. 5. Serve the crispy bread chunks alongside hot soup for dipping or as a garnish. Enjoy!

Chapter 4
Poultry

Herbed Roast Chicken Breast

Prep time: 10 minutes | Cook time: 25 minutes | Serves 2 to 4

2 tablespoons salted butter or ghee, at room temperature
1 teaspoon dried Italian seasoning, crushed
½ teaspoon kosher salt
½ teaspoon smoked paprika
¼ teaspoon black pepper
2 bone-in, skin-on chicken breast halves (about 10 ounces / 283 g each)
Lemon wedges, for serving

1. In a small bowl, stir together the butter, Italian seasoning, salt, paprika, and pepper until thoroughly combined. 2. Using a small sharp knife, carefully loosen the skin on each chicken breast half, starting at the thin end of each. Very carefully separate the skin from the flesh, leaving the skin attached at the thick end of each breast. Divide the herb butter into quarters. Rub one-quarter of the butter onto the flesh of each breast. Fold and lightly press the skin back onto each breast. Rub the remaining butter onto the skin of each breast. 3. Place the chicken in the air fryer basket. Set the air fryer to 375°F (191°C) for 25 minutes. Use a meat thermometer to ensure the chicken breasts have reached an internal temperature of 165°F (74°C). 4. Transfer the chicken to a cutting board. Lightly cover with aluminum foil and let rest for 5 to 10 minutes. 5. Serve with lemon wedges.

Basil Chicken Pizzas

Prep time: 10 minutes | Cook time: 12 minutes | Serves 4

1 pound (454 g) ground chicken thighs
¼ teaspoon salt
⅛ teaspoon ground black pepper
¼ cup basil pesto
1 cup shredded Mozzarella cheese
4 grape tomatoes, sliced

1. Cut four squares of parchment paper to fit into your air fryer basket. 2. Place ground chicken in a large bowl and mix with salt and pepper. Divide mixture into four equal sections. 3. Wet your hands with water to prevent sticking, then press each section into a 6-inch circle onto a piece of ungreased parchment. Place each chicken crust into air fryer basket, working in batches if needed. 4. Adjust the temperature to 350°F (177°C) and air fry for 10 minutes, turning crusts halfway through cooking. 5. Spread 1 tablespoon pesto across the top of each crust, then sprinkle with ¼ cup Mozzarella and top with 1 sliced tomato. Continue cooking at 350°F (177°C) for 2 minutes. Cheese will be melted and brown when done. Serve warm.

Classic Whole Chicken

Prep time: 5 minutes | Cook time: 50 minutes | Serves 4

Oil, for spraying
1 (4-pound / 1.8-kg) whole chicken, giblets removed
1 tablespoon olive oil
1 teaspoon paprika
½ teaspoon granulated garlic
½ teaspoon salt
½ teaspoon freshly ground black pepper
¼ teaspoon finely chopped fresh parsley, for garnish

1. Line the air fryer basket with parchment and spray lightly with oil. 2. Pat the chicken dry with paper towels. Rub it with the olive oil until evenly coated. 3. In a small bowl, mix together the paprika, garlic, salt, and black pepper and sprinkle it evenly over the chicken. 4. Place the chicken in the prepared basket, breast-side down. 5. Air fry at 360°F (182°C) for 30 minutes, flip, and cook for another 20 minutes, or until the internal temperature reaches 165°F (74°C) and the juices run clear. 6. Sprinkle with the parsley before serving.

Gochujang Chicken Wings

Prep time: 15 minutes | Cook time: 25 minutes | Serves 4

Wings:
2 pounds (907 g) chicken wings
1 teaspoon kosher salt
1 teaspoon black pepper or gochugaru (Korean red pepper)

Sauce:
2 tablespoons gochujang (Korean chile paste)
1 tablespoon mayonnaise
1 tablespoon toasted sesame oil
1 tablespoon minced fresh ginger
1 tablespoon minced garlic
1 teaspoon sugar
1 teaspoon agave nectar or honey

For Serving
1 teaspoon sesame seeds
¼ cup chopped scallions

1. For the wings: Season the wings with the salt and pepper and place in the air fryer basket. Set the air fryer to 400°F (204°C) for 20 minutes, turning the wings halfway through the cooking time. 2. Meanwhile, for the sauce: In a small bowl, combine the gochujang, mayonnaise, sesame oil, ginger, garlic, sugar, and agave; set aside. 3. As you near the 20-minute mark, use a meat thermometer to check the meat. When the wings reach 160°F (71°C), transfer them to a large bowl. Pour about half the sauce on the wings; toss to coat (serve the remaining sauce as a dip). 4. Return the wings to the air fryer basket and cook for 5 minutes, until the sauce has glazed. 5. Transfer the wings to a serving platter. Sprinkle with the sesame seeds and scallions. Serve with the reserved sauce on the side for dipping.

Almond-Crusted Chicken

Prep time: 15 minutes | Cook time: 25 minutes | Serves 4

¼ cup slivered almonds
2 (6-ounce / 170-g) boneless, skinless chicken breasts
2 tablespoons full-fat mayonnaise
1 tablespoon Dijon mustard

1. Pulse the almonds in a food processor or chop until finely chopped. Place almonds evenly on a plate and set aside. 2. Completely slice each chicken breast in half lengthwise. 3. Mix the mayonnaise and mustard in a small bowl and then coat chicken with the mixture. 4. Lay each piece of chicken in the chopped almonds to fully coat. Carefully move the pieces into the air fryer basket. 5. Adjust the temperature to 350°F (177°C) and air fry for 25 minutes. 6. Chicken will be done when it has reached an internal temperature of 165°F (74°C) or more. Serve warm.

Peruvian Herb-Crusted Chicken

Prep time: 30 minutes | Cook time: 15 minutes | Serves 4

Chicken:
4 boneless, skinless chicken thighs (about 1½ pounds / 680 g)
2 teaspoons grated lemon zest
2 tablespoons fresh lemon juice
1 tablespoon extra-virgin olive oil
1 serrano chile, seeded and minced
1 teaspoon ground cumin
½ teaspoon dried oregano, crushed
½ teaspoon kosher salt

Sauce:
1 cup fresh cilantro leaves
1 jalapeño, seeded and coarsely chopped
1 garlic clove, minced
1 tablespoon extra-virgin olive oil
2½ teaspoons fresh lime juice
¼ teaspoon kosher salt
⅓ cup mayonnaise

1. For the chicken: Use a fork to pierce the chicken all over to allow the marinade to penetrate better. In a small bowl, combine the lemon zest, lemon juice, olive oil, serrano, cumin, oregano, and salt. Place the chicken in a large bowl or large resealable plastic bag. Pour the marinade over the chicken. Toss to coat. Marinate at room temperature for 30 minutes, or cover and refrigerate for up to 24 hours. 2. Place the chicken in the air fryer basket. (Discard remaining marinade.) Set the air fryer to 350°F (177°C) for 15 minutes, turning halfway through the cooking time. 3. Meanwhile, for the sauce: Combine the cilantro, jalapeño, garlic, olive oil, lime juice, and salt in a blender. Blend until combined. Add the mayonnaise and blend until puréed. Transfer to a small bowl. Cover and chill until ready to serve. 4. At the end of the cooking time, use a meat thermometer to ensure the chicken has reached an internal temperature of 165°F (74°C). Serve the chicken with the sauce.

Spanish Chicken and Mini Sweet Pepper Baguette

Prep time: 10 minutes | Cook time: 20 minutes | Serves 2

1¼ pounds (567 g) assorted small chicken parts, breasts cut into halves
¼ teaspoon salt
¼ teaspoon ground black pepper
2 teaspoons olive oil
½ pound (227 g) mini sweet peppers
¼ cup light mayonnaise
¼ teaspoon smoked paprika
½ clove garlic, crushed
Baguette, for serving
Cooking spray

1. Preheat air fryer to 375°F (191°C). Spritz the air fryer basket with cooking spray. 2. Toss the chicken with salt, ground black pepper, and olive oil in a large bowl. 3. Arrange the sweet peppers and chicken in the preheated air fryer and air fry for 10 minutes, then transfer the peppers on a plate. 4. Flip the chicken and air fry for 10 more minutes or until well browned. 5. Meanwhile, combine the mayo, paprika, and garlic in a small bowl. Stir to mix well. 6. Assemble the baguette with chicken and sweet pepper, then spread with mayo mixture and serve.

Turkey and Cranberry Wraps

Prep time: 7 minutes | Cook time: 4 to 8 minutes | Serves 4

6 low-sodium whole-wheat tortillas
⅓ cup shredded low-sodium low-fat Swiss cheese
¾ cup shredded cooked low-sodium turkey breast
2 tablespoons cranberry sauce
2 tablespoons dried cranberries
½ teaspoon dried basil
Olive oil spray, for spraying the tortillas

1. Preheat the air fryer to 400°F (204°C). 2. Put 3 tortillas on a work surface. 3. Evenly divide the Swiss cheese, turkey, cranberry sauce, and dried cranberries among the tortillas. Sprinkle with the basil and top with the remaining tortillas. 4. Spray the outsides of the tortillas with olive oil spray. 5. One at a time, air fry the quesadillas in the air fryer for 4 to 8 minutes, or until crisp and the cheese is melted. Cut into quarters and serve.

Bacon-Wrapped Stuffed Chicken Breasts

Prep time: 15 minutes | Cook time: 30 minutes | Serves 4

½ cup chopped frozen spinach, thawed and squeezed dry
¼ cup cream cheese, softened
¼ cup grated Parmesan cheese
1 jalapeño, seeded and chopped
½ teaspoon kosher salt
1 teaspoon black pepper
2 large boneless, skinless chicken breasts, butterflied and pounded to ½-inch thickness
4 teaspoons salt-free Cajun seasoning
6 slices bacon

1. In a small bowl, combine the spinach, cream cheese, Parmesan cheese, jalapeño, salt, and pepper. Stir until well combined. 2. Place the butterflied chicken breasts on a flat surface. Spread the cream cheese mixture evenly across each piece of chicken. Starting with the narrow end, roll up each chicken breast, ensuring the filling stays inside. Season chicken with the Cajun seasoning, patting it in to ensure it sticks to the meat. 3. Wrap each breast in 3 slices of bacon. Place in the air fryer basket. Set the air fryer to 350°F (177°C) for 30 minutes. Use a meat thermometer to ensure the chicken has reached an internal temperature of 165°F (74°C). 4. Let the chicken stand 5 minutes before slicing each rolled-up breast in half to serve.

Teriyaki-Glazed Chicken Thighs with Lemon Peas

Prep time: 30 minutes | Cook time: 34 minutes | Serves 4

¼ cup chicken broth
½ teaspoon grated fresh ginger
⅛ teaspoon red pepper flakes
1½ tablespoons soy sauce
4 (5 ounces / 142 g) bone-in chicken thighs, trimmed
1 tablespoon mirin
½ teaspoon cornstarch
1 tablespoon sugar
6 ounces (170 g) snow peas, strings removed
⅛ teaspoon lemon zest
1 garlic clove, minced
¼ teaspoon salt
Ground black pepper, to taste
½ teaspoon lemon juice

1. Combine the broth, ginger, pepper flakes, and soy sauce in a large bowl. Stir to mix well. 2. Pierce 10 to 15 holes into the chicken skin. Put the chicken in the broth mixture and toss to coat well. Let sit for 10 minutes to marinate. 3. Preheat the air fryer to 400°F (205°C). 4. Transfer the marinated chicken on a plate and pat dry with paper towels. 5. Scoop 2 tablespoons of marinade in a microwave-safe bowl and combine with mirin, cornstarch and sugar. Stir to mix well. Microwave for 1 minute or until frothy and has a thick consistency. Set aside. 6. Arrange the chicken in the preheated air fryer, skin side up, and air fry for 25 minutes or until the internal temperature of the chicken reaches at least 165°F (74°C). Gently turn the chicken over halfway through. 7. When the frying is complete, brush the chicken skin with marinade mixture. Air fryer the chicken for 5 more minutes or until glazed. 8. Remove the chicken from the air fryer and reserve ½ teaspoon of chicken fat remains in the air fryer. Allow the chicken to cool for 10 minutes. 9. Meanwhile, combine the reserved chicken fat, snow peas, lemon zest, garlic, salt, and ground black pepper in a small bowl. Toss to coat well. 10. Transfer the snow peas in the air fryer and air fry for 3 minutes or until soft. Remove the peas from the air fryer and toss with lemon juice. 11. Serve the chicken with lemony snow peas.

Buttermilk Breaded Chicken

Prep time: 7 minutes | Cook time: 20 to 25 minutes | Serves 4

1 cup all-purpose flour
2 teaspoons paprika
Pinch salt
Freshly ground black pepper, to taste
⅓ cup buttermilk
2 eggs
2 tablespoons extra-virgin olive oil
1½ cups bread crumbs
6 chicken pieces, drumsticks, breasts, and thighs, patted dry
Cooking oil spray

1. In a shallow bowl, stir together the flour, paprika, salt, and pepper. 2. In another bowl, beat the buttermilk and eggs until smooth. 3. In a third bowl, stir together the olive oil and bread crumbs until mixed. 4. Dredge the chicken in the flour, dip in the eggs to coat, and finally press into the bread crumbs, patting the crumbs firmly onto the chicken skin. 5. Insert the crisper plate into the basket and the basket into the unit. Preheat the unit by selecting AIR FRY, setting the temperature to 375°F (191°C), and setting the time to 3 minutes. Select START/STOP to begin. 6. Once the unit is preheated, spray the crisper plate with cooking oil. Place the chicken into the basket. 7. Select AIR FRY, set the temperature to 375°F (191°C), and set the time to 25 minutes. Select START/STOP to begin. 8. After 10 minutes, flip the chicken. Resume cooking. After 10 minutes more, check the chicken. If a food thermometer inserted into the chicken registers 165°F (74°C) and the chicken is brown and crisp, it is done. Otherwise, resume cooking for up to 5 minutes longer. 9. When the cooking is complete, let cool for 5 minutes, then serve.

Cheesy Peanut-Crusted Chicken Strips

Prep time: 10 minutes | Cook time: 25 minutes | Serves 4

½ cup grated Parmesan cheese
½ teaspoon garlic powder
1 teaspoon red pepper flakes
Sea salt and ground black pepper, to taste
2 tablespoons peanut oil
1½ pounds (680 g) chicken tenderloins
2 tablespoons peanuts, roasted and roughly chopped
Cooking spray

1. Preheat the air fryer to 360ºF (182ºC). Spritz the air fryer basket with cooking spray. 2. Combine the Parmesan cheese, garlic powder, red pepper flakes, salt, black pepper, and peanut oil in a large bow. Stir to mix well. 3. Dip the chicken tenderloins in the cheese mixture, then press to coat well. Shake the excess off. 4. Transfer the chicken tenderloins in the air fryer basket. Air fry for 12 minutes or until well browned. Flip the tenderloin halfway through. You may need to work in batches to avoid overcrowding. 5. Transfer the chicken tenderloins on a large plate and top with roasted peanuts before serving.

Pickle Brined Fried Chicken

Prep time: 30 minutes | Cook time: 47 minutes | Serves 4

4 bone-in, skin-on chicken legs, cut into drumsticks and thighs (about 3½ pounds / 1.6 kg)
Pickle juice from 1 (24 ounces / 680 g) jar kosher dill pickles
½ cup flour
Salt and freshly ground black pepper, to taste
2 eggs
1 cup fine bread crumbs
1 teaspoon salt
1 teaspoon freshly ground black pepper
½ teaspoon ground paprika
⅛ teaspoon ground cayenne pepper
Vegetable or canola oil

1. Place the chicken in a shallow dish and pour the pickle juice over the top. Cover and transfer the chicken to the refrigerator to brine in the pickle juice for 3 to 8 hours. 2. When you are ready to cook, remove the chicken from the refrigerator to let it come to room temperature while you set up a dredging station. Place the flour in a shallow dish and season well with salt and freshly ground black pepper. Whisk the eggs in a second shallow dish. In a third shallow dish, combine the bread crumbs, salt, pepper, paprika and cayenne pepper. 3. Preheat the air fryer to 370ºF (188ºC). 4. Remove the chicken from the pickle brine and gently dry it with a clean kitchen towel. Dredge each piece of chicken in the flour, then dip it into the egg mixture, and finally press it into the bread crumb mixture to coat all sides of the chicken. Place the breaded chicken on a plate or baking sheet and spray each piece all over with vegetable oil. 5. Air fry the chicken in two batches. Place two chicken thighs and two drumsticks into the air fryer basket. Air fry for 10 minutes. Then, gently turn the chicken pieces over and air fry for another 10 minutes. Remove the chicken pieces and let them rest on plate, do not cover. Repeat with the second batch of chicken, air frying for 20 minutes, turning the chicken over halfway through. 6. Lower the temperature of the air fryer to 340ºF (171ºC). Place the first batch of chicken on top of the second batch already in the basket and air fry for an additional 7 minutes. Serve warm and enjoy.

Avocado and Chicken Cobb Salad

Prep time: 15 minutes | Cook time: 8 minutes | Serves 4

8 slices reduced-sodium bacon
8 chicken breast tenders (about 1½ pounds / 680 g)
8 cups chopped romaine lettuce
1 cup cherry tomatoes, halved
¼ red onion, thinly sliced
2 hard-boiled eggs, peeled and sliced

Avocado-Lime Dressing:
½ cup plain Greek yogurt
¼ cup almond milk
½ avocado
Juice of ½ lime
3 scallions, coarsely chopped
1 clove garlic
2 tablespoons fresh cilantro
⅛ teaspoon ground cumin
Salt and freshly ground black pepper, to taste

1. Preheat the air fryer to 400ºF (204ºC). 2. Wrap a piece of bacon around each piece of chicken and secure with a toothpick. Working in batches if necessary, arrange the bacon-wrapped chicken in a single layer in the air fryer basket. Air fry for 8 minutes until the bacon is browned and a thermometer inserted into the thickest piece of chicken register 165ºF (74ºC). Let cool for a few minutes, then slice into bite-size pieces. 3. To make the dressing: In a blender or food processor, combine the yogurt, milk, avocado, lime juice, scallions, garlic, cilantro, and cumin. Purée until smooth. Season to taste with salt and freshly ground pepper. 4. To assemble the salad, in a large bowl, combine the lettuce, tomatoes, and onion. Drizzle the dressing over the vegetables and toss gently until thoroughly combined. Arrange the chicken and eggs on top just before serving.

Dijon Mustard Lemon Chicken

Prep time: 30 minutes | Cook time: 13 to 16 minutes | Serves 6

½ cup sugar-free mayonnaise
1 tablespoon Dijon mustard
1 tablespoon freshly squeezed lemon juice (optional)
1 tablespoon coconut aminos
1 teaspoon Italian seasoning
1 teaspoon sea salt
½ teaspoon freshly ground black pepper
¼ teaspoon cayenne pepper
1½ pounds (680 g) boneless, skinless chicken breasts or thighs

1. In a small bowl, combine the mayonnaise, mustard, lemon juice (if using), coconut aminos, Italian seasoning, salt, black pepper, and cayenne pepper. 2. Place the chicken in a shallow dish or large zip-top plastic bag. Add the marinade, making sure all the pieces are coated. Cover and refrigerate for at least 30 minutes or up to 4 hours. 3. Set the air fryer to 400°F (204°C). Arrange the chicken in a single layer in the air fryer basket, working in batches if necessary. Air fry for 7 minutes. Flip the chicken and continue cooking for 6 to 9 minutes more, until an instant-read thermometer reads 160°F (71°C).

Crispy Duck with Cherry Sauce

Prep time: 10 minutes | Cook time: 33 minutes | Serves 2 to 4

1 whole duck (up to 5 pounds / 2.3 kg), split in half, back and rib bones removed
Cherry Sauce:
1 tablespoon butter
1 shallot, minced
½ cup sherry
¾ cup cherry preserves
1 cup chicken stock
1 teaspoon white wine vinegar
1 teaspoon olive oil
Salt and freshly ground black pepper, to taste

1 teaspoon fresh thyme leaves
Salt and freshly ground black pepper, to taste

1. Preheat the air fryer to 400°F (204°C). 2. Trim some of the fat from the duck. Rub olive oil on the duck and season with salt and pepper. Place the duck halves in the air fryer basket, breast side up and facing the center of the basket. 3. Air fry the duck for 20 minutes. Turn the duck over and air fry for another 6 minutes. 4. While duck is air frying, make the cherry sauce. Melt the butter in a large sauté pan. Add the shallot and sauté until it is just starting to brown, about 2 to 3 minutes. Add the sherry and deglaze the pan by scraping up any brown bits from the bottom of the pan. Simmer the liquid for a few minutes, until it has reduced by half. Add the cherry preserves, chicken stock and white wine vinegar. Whisk well to combine all the ingredients. Simmer the sauce until it thickens and coats the back of a spoon, about 5 to 7 minutes. Season with salt and pepper and stir in the fresh thyme leaves. 5. When the air fryer timer goes off, spoon some cherry sauce over the duck and continue to air fry at 400°F (204°C) for 4 more minutes. Then, turn the duck halves back over so that the breast side is facing up. Spoon more cherry sauce over the top of the duck, covering the skin completely. Air fry for 3 more minutes and then remove the duck to a plate to rest for a few minutes. 6. Serve the duck in halves, or cut each piece in half again for a smaller serving. Spoon any additional sauce over the duck or serve it on the side.

Herb-Rolled Chicken Breasts

Prep time: 10 minutes | Cook time: 15 minutes | Serves 4

½ cup fresh parsley leaves
¼ cup roughly chopped fresh chives
4 cloves garlic, peeled
2 tablespoons lemon juice
3 teaspoons fine sea salt
1 teaspoon dried rubbed sage
1 teaspoon fresh rosemary leaves
1 teaspoon ground fennel
½ teaspoon red pepper flakes
4 (4-ounce / 113-g) boneless, skinless chicken breasts, pounded to ¼ inch thick
8 slices bacon
Sprigs of fresh rosemary, for garnish (optional)

1. Spray the air fryer basket with avocado oil. Preheat the air fryer to 340°F (171°C). 2. Place the parsley, chives, garlic, lemon juice, salt, sage, rosemary, fennel, and red pepper flakes in a food processor and purée until a smooth paste forms. 3. Place the chicken breasts on a cutting board and rub the paste all over the tops. With a short end facing you, roll each breast up like a jelly roll to make a log and secure it with toothpicks. 4. Wrap 2 slices of bacon around each chicken breast log to cover the entire breast. Secure the bacon with toothpicks. 5. Place the chicken breast logs in the air fryer basket and air fry for 5 minutes, flip the logs over, and cook for another 5 minutes. Increase the heat to 390°F (199°C) and cook until the bacon is crisp, about 5 minutes more. 6. Remove the toothpicks and garnish with fresh rosemary sprigs, if desired, before serving. Store leftovers in an airtight container in the refrigerator for up to 4 days or in the freezer for up to a month. Reheat in a preheated 350°F (177°C) air fryer for 5 minutes, then increase the heat to 390°F (199°C) and cook for 2 minutes to crisp the bacon.

Cranberry Curry Chicken

Prep time: 12 minutes | Cook time: 18 minutes | Serves 4

3 (5-ounce / 142-g) low-sodium boneless, skinless chicken breasts, cut into 1½-inch cubes
2 teaspoons olive oil
2 tablespoons cornstarch
1 tablespoon curry powder
1 tart apple, chopped
½ cup low-sodium chicken broth
⅓ cup dried cranberries
2 tablespoons freshly squeezed orange juice
Brown rice, cooked (optional)

1. Preheat the air fryer to 380°F (193°C). 2. In a medium bowl, mix the chicken and olive oil. Sprinkle with the cornstarch and curry powder. Toss to coat. Stir in the apple and transfer to a metal pan. Bake in the air fryer for 8 minutes, stirring once during cooking. 3. Add the chicken broth, cranberries, and orange juice. Bake for about 10 minutes more, or until the sauce is slightly thickened and the chicken reaches an internal temperature of 165°F (74°C) on a meat thermometer. Serve over hot cooked brown rice, if desired.

Herb-Buttermilk Chicken Breast

Prep time: 5 minutes | Cook time: 40 minutes | Serves 2

1 large bone-in, skin-on chicken breast
1 cup buttermilk
1½ teaspoons dried parsley
1½ teaspoons dried chives
¾ teaspoon kosher salt
½ teaspoon dried dill
½ teaspoon onion powder
¼ teaspoon garlic powder
¼ teaspoon dried tarragon
Cooking spray

1. Place the chicken breast in a bowl and pour over the buttermilk, turning the chicken in it to make sure it's completely covered. Let the chicken stand at room temperature for at least 20 minutes or in the refrigerator for up to 4 hours. 2. Meanwhile, in a bowl, stir together the parsley, chives, salt, dill, onion powder, garlic powder, and tarragon. 3. Preheat the air fryer to 300°F (149°C). 4. Remove the chicken from the buttermilk, letting the excess drip off, then place the chicken skin-side up directly in the air fryer. Sprinkle the seasoning mix all over the top of the chicken breast, then let stand until the herb mix soaks into the buttermilk, at least 5 minutes. 5. Spray the top of the chicken with cooking spray. Bake for 10 minutes, then increase the temperature to 350°F (177°C) and bake until an instant-read thermometer inserted into the thickest part of the breast reads 160°F (71°C) and the chicken is deep golden brown, 30 to 35 minutes. 6. Transfer the chicken breast to a cutting board, let rest for 10 minutes, then cut the meat off the bone and cut into thick slices for serving.

Fajita Chicken Rolls

Prep time: 15 minutes | Cook time: 25 minutes | Serves 4

2 (6-ounce / 170-g) boneless, skinless chicken breasts
¼ medium white onion, peeled and sliced
1 medium green bell pepper, seeded and sliced
1 tablespoon coconut oil
2 teaspoons chili powder
1 teaspoon ground cumin
½ teaspoon garlic powder

1. Slice each chicken breast completely in half lengthwise into two even pieces. Using a meat tenderizer, pound out the chicken until it's about ¼-inch thickness. 2. Lay each slice of chicken out and place three slices of onion and four slices of green pepper on the end closest to you. Begin rolling the peppers and onions tightly into the chicken. Secure the roll with either toothpicks or a couple pieces of butcher's twine. 3. Drizzle coconut oil over chicken. Sprinkle each side with chili powder, cumin, and garlic powder. Place each roll into the air fryer basket. 4. Adjust the temperature to 350°F (177°C) and air fry for 25 minutes. 5. Serve warm.

Fiesta Chicken Plate

Prep time: 15 minutes | Cook time: 12 to 15 minutes | Serves 4

1 pound (454 g) boneless, skinless chicken breasts (2 large breasts)
2 tablespoons lime juice
1 teaspoon cumin
½ teaspoon salt
½ cup grated Pepper Jack cheese
1 (16-ounce / 454-g) can refried beans
½ cup salsa
2 cups shredded lettuce
1 medium tomato, chopped
2 avocados, peeled and sliced
1 small onion, sliced into thin rings
Sour cream
Tortilla chips (optional)

1. Split each chicken breast in half lengthwise. 2. Mix lime juice, cumin, and salt together and brush on all surfaces of chicken breasts. 3. Place in air fryer basket and air fry at 390°F (199°C) for 12 to 15 minutes, until well done. 4. Divide the cheese evenly over chicken breasts and cook for an additional minute to melt cheese. 5. While chicken is cooking, heat refried beans on stovetop or in microwave. 6. When ready to serve, divide beans among 4 plates. Place chicken breasts on top of beans and spoon salsa over. Arrange the lettuce, tomatoes, and avocados artfully on each plate and scatter with the onion rings. 7. Pass sour cream at the table and serve with tortilla chips if desired.

Chicken Schnitzel Dogs

Prep time: 15 minutes | Cook time: 8 to 10 minutes | Serves 4

½ cup flour
½ teaspoon salt
1 teaspoon marjoram
1 teaspoon dried parsley flakes
½ teaspoon thyme
1 egg
1 teaspoon lemon juice
1 teaspoon water
1 cup bread crumbs
4 chicken tenders, pounded thin
Oil for misting or cooking spray
4 whole-grain hotdog buns
4 slices Gouda cheese
1 small Granny Smith apple, thinly sliced
½ cup shredded Napa cabbage
Coleslaw dressing

1. In a shallow dish, mix together the flour, salt, marjoram, parsley, and thyme. 2. In another shallow dish, beat together egg, lemon juice, and water. 3. Place bread crumbs in a third shallow dish. 4. Cut each of the flattened chicken tenders in half lengthwise. 5. Dip flattened chicken strips in flour mixture, then egg wash. Let excess egg drip off and roll in bread crumbs. Spray both sides with oil or cooking spray. 6. Air fry at 390°F (199°C) for 5 minutes. Spray with oil, turn over, and spray other side. 7. Cook for 3 to 5 minutes more, until well done and crispy brown. 8. To serve, place 2 schnitzel strips on bottom of each hotdog bun. Top with cheese, sliced apple, and cabbage. Drizzle with coleslaw dressing and top with other half of bun.

Grilled BBQ Chicken

Prep time: 10 minutes | Cook time: 18 to 20 minutes | Serves 4

⅓ cup no-salt-added tomato sauce
2 tablespoons low-sodium grainy mustard
2 tablespoons apple cider vinegar
1 tablespoon honey
2 garlic cloves, minced
1 jalapeño pepper, minced
3 tablespoons minced onion
4 (5 ounces / 142 g) low-sodium boneless, skinless chicken breasts

1. Preheat the air fryer to 370°F (188°C). 2. In a small bowl, stir together the tomato sauce, mustard, cider vinegar, honey, garlic, jalapeño, and onion. 3. Brush the chicken breasts with some sauce and air fry for 10 minutes. 4. Remove the air fryer basket and turn the chicken; brush with more sauce. Air fry for 5 minutes more. 5. Remove the air fryer basket and turn the chicken again; brush with more sauce. Air fry for 3 to 5 minutes more, or until the chicken reaches an internal temperature of 165°F (74°C) on a meat thermometer. Discard any remaining sauce. Serve immediately.

Easy Cajun Chicken Drumsticks

Prep time: 5 minutes | Cook time: 40 minutes | Serves 5

1 tablespoon olive oil
10 chicken drumsticks
1½ tablespoons Cajun seasoning
Salt and ground black pepper, to taste

1. Preheat the air fryer to 390°F (199°C). Grease the air fryer basket with olive oil. 2. On a clean work surface, rub the chicken drumsticks with Cajun seasoning, salt, and ground black pepper. 3. Arrange the seasoned chicken drumsticks in a single layer in the air fryer. You need to work in batches to avoid overcrowding. 4. Air fry for 18 minutes or until lightly browned. Flip the drumsticks halfway through. 5. Remove the chicken drumsticks from the air fryer. Serve immediately.

Grilled Cilantro Chicken Kebabs

Prep time: 30 minutes | Cook time: 10 minutes | Serves 4

Chutney:

½ cup unsweetened shredded coconut
½ cup hot water
2 cups fresh cilantro leaves, roughly chopped
¼ cup fresh mint leaves, roughly chopped
6 cloves garlic, roughly chopped
1 jalapeño, seeded and roughly chopped
¼ to ¾ cup water, as needed
Juice of 1 lemon

Chicken:

1 pound (454 g) boneless, skinless chicken thighs, cut crosswise into thirds
Olive oil spray

1. For the chutney: In a blender or food processor, combine the coconut and hot water; set aside to soak for 5 minutes. 2. To the processor, add the cilantro, mint, garlic, and jalapeño, along with ¼ cup water. Blend at low speed, stopping occasionally to scrape down the sides. Add the lemon juice. With the blender or processor running, add only enough additional water to keep the contents moving. Turn the blender to high once the contents are moving freely and blend until the mixture is puréed. 3. For the chicken: Place the chicken pieces in a large bowl. Add ¼ cup of the chutney and mix well to coat. Set aside the remaining chutney to use as a dip. Marinate the chicken for 15 minutes at room temperature. 4. Spray the air fryer basket with olive oil spray. Arrange the chicken in the air fryer basket. Set the air fryer to 350°F (177°C) for 10 minutes. Use a meat thermometer to ensure that the chicken has reached an internal temperature of 165°F (74°C). 5. Serve the chicken with the remaining chutney.

Chapter 4 Poultry | 33

Garlic-Infused Soy Chicken

Prep time: 10 minutes | Cook time: 30 minutes | Serves 1 to 2

2 tablespoons chicken stock
2 tablespoons reduced-sodium soy sauce
1½ tablespoons sugar
4 garlic cloves, smashed and peeled
2 large scallions, cut into 2- to 3-inch batons, plus more, thinly sliced, for garnish
2 bone-in, skin-on chicken thighs (7 to 8 ounces / 198 to 227 g each)

1. Preheat the air fryer to 375°F (191°C). 2. In a metal cake pan, combine the chicken stock, soy sauce, and sugar and stir until the sugar dissolves. Add the garlic cloves, scallions, and chicken thighs, turning the thighs to coat them in the marinade, then resting them skin-side up. Place the pan in the air fryer and bake, flipping the thighs every 5 minutes after the first 10 minutes, until the chicken is cooked through and the marinade is reduced to a sticky glaze over the chicken, about 30 minutes. 3. Remove the pan from the air fryer and serve the chicken thighs warm, with any remaining glaze spooned over top and sprinkled with more sliced scallions.

Italian Chicken with Sauce

Prep time: 15 minutes | Cook time: 20 minutes | Serves 4

2 large skinless chicken breasts (about 1¼ pounds / 567 g)
Salt and freshly ground black pepper
½ cup almond meal
½ cup grated Parmesan cheese
2 teaspoons Italian seasoning
1 egg, lightly beaten
1 tablespoon olive oil
1 cup no-sugar-added marinara sauce
4 slices Mozzarella cheese or ½ cup shredded Mozzarella

1. Preheat the air fryer to 360°F (182°C). 2. Slice the chicken breasts in half horizontally to create 4 thinner chicken breasts. Working with one piece at a time, place the chicken between two pieces of parchment paper and pound with a meat mallet or rolling pin to flatten to an even thickness. Season both sides with salt and freshly ground black pepper. 3. In a large shallow bowl, combine the almond meal, Parmesan, and Italian seasoning; stir until thoroughly combined. Place the egg in another large shallow bowl. 4. Dip the chicken in the egg, followed by the almond meal mixture, pressing the mixture firmly into the chicken to create an even coating. 5. Working in batches if necessary, arrange the chicken breasts in a single layer in the air fryer basket and coat both sides lightly with olive oil. Pausing halfway through the cooking time to flip the chicken, air fry for 15 minutes, or until a thermometer inserted into the thickest part registers 165°F (74°C). 6. Spoon the marinara sauce over each piece of chicken and top with the Mozzarella cheese. Air fry for an additional 3 to 5 minutes until the cheese is melted.

Spiced Thai Curry Meatballs

Prep time: 10 minutes | Cook time: 10 minutes | Serves 4

1 pound (454 g) ground chicken
¼ cup chopped fresh cilantro
1 teaspoon chopped fresh mint
1 tablespoon fresh lime juice
1 tablespoon Thai red, green, or yellow curry paste
1 tablespoon fish sauce
2 garlic cloves, minced
2 teaspoons minced fresh ginger
½ teaspoon kosher salt
½ teaspoon black pepper
¼ teaspoon red pepper flakes

1. Preheat the air fryer to 400°F (204°C). 2. In a large bowl, gently mix the ground chicken, cilantro, mint, lime juice, curry paste, fish sauce, garlic, ginger, salt, black pepper, and red pepper flakes until thoroughly combined. 3. Form the mixture into 16 meatballs. Place the meatballs in a single layer in the air fryer basket. Air fry for 10 minutes, turning the meatballs halfway through the cooking time. Use a meat thermometer to ensure the meatballs have reached an internal temperature of 165°F (74°C). Serve immediately.

Chicken Drumsticks with Barbecue-Honey Sauce

Prep time: 5 minutes | Cook time: 40 minutes | Serves 5

1 tablespoon olive oil
10 chicken drumsticks
Chicken seasoning or rub, to taste
Salt and ground black pepper, to taste
1 cup barbecue sauce
¼ cup honey

1. Preheat the air fryer to 390°F (199°C). Grease the air fryer basket with olive oil. 2. Rub the chicken drumsticks with chicken seasoning or rub, salt and ground black pepper on a clean work surface. 3. Arrange the chicken drumsticks in a single layer in the air fryer, then air fry for 18 minutes or until lightly browned. Flip the drumsticks halfway through. You may need to work in batches to avoid overcrowding. 4. Meanwhile, combine the barbecue sauce and honey in a small bowl. Stir to mix well. 5. Remove the drumsticks from the air fryer and baste with the sauce mixture to serve.

Hoisin-Glazed Turkey Sliders

Prep time: 30 minutes | Cook time: 20 minutes | Serves 4

Olive oil
1 pound (454 g) lean ground turkey
¼ cup whole-wheat bread crumbs
¼ cup hoisin sauce
2 tablespoons soy sauce
4 whole-wheat buns

1. Spray the air fryer basket lightly with olive oil. 2. In a large bowl, mix together the turkey, bread crumbs, hoisin sauce, and soy sauce. 3. Form the mixture into 4 equal patties. Cover with plastic wrap and refrigerate the patties for 30 minutes. 4. Place the patties in the air fryer basket in a single layer. Spray the patties lightly with olive oil. 5. Air fry at 370ºF (188ºC) for 10 minutes. Flip the patties over, lightly spray with olive oil, and cook until golden brown, an additional 5 to 10 minutes. 6. Place the patties on buns and top with your choice of low-calorie burger toppings like sliced tomatoes, onions, and cabbage slaw.

Chicken Chimichangas

Prep time: 20 minutes | Cook time: 8 to 10 minutes | Serves 4

2 cups cooked chicken, shredded
2 tablespoons chopped green chiles
½ teaspoon oregano
½ teaspoon cumin
½ teaspoon onion powder
Chimichanga Sauce:
2 tablespoons butter
2 tablespoons flour
1 cup chicken broth
¼ cup light sour cream
¼ teaspoon garlic powder
Salt and pepper, to taste
8 flour tortillas (6- or 7-inch diameter)
Oil for misting or cooking spray
¼ teaspoon salt
2 ounces (57 g) Pepper Jack or Monterey Jack cheese, shredded

1. Make the sauce by melting butter in a saucepan over medium-low heat. Stir in flour until smooth and slightly bubbly. Gradually add broth, stirring constantly until smooth. Cook and stir 1 minute, until the mixture slightly thickens. Remove from heat and stir in sour cream and salt. Set aside. 2. In a medium bowl, mix together the chicken, chiles, oregano, cumin, onion powder, garlic, salt, and pepper. Stir in 3 to 4 tablespoons of the sauce, using just enough to make the filling moist but not soupy. 3. Divide filling among the 8 tortillas. Place filling down the center of tortilla, stopping about 1 inch from edges. Fold one side of tortilla over filling, fold the two sides in, and then roll up. Mist all sides with oil or cooking spray. 4. Place chimichangas in air fryer basket seam side down. To fit more into the basket, you can stand them on their sides with the seams against the sides of the basket. 5. Air fry at 360ºF (182ºC) for 8 to 10 minutes or until heated through and crispy brown outside. 6. Add the shredded cheese to the remaining sauce. Stir over low heat, warming just until the cheese melts. Don't boil or sour cream may curdle. 7. Drizzle the sauce over the chimichangas.

BitesPeach-Cherry Glazed Chicken

Prep time: 8 minutes | Cook time: 14 to 16 minutes | Serves 4

⅓ cup peach preserves
1 teaspoon ground rosemary
½ teaspoon black pepper
½ teaspoon salt
½ teaspoon marjoram
1 teaspoon light olive oil
1 pound (454 g) boneless chicken breasts, cut in 1½-inch chunks
Oil for misting or cooking spray
1 (10-ounce / 283-g) package frozen unsweetened dark cherries, thawed and drained

1. In a medium bowl, mix together peach preserves, rosemary, pepper, salt, marjoram, and olive oil. 2. Stir in chicken chunks and toss to coat well with the preserve mixture. 3. Spray the air fryer basket with oil or cooking spray and lay chicken chunks in basket. 4. Air fry at 390ºF (199ºC) for 7 minutes. Stir. Cook for 6 to 8 more minutes or until chicken juices run clear. 5. When chicken has cooked through, scatter the cherries over and cook for additional minute to heat cherries.

Sweet Apricot Turkey Fillets

Prep time: 20 minutes | Cook time: 30 minutes | Serves 4

Olive oil
¼ cup sugar-free apricot preserves
½ tablespoon spicy brown mustard
1½ pounds (680 g) turkey breast tenderloin
Salt and freshly ground black pepper, to taste

1. Spray the air fryer basket lightly with olive oil. 2. In a small bowl, combine the apricot preserves and mustard to make a paste. 3. Season the turkey with salt and pepper. Spread the apricot paste all over the turkey. 4. Place the turkey in the air fryer basket and lightly spray with olive oil. 5. Air fry at 370ºF (188ºC) for 15 minutes. Flip the turkey over and lightly spray with olive oil. Air fry until the internal temperature reaches at least 170ºF (77ºC), an additional 10 to 15 minutes. 6. Let the turkey rest for 10 minutes before slicing and serving.

Spicy Cajun Chicken Tenders

Prep time: 10 minutes | Cook time: 17 minutes | Serves 4

2 teaspoons paprika
1 teaspoon chili powder
½ teaspoon garlic powder
½ teaspoon dried thyme
¼ teaspoon onion powder
⅛ teaspoon ground cayenne pepper
2 tablespoons coconut oil
1 pound (454 g) boneless, skinless chicken tenders
¼ cup full-fat ranch dressing

1. In a small bowl, combine all seasonings. 2. Drizzle oil over chicken tenders and then generously coat each tender in the spice mixture. Place tenders into the air fryer basket. 3. Adjust the temperature to 375°F (191°C) and air fry for 17 minutes. 4. Tenders will be 165°F (74°C) internally when fully cooked. Serve with ranch dressing for dipping.

Skewers

Prep time: 35 minutes | Cook time: 25 minutes | Serves 4

¼ cup olive oil
1 teaspoon garlic powder
1 teaspoon onion powder
1 teaspoon ground cumin
½ teaspoon dried oregano
½ teaspoon dried basil
¼ cup lemon juice
1 tablespoon apple cider vinegar
Olive oil cooking spray
1 pound (454 g) boneless skinless chicken thighs, cut into 1-inch pieces
1 red bell pepper, cut into 1-inch pieces
1 red onion, cut into 1-inch pieces
1 zucchini, cut into 1-inch pieces
12 cherry tomatoes

1. In a large bowl, mix together the olive oil, garlic powder, onion powder, cumin, oregano, basil, lemon juice, and apple cider vinegar. 2. Spray six skewers with olive oil cooking spray. 3. On each skewer, slide on a piece of chicken, then a piece of bell pepper, onion, zucchini, and finally a tomato and then repeat. Each skewer should have at least two pieces of each item. 4. Once all of the skewers are prepared, place them in a 9-by-13-inch baking dish and pour the olive oil marinade over the top of the skewers. Turn each skewer so that all sides of the chicken and vegetables are coated. 5. Cover the dish with plastic wrap and place it in the refrigerator for 30 minutes. 6. After 30 minutes, preheat the air fryer to 380°F(193°C). (If using a grill attachment, make sure it is inside the air fryer during preheating.) 7. Remove the skewers from the marinade and lay them in a single layer in the air fryer basket. If the air fryer has a grill attachment, you can also lay them on this instead. 8. Cook for 10 minutes. Rotate the kebabs, then cook them for 15 minutes more. 9. Remove the skewers from the air fryer and let them rest for 5 minutes before serving.

Tomato and Bacon Chicken Bake

Prep time: 30 minutes | Cook time: 18 minutes | Serves 6

2 leeks, sliced
2 large-sized tomatoes, chopped
3 cloves garlic, minced
½ teaspoon dried oregano
6 chicken legs, boneless and skinless
½ teaspoon smoked cayenne pepper
2 tablespoons olive oil
A freshly ground nutmeg

1. In a mixing dish, thoroughly combine all ingredients, minus the leeks. Place in the refrigerator and let it marinate overnight. 2. Lay the leeks onto the bottom of the air fryer basket. Top with the chicken legs. 3. Roast chicken legs at 375°F (191°C) for 18 minutes, turning halfway through. Serve with hoisin sauce.

Tortilla Crusted Chicken Breast

Prep time: 10 minutes | Cook time: 12 minutes | Serves 2

⅓ cup flour
1 teaspoon salt
1½ teaspoons chili powder
1 teaspoon ground cumin
Freshly ground black pepper, to taste
1 egg, beaten
¾ cup coarsely crushed yellow corn tortilla chips
2 (3 to 4 ounces / 85 to 113 g) boneless chicken breasts
Vegetable oil
½ cup salsa
½ cup crumbled queso fresco
Fresh cilantro leaves
Sour cream or guacamole (optional)

1. Set up a dredging station with three shallow dishes. Combine the flour, salt, chili powder, cumin and black pepper in the first shallow dish. Beat the egg in the second shallow dish. Place the crushed tortilla chips in the third shallow dish. 2. Dredge the chicken in the spiced flour, covering all sides of the breast. Then dip the chicken into the egg, coating the chicken completely. Finally, place the chicken into the tortilla chips and press the chips onto the chicken to make sure they adhere to all sides of the breast. Spray the coated chicken breasts on both sides with vegetable oil. 3. Preheat the air fryer to 380°F (193°C). 4. Air fry the chicken for 6 minutes. Then turn the chicken breasts over and air fry for another 6 minutes. (Increase the cooking time if you are using chicken breasts larger than 3 to 4 ounces / 85 to 113 g.) 5. When the

chicken has finished cooking, serve each breast with a little salsa, the crumbled queso fresco and cilantro as the finishing touch. Serve some sour cream and/or guacamole at the table, if desired.

Traditional Grilled Chicken Chicken with Bacon and Tomato

Prep time: 25 minutes | Cook time: 10 minutes | Serves 4

4 medium-sized skin-on chicken drumsticks	2 garlic cloves, crushed
1½ teaspoons herbs de Provence	12 ounces (340 g) crushed canned tomatoes
Salt and pepper, to taste	1 small-size leek, thinly sliced
1 tablespoon rice vinegar	2 slices smoked bacon, chopped
2 tablespoons olive oil	

1. Sprinkle the chicken drumsticks with herbs de Provence, salt and pepper; then, drizzle them with rice vinegar and olive oil. 2. Cook in the baking pan at 360°F (182°C) for 8 to 10 minutes. Pause the air fryer; stir in the remaining ingredients and continue to cook for 15 minutes longer; make sure to check them periodically. Bon appétit!

Korean Honey Wings

Prep time: 10 minutes | Cook time: 25 minutes per batch | Serves 4

¼ cup gochujang, or red pepper paste	2 teaspoons ground ginger
¼ cup mayonnaise	3 pounds (1.4 kg) whole chicken wings
2 tablespoons honey	Olive oil spray
1 tablespoon sesame oil	1 teaspoon salt
2 teaspoons minced garlic	½ teaspoon freshly ground black pepper
1 tablespoon sugar	

1. In a large bowl, whisk the gochujang, mayonnaise, honey, sesame oil, garlic, sugar, and ginger. Set aside. 2. Insert the crisper plate into the basket and the basket into the unit. Preheat the unit by selecting AIR FRY, setting the temperature to 400°F (204°C), and setting the time to 3 minutes. Select START/STOP to begin. 3. To prepare the chicken wings, cut the wings in half. The meatier part is the drumette. Cut off and discard the wing tip from the flat part (or save the wing tips in the freezer to make chicken stock). 4. Once the unit is preheated, spray the crisper plate with olive oil. Working in batches, place half the chicken wings into the basket, spray them with olive oil, and sprinkle with the salt and pepper. 5. Select AIR FRY, set the temperature to 400°F (204°C), and set the time to 20 minutes. Select START/STOP to begin. 6. After 10 minutes, remove the basket, flip the wings, and spray them with more olive oil. Reinsert the basket to resume cooking. 7. Cook the wings to an internal temperature of 165°F (74°C), then transfer them to the bowl with the prepared sauce and toss to coat. 8. Repeat steps 4, 5, 6, and 7 for the remaining chicken wings. 9. Return the coated wings to the basket and air fry for 4 to 6 minutes more until the sauce has glazed the wings and the chicken is crisp. After 3 minutes, check the wings to make sure they aren't burning. Serve hot.

Chicken Thighs in Waffles

Prep time: 1 hour 20 minutes | Cook time: 40 minutes | Serves 4

For the chicken:

4 chicken thighs, skin on	1 teaspoon kosher salt
1 cup low-fat buttermilk	½ teaspoon freshly ground black pepper
½ cup all-purpose flour	¼ cup honey, for serving
½ teaspoon garlic powder	Cooking spray
½ teaspoon mustard powder	

For the waffles:

½ cup all-purpose flour	1 teaspoon baking powder
½ cup whole wheat pastry flour	2 tablespoons canola oil
1 large egg, beaten	½ teaspoon kosher salt
1 cup low-fat buttermilk	1 tablespoon granulated sugar

1. Combine the chicken thighs with buttermilk in a large bowl. Wrap the bowl in plastic and refrigerate to marinate for at least an hour. 2. Preheat the air fryer to 360°F (182°C). Spritz the air fryer basket with cooking spray. 3. Combine the flour, mustard powder, garlic powder, salt, and black pepper in a shallow dish. Stir to mix well. 4. Remove the thighs from the buttermilk and pat dry with paper towels. Sit the bowl of buttermilk aside. 5. Dip the thighs in the flour mixture first, then into the buttermilk, and then into the flour mixture. Shake the excess off. 6. Arrange 2 thighs in the preheated air fryer and spritz with cooking spray. Air fryer for 20 minutes or until an instant-read thermometer inserted in the thickest part of the chicken thighs registers at least 165°F (74°C). flip the thighs halfway through. Repeat with remaining thighs. 7. Meanwhile, make the waffles: combine the ingredients for the waffles in a large bowl. Stir to mix well, then arrange the mixture in a waffle iron and cook until a golden and fragrant waffle forms. 8. Remove the waffles from the waffle iron and slice into 4 pieces. Remove the chicken thighs from the air fryer and allow to cool for 5 minutes. 9. Arrange each chicken thigh on each waffle piece and drizzle with 1 tablespoon of honey. Serve warm.

Chapter 5
Beef, Pork, and Lamb

Sumptuous Pizza Tortilla Rolls

Prep time: 10 minutes | Cook time: 6 minutes | Serves 4

1 teaspoon butter
½ medium onion, slivered
½ red or green bell pepper, julienned
4 ounces (113 g) fresh white mushrooms, chopped
½ cup pizza sauce
8 flour tortillas
8 thin slices deli ham
24 pepperoni slices
1 cup shredded Mozzarella cheese
Cooking spray

1. Preheat the air fryer to 390°F (199°C). 2. Put butter, onions, bell pepper, and mushrooms in a baking pan. Bake in the preheated air fryer for 3 minutes. Stir and cook 3 to 4 minutes longer until just crisp and tender. Remove pan and set aside. 3. To assemble rolls, spread about 2 teaspoons of pizza sauce on one half of each tortilla. Top with a slice of ham and 3 slices of pepperoni. Divide sautéed vegetables among tortillas and top with cheese. 4. Roll up tortillas, secure with toothpicks if needed, and spray with oil. 5. Put 4 rolls in air fryer basket and air fry for 4 minutes. Turn and air fry 4 minutes, until heated through and lightly browned. 6. Repeat step 4 to air fry remaining pizza rolls. 7. Serve immediately.

Mint and Chile Indian-Style Kebabs

Prep time: 30 minutes | Cook time: 15 minutes | Serves 4

1 pound (454 g) ground lamb
½ cup finely minced onion
¼ cup chopped fresh mint
¼ cup chopped fresh cilantro
1 tablespoon minced garlic
½ teaspoon ground turmeric
½ teaspoon cayenne pepper
¼ teaspoon ground cardamom
¼ teaspoon ground cinnamon
1 teaspoon kosher salt

1. In the bowl of a stand mixer fitted with the paddle attachment, combine the lamb, onion, mint, cilantro, garlic, turmeric, cayenne, cardamom, cinnamon, and salt. Mix on low speed until you have a sticky mess of spiced meat. If you have time, let the mixture stand at room temperature for 30 minutes (or cover and refrigerate for up to a day or two, until you're ready to make the kebabs). 2. Divide the meat into eight equal portions. Form each into a long sausage shape. Place the kebabs in a single layer in the air fryer basket. Set the air fryer to 350°F (177°C) for 10 minutes. Increase the air fryer temperature to 400°F (204°C) and cook for 3 to 4 minutes more to brown the kebabs. Use a meat thermometer to ensure the kebabs have reached an internal temperature of 160°F / 71°C (medium).

Juicy Beef Chuck Cheeseburgers

Prep time: 10 minutes | Cook time: 15 minutes | Serves 4

¾ pound (340 g) ground beef chuck
1 envelope onion soup mix
Kosher salt and freshly ground black pepper, to taste
1 teaspoon paprika
4 slices Monterey Jack cheese
4 ciabatta rolls

1. In a bowl, stir together the ground chuck, onion soup mix, salt, black pepper, and paprika to combine well. 2. Preheat the air fryer to 385°F (196°C). 3. Take four equal portions of the mixture and mold each one into a patty. Transfer to the air fryer and air fry for 10 minutes. 4. Put the slices of cheese on the top of the burgers. 5. Air fry for another minute before serving on ciabatta rolls.

Air Fried Beef Satay with Peanut Dipping Sauce

Prep time: 30 minutes | Cook time: 5 to 7 minutes | Serves 4

8 ounces (227 g) London broil, sliced into 8 strips
2 teaspoons curry powder
½ teaspoon kosher salt
Cooking spray

Peanut Dipping sauce:

2 tablespoons creamy peanut butter
1 tablespoon reduced-sodium soy sauce
2 teaspoons rice vinegar
1 teaspoon honey
1 teaspoon grated ginger

Special Equipment:

4 bamboo skewers, cut into halves and soaked in water for 20 minutes to keep them from burning while cooking

1. Preheat the air fryer to 360°F (182°C). Spritz the air fryer basket with cooking spray. 2. In a bowl, place the London broil strips and sprinkle with the curry powder and kosher salt to season. Thread the strips onto the soaked skewers. 3. Arrange the skewers in the prepared air fryer basket and spritz with cooking spray. Air fry for 5 to 7 minutes, or until the beef is well browned, turning halfway through. 4. In the meantime, stir together the peanut butter, soy sauce, rice vinegar, honey, and ginger in a bowl to make the dipping sauce. 5. Transfer the beef to the serving dishes and let rest for 5 minutes. Serve with the peanut dipping sauce on the side.

Italian-Style Rolled Steaks

Prep time: 30 minutes | Cook time: 9 minutes | Serves 4

1 tablespoon vegetable oil	thick
2 cloves garlic, minced	1 (10-ounce / 283-g) package frozen spinach, thawed and squeezed dry
2 teaspoons dried Italian seasoning	½ cup diced jarred roasted red pepper
1 teaspoon kosher salt	1 cup shredded Mozzarella cheese
1 teaspoon black pepper	
1 pound (454 g) flank or skirt steak, ¼ to ½ inch	

1. In a large bowl, combine the oil, garlic, Italian seasoning, salt, and pepper. Whisk to combine. Add the steak to the bowl, turning to ensure the entire steak is covered with the seasonings. Cover and marinate at room temperature for 30 minutes or in the refrigerator for up to 24 hours. 2. Lay the steak on a flat surface. Spread the spinach evenly over the steak, leaving a ¼-inch border at the edge. Evenly top each steak with the red pepper and cheese. 3. Starting at a long end, roll up the steak as tightly as possible, ending seam side down. Use 2 or 3 wooden toothpicks to hold the roll together. Using a sharp knife, cut the roll in half so that it better fits in the air fryer basket. 4. Place the steak roll, seam side down, in the air fryer basket. Set the air fryer to 400°F (204°C) for 9 minutes. Use a meat thermometer to ensure the steak has reached an internal temperature of 145°F (63°C). (It is critical to not overcook flank steak, so as to not toughen the meat.) 5. Let the steak rest for 10 minutes before cutting into slices to serve.

Kielbasa Sausage with Pineapple and Bell Peppers

Prep time: 15 minutes | Cook time: 10 minutes | Serves 2 to 4

¾ pound (340 g) kielbasa sausage, cut into ½-inch slices	1 cup bell pepper chunks
	1 tablespoon barbecue seasoning
1 (8-ounce / 227-g) can pineapple chunks in juice, drained	1 tablespoon soy sauce
	Cooking spray

1. Preheat the air fryer to 390°F (199°C). Spritz the air fryer basket with cooking spray. 2. Combine all the ingredients in a large bowl. Toss to mix well. 3. Pour the sausage mixture in the preheated air fryer. 4. Air fry for 10 minutes or until the sausage is lightly browned and the bell pepper and pineapple are soft. Shake the basket halfway through. Serve immediately.

Golden Air-Fried Venison

Prep time: 30 minutes | Cook time: 20 minutes | Serves 6

¼ cup minced yellow onion	½ teaspoon black pepper
2 tablespoons sugar	1½ pounds (680 g) boneless pork shoulder, cut into ½-inch-thick slices
2 tablespoons vegetable oil	
1 tablespoon minced garlic	¼ cup chopped salted roasted peanuts
1 tablespoon fish sauce	
1 tablespoon minced fresh lemongrass	2 tablespoons chopped fresh cilantro or parsley
2 teaspoons dark soy sauce	

1. In a large bowl, combine the onion, sugar, vegetable oil, garlic, fish sauce, lemongrass, soy sauce, and pepper. Add the pork and toss to coat. Marinate at room temperature for 30 minutes, or cover and refrigerate for up to 24 hours. 2. Arrange the pork slices in the air fryer basket; discard the marinade. Set the air fryer to 400°F (204°C) for 20 minutes, turning the pork halfway through the cooking time. 3. Transfer the pork to a serving platter. Sprinkle with the peanuts and cilantro and serve.

Deconstructed Chicago Dogs

Prep time: 10 minutes | Cook time: 7 minutes | Serves 4

4 hot dogs	dice
2 large dill pickles	4 pickled sport peppers, diced
¼ cup diced onions	
1 tomato, cut into ½-inch	

For Garnish (Optional):

Brown mustard	Poppy seeds
Celery salt	

1. Spray the air fryer basket with avocado oil. Preheat the air fryer to 400°F (204°C). 2. Place the hot dogs in the air fryer basket and air fry for 5 to 7 minutes, until hot and slightly crispy. 3. While the hot dogs cook, quarter one of the dill pickles lengthwise, so that you have 4 pickle spears. Finely dice the other pickle. 4. When the hot dogs are done, transfer them to a serving platter and arrange them in a row, alternating with the pickle spears. Top with the diced pickles, onions, tomato, and sport peppers. Drizzle brown mustard on top and garnish with celery salt and poppy seeds, if desired. 5. Best served fresh. Store leftover hot dogs in an airtight container in the refrigerator for up to 3 days. Reheat in a preheated 390°F (199°C) air fryer for 2 minutes, or until warmed through.

Greek Pork with Tzatziki Sauce

Prep time: 30 minutes | Cook time: 50 minutes | Serves 4

Greek Pork:
2 pounds (907 g) pork sirloin roast
Salt and black pepper, to taste
1 teaspoon smoked paprika
½ teaspoon mustard seeds
½ teaspoon celery seeds
Tzatziki:
½ cucumber, finely chopped and squeezed
1 cup full-fat Greek yogurt
1 garlic clove, minced
1 tablespoon extra-virgin olive oil
1 teaspoon fennel seeds
1 teaspoon Ancho chili powder
1 teaspoon turmeric powder
½ teaspoon ground ginger
2 tablespoons olive oil
2 cloves garlic, finely chopped

1 teaspoon balsamic vinegar
1 teaspoon minced fresh dill
A pinch of salt

1. Toss all ingredients for Greek pork in a large mixing bowl. Toss until the meat is well coated. 2. Cook in the preheated air fryer at 360ºF (182ºC) for 30 minutes; turn over and cook another 20 minutes. 3. Meanwhile, prepare the tzatziki by mixing all the tzatziki ingredients. Place in your refrigerator until ready to use. 4. Serve the pork sirloin roast with the chilled tzatziki on the side. Enjoy!

Cheese-Topped Low-Carb Lasagna

Prep time: 10 minutes | Cook time: 10 minutes | Serves 4

Meat Layer:
Extra-virgin olive oil
1 pound (454 g) 85% lean ground beef
1 cup prepared marinara sauce
Cheese Layer:
8 ounces (227 g) ricotta cheese
1 cup shredded Mozzarella cheese
½ cup grated Parmesan cheese

¼ cup diced celery
¼ cup diced red onion
½ teaspoon minced garlic
Kosher salt and black pepper, to taste

2 large eggs
1 teaspoon dried Italian seasoning, crushed
½ teaspoon each minced garlic, garlic powder, and black pepper

1. For the meat layer: Grease a cake pan with 1 teaspoon olive oil. 2. In a large bowl, combine the ground beef, marinara, celery, onion, garlic, salt, and pepper. Place the seasoned meat in the pan. 3. Place the pan in the air fryer basket. Set the air fryer to 375ºF (191ºC) for 10 minutes. 4. Meanwhile, for the cheese layer: In a medium bowl, combine the ricotta, half the Mozzarella, the Parmesan, lightly beaten eggs, Italian seasoning, minced garlic, garlic powder, and pepper. Stir until well blended. 5. At the end of the cooking time, spread the cheese mixture over the meat mixture. Sprinkle with the remaining ½ cup Mozzarella. Set the air fryer to 375ºF (191ºC) for 10 minutes, or until the cheese is browned and bubbling. 6. At the end of the cooking time, use a meat thermometer to ensure the meat has reached an internal temperature of 160ºF (71ºC). 7. Drain the fat and liquid from the pan. Let stand for 5 minutes before serving.

Bone-in Pork Chops

Prep time: 5 minutes | Cook time: 10 to 12 minutes | Serves 2

1 pound (454 g) bone-in pork chops
1 tablespoon avocado oil
1 teaspoon smoked paprika
½ teaspoon onion powder
¼ teaspoon cayenne pepper
Sea salt and freshly ground black pepper, to taste

1. Brush the pork chops with the avocado oil. In a small dish, mix together the smoked paprika, onion powder, cayenne pepper, and salt and black pepper to taste. Sprinkle the seasonings over both sides of the pork chops. 2. Set the air fryer to 400ºF (204ºC). Place the chops in the air fryer basket in a single layer, working in batches if necessary. Air fry for 10 to 12 minutes, until an instant-read thermometer reads 145ºF (63ºC) at the chops' thickest point. 3. Remove the chops from the air fryer and allow them to rest for 5 minutes before serving.

Italian Sausage and Cheese Meatballs

Prep time: 10 minutes | Cook time: 20 minutes | Serves 4

½ pound (227 g) bulk Italian sausage
½ pound (227 g) 85% lean ground beef
½ cup shredded sharp
Cheddar cheese
½ teaspoon onion powder
½ teaspoon garlic powder
½ teaspoon black pepper

1. In a large bowl, gently mix the sausage, ground beef, cheese, onion powder, garlic powder, and pepper until well combined. 2. Form the mixture into 16 meatballs. Place the meatballs in a single layer in the air fryer basket. Set the air fryer to 350ºF (177ºC) for 20 minutes, turning the meatballs halfway through the cooking time. Use a meat thermometer to ensure the meatballs have reached an internal temperature of 160ºF / 71ºC (medium).

Broccoli Pork Teriyaki Stir-Fry

Prep time: 10 minutes | Cook time: 13 minutes | Serves 4

1 head broccoli, trimmed into florets	tenderloin, trimmed and cut into 1-inch pieces
1 tablespoon extra-virgin olive oil	½ cup teriyaki sauce, divided
¼ teaspoon sea salt	Olive oil spray
¼ teaspoon freshly ground black pepper	2 cups cooked brown rice
1 pound (454 g) pork	Sesame seeds, for garnish

1. Insert the crisper plate into the basket and the basket into the unit. Preheat the unit by selecting AIR ROAST, setting the temperature to 400°F (204°C), and setting the time to 3 minutes. Select START/STOP to begin. 2. In a large bowl, toss together the broccoli, olive oil, salt, and pepper. 3. In a medium bowl, toss together the pork and 3 tablespoons of teriyaki sauce to coat the meat. 4. Once the unit is preheated, spray the crisper plate with olive oil. Put the broccoli and pork into the basket. Spray them with olive oil and drizzle with 1 tablespoon of teriyaki sauce. 5. Select AIR ROAST, set the temperature to 400°F (204°C), and set the time to 13 minutes. Select START/STOP to begin. 6. After 10 to 12 minutes, the broccoli is tender and light golden brown and a food thermometer inserted into the pork should register 145°F (63°C). Remove the basket and drizzle the broccoli and pork with the remaining ¼ cup of teriyaki sauce and toss to coat. Reinsert the basket to resume cooking for 1 minute. 7. When the cooking is complete, serve immediately over the hot cooked rice, if desired, garnished with the sesame seeds.

Herbed Milanese Pork Cutlets

Prep time: 10 minutes | Cook time: 12 minutes | Serves 4

4 (1-inch) boneless pork chops	¾ cup powdered Parmesan cheese
Fine sea salt and ground black pepper, to taste	Chopped fresh parsley, for garnish
2 large eggs	Lemon slices, for serving

1. Spray the air fryer basket with avocado oil. Preheat the air fryer to 400°F (204°C). 2. Place the pork chops between 2 sheets of plastic wrap and pound them with the flat side of a meat tenderizer until they're ¼ inch thick. Lightly season both sides of the chops with salt and pepper. 3. Lightly beat the eggs in a shallow bowl. Divide the Parmesan cheese evenly between 2 bowls and set the bowls in this order: Parmesan, eggs, Parmesan. Dredge a chop in the first bowl of Parmesan, then dip it in the eggs, and then dredge it again in the second bowl of Parmesan, making sure both sides and all edges are well coated. Repeat with the remaining chops. 4. Place the chops in the air fryer basket and air fry for 12 minutes, or until the internal temperature reaches 145°F (63°C), flipping halfway through. 5. Garnish with fresh parsley and serve immediately with lemon slices. Store leftovers in an airtight container in the refrigerator for up to 3 days. Reheat in a preheated 390°F (199°C) air fryer for 5 minutes, or until warmed through.

Vietnamese Shaking Beef

Prep time: 50 minutes | Cook time: 8 minutes | Serves 4

For the Meat:

2 teaspoons soy sauce	1 teaspoon toasted sesame oil
4 garlic cloves, minced	1½ pounds (680 g) top sirloin steak, cut into 1-inch cubes
1 teaspoon kosher salt	
2 teaspoons sugar	
¼ teaspoon ground black pepper	Cooking spray

For the Salad:

1 head Bibb lettuce, leaves separated and torn into large pieces	2 tablespoons apple cider vinegar
¼ cup fresh mint leaves	1 garlic clove, minced
½ cup halved grape tomatoes	2 teaspoons sugar
½ red onion, halved and thinly sliced	¼ teaspoon kosher salt
	¼ teaspoon ground black pepper
	2 tablespoons vegetable oil

For Serving:

Lime wedges, for garnish	cracked black pepper, to taste
Coarse salt and freshly	

1. Combine the ingredients for the meat, except for the steak, in a large bowl. Stir to mix well. 2. Dunk the steak cubes in the bowl and press to coat. Wrap the bowl in plastic and marinate under room temperature for at least 30 minutes. 3. Preheat the air fryer to 450°F (232°C). Spritz the air fryer basket with cooking spray. 4. Discard the marinade and transfer the steak cubes in the preheated air fryer basket. You need to air fry in batches to avoid overcrowding. 5. Air fry for 4 minutes or until the steak cubes are lightly browned but still have a little pink. Shake the basket halfway through the cooking time. 6. Meanwhile, combine the ingredients for the salad in a separate large bowl. Toss to mix well. 7. Pour the salad in a large serving bowl and top with the steak cubes. Squeeze the lime wedges over and sprinkle with salt and black pepper before serving.

Cube Steak Roll-Ups

Prep time: 30 minutes | Cook time: 8 to 10 minutes | Serves 4

4 cube steaks (6 ounces / 170 g each)	½ cup finely chopped yellow onion
1 (16-ounce / 454-g) bottle Italian dressing	½ cup finely chopped green bell pepper
1 teaspoon salt	½ cup finely chopped mushrooms
½ teaspoon freshly ground black pepper	1 to 2 tablespoons oil

1. In a large resealable bag or airtight storage container, combine the steaks and Italian dressing. Seal the bag and refrigerate to marinate for 2 hours. 2. Remove the steaks from the marinade and place them on a cutting board. Discard the marinade. Evenly season the steaks with salt and pepper. 3. In a small bowl, stir together the onion, bell pepper, and mushrooms. Sprinkle the onion mixture evenly over the steaks. Roll up the steaks, jelly roll-style, and secure with toothpicks. 4. Preheat the air fryer to 400ºF (204ºC). 5. Place the steaks in the air fryer basket. 6. Cook for 4 minutes. Flip the steaks and spritz them with oil. Cook for 4 to 6 minutes more until the internal temperature reaches 145ºF (63ºC). Let rest for 5 minutes before serving.

Fajita-Spiced Meatball Wraps

Prep time: 10 minutes | Cook time: 10 minutes | Serves 4

1 pound (454 g) ground beef (85% lean)	bell peppers
½ cup salsa, plus more for serving if desired	1 large egg, beaten
	1 teaspoon fine sea salt
¼ cup chopped onions	½ teaspoon chili powder
¼ cup diced green or red	½ teaspoon ground cumin
	1 clove garlic, minced

For Serving (Optional):
8 leaves Boston lettuce	Lime slices
Pico de gallo or salsa	

1. Spray the air fryer basket with avocado oil. Preheat the air fryer to 350ºF (177ºC). 2. In a large bowl, mix together all the ingredients until well combined. 3. Shape the meat mixture into eight 1-inch balls. Place the meatballs in the air fryer basket, leaving a little space between them. Air fry for 10 minutes, or until cooked through and no longer pink inside and the internal temperature reaches 145ºF (63ºC). 4. Serve each meatball on a lettuce leaf, topped with pico de gallo or salsa, if desired. Serve with lime slices if desired. 5. Store leftovers in an airtight container in the fridge for 3 days or in the freezer for up to a month. Reheat in a preheated 350ºF (177ºC) air fryer for 4 minutes, or until heated through.

Bean and Beef Meatball Taco Pizza

Prep time: 10 minutes | Cook time: 7 to 9 minutes per batch | Serves 4

¾ cup refried beans (from a 16-ounce / 454-g can)	4 whole-wheat pita breads
	1 cup shredded pepper Jack cheese
½ cup salsa	½ cup shredded Colby cheese
10 frozen precooked beef meatballs, thawed and sliced	
	Cooking oil spray
1 jalapeño pepper, sliced	⅓ cup sour cream

1. In a medium bowl, stir together the refried beans, salsa, meatballs, and jalapeño. 2. Insert the crisper plate into the basket and the basket into the unit. Preheat the unit by selecting BAKE, setting the temperature to 375ºF (191ºC), and setting the time to 3 minutes. Select START/STOP to begin. 3. Top the pitas with the refried bean mixture and sprinkle with the cheeses. 4. Once the unit is preheated, spray the crisper plate with cooking oil. Working in batches, place the pizzas into the basket. Select BAKE, set the temperature to 375ºF (191ºC), and set the time to 9 minutes. Select START/STOP to begin. 5. After about 7 minutes, check the pizzas. They are done when the cheese is melted and starts to brown. If not ready, resume cooking. 6. When the cooking is complete, top each pizza with a dollop of sour cream and serve warm.

Extra Bacon and Meat Combo

Prep time: 5 minutes | Cook time: 1 hour | Serves 4

30 slices thick-cut bacon	10 ounces (283 g) pork sausage
4 ounces (113 g) Cheddar cheese, shredded	
12 ounces (340 g) steak	Salt and ground black pepper, to taste

1. Preheat the air fryer to 400ºF (204ºC). 2. Lay out 30 slices of bacon in a woven pattern and bake for 20 minutes until crisp. Put the cheese in the center of the bacon. 3. Combine the steak and sausage to form a meaty mixture. 4. Lay out the meat in a rectangle of similar size to the bacon strips. Season with salt and pepper. 5. Roll the meat into a tight roll and refrigerate. 6. Preheat the air fryer to 400ºF (204ºC). 7. Make a 7×7 bacon weave and roll the bacon weave over the meat, diagonally. 8. Bake for 60 minutes or until the internal temperature reaches at least 165ºF (74ºC). 9. Let rest for 5 minutes before serving.

Nigerian Peanut-Crusted Flank Steak

Prep time: 30 minutes | Cook time: 8 minutes | Serves 4

Suya Spice Mix:
¼ cup dry-roasted peanuts
1 teaspoon cumin seeds
1 teaspoon garlic powder
1 teaspoon smoked paprika
½ teaspoon ground ginger
1 teaspoon kosher salt
½ teaspoon cayenne pepper

Steak:
1 pound (454 g) flank steak
2 tablespoons vegetable oil

1. For the spice mix: In a clean coffee grinder or spice mill, combine the peanuts and cumin seeds. Process until you get a coarse powder. (Do not overprocess or you will wind up with peanut butter! Alternatively, you can grind the cumin with ⅓ cup ready-made peanut powder, such as PB2, instead of the peanuts.) 2. Pour the peanut mixture into a small bowl, add the garlic powder, paprika, ginger, salt, and cayenne, and stir to combine. This recipe makes about ½ cup suya spice mix. Store leftovers in an airtight container in a cool, dry place for up to 1 month. 3. For the steak: Cut the flank steak into ½-inch-thick slices, cutting against the grain and at a slight angle. Place the beef strips in a resealable plastic bag and add the oil and 2½ to 3 tablespoons of the spice mixture. Seal the bag and massage to coat all of the meat with the oil and spice mixture. Marinate at room temperature for 30 minutes or in the refrigerator for up to 24 hours. 4. Place the beef strips in the air fryer basket. Set the air fryer to 400ºF (204ºC) for 8 minutes, turning the strips halfway through the cooking time. 5. Transfer the meat to a serving platter. Sprinkle with additional spice mix, if desired.

Golden Lemon Pork Schnitzel

Prep time: 15 minutes | Cook time: 15 minutes | Serves 4

4 thin boneless pork loin chops
2 tablespoons lemon juice
½ cup flour
¼ teaspoon marjoram
1 teaspoon salt
1 cup panko breadcrumbs
2 eggs
Lemon wedges, for serving
Cooking spray

1. Preheat the air fryer to 390ºF (199ºC) and spritz with cooking spray. 2. On a clean work surface, drizzle the pork chops with lemon juice on both sides. 3. Combine the flour with marjoram and salt on a shallow plate. Pour the breadcrumbs on a separate shallow dish. Beat the eggs in a large bowl. 4. Dredge the pork chops in the flour, then dunk in the beaten eggs to coat well. Shake the excess off and roll over the breadcrumbs. 5. Arrange the chops in the preheated air fryer and spritz with cooking spray. Air fry for 15 minutes or until the chops are golden and crispy. Flip the chops halfway through. Squeeze the lemon wedges over the fried chops and serve immediately.

Pork Loin Roast

Prep time: 30 minutes | Cook time: 55 minutes | Serves 6

1½ pounds (680 g) boneless pork loin roast, washed
1 teaspoon mustard seeds
1 teaspoon garlic powder
1 teaspoon porcini powder
1 teaspoon shallot powder
¾ teaspoon sea salt flakes
1 teaspoon red pepper flakes, crushed
2 dried sprigs thyme, crushed
2 tablespoons lime juice

1. Firstly, score the meat using a small knife; make sure to not cut too deep. 2. In a small-sized mixing dish, combine all seasonings in the order listed above; mix to combine well. 3. Massage the spice mix into the pork meat to evenly distribute. Drizzle with lemon juice. 4. Set the air fryer to 360ºF (182ºC). Place the pork in the air fryer basket; roast for 25 to 30 minutes. Pause the machine, check for doneness and cook for 25 minutes more.

Bacon Wrapped Pork with Apple Gravy

Prep time: 10 minutes | Cook time: 25 minutes | Serves 4

Pork:
1 tablespoons Dijon mustard
1 pork tenderloin
3 strips bacon

Apple Gravy:
3 tablespoons ghee, divided
1 small shallot, chopped
2 apples
1 tablespoon almond flour
1 cup vegetable broth
½ teaspoon Dijon mustard

1. Preheat the air fryer to 360ºF (182ºC). 2. Spread Dijon mustard all over tenderloin and wrap with strips of bacon. 3. Put into air fryer and air fry for 12 minutes. Use a meat thermometer to check for doneness. 4. To make sauce, heat 1 tablespoons of ghee in a pan and add shallots. Cook for 1 minute. 5. Then add apples, cooking for 4 minutes until softened. 6. Add flour and 2 tablespoons of ghee to make a roux. Add broth and mustard, stirring well to combine. 7. When sauce starts to bubble, add 1 cup of sautéed apples, cooking until sauce thickens. 8. Once pork tenderloin is cooked, allow to sit 8 minutes to rest before slicing. 9. Serve topped with apple gravy.

Grilled Ribeye with Rosemary

Prep time: 10 minutes | Cook time: 15 minutes | Serves 2

¼ cup butter
1 clove garlic, minced
Salt and ground black pepper, to taste
1½ tablespoons balsamic vinegar
¼ cup rosemary, chopped
2 ribeye steaks

1. Melt the butter in a skillet over medium heat. Add the garlic and fry until fragrant. 2. Remove the skillet from the heat and add the salt, pepper, and vinegar. Allow it to cool. 3. Add the rosemary, then pour the mixture into a Ziploc bag. 4. Put the ribeye steaks in the bag and shake well, coating the meat well. Refrigerate for an hour, then allow to sit for a further twenty minutes. 5. Preheat the air fryer to 400°F (204°C). 6. Air fry the ribeye steaks for 15 minutes. 7. Take care when removing the steaks from the air fryer and plate up. 8. Serve immediately.

Meatballs with Zucchini Noodles

Prep time: 30 minutes | Cook time: 11 to 13 minutes | Serves 6

1 pound (454 g) ground beef
1½ teaspoons sea salt, plus more for seasoning
1 large egg, beaten
1 teaspoon gelatin
¾ cup Parmesan cheese
2 teaspoons minced garlic
1 teaspoon Italian seasoning
Freshly ground black pepper, to taste
Avocado oil spray
Keto-friendly marinara sauce, for serving
6 ounces (170 g) zucchini noodles, made using a spiralizer or store-bought

1. Place the ground beef in a large bowl, and season with the salt. 2. Place the egg in a separate bowl and sprinkle with the gelatin. Allow to sit for 5 minutes. 3. Stir the gelatin mixture, then pour it over the ground beef. Add the Parmesan, garlic, and Italian seasoning. Season with salt and pepper. 4. Form the mixture into 1½-inch meatballs and place them on a plate; cover with plastic wrap and refrigerate for at least 1 hour or overnight. 5. Spray the meatballs with oil. Set the air fryer to 400°F (204°C) and arrange the meatballs in a single layer in the air fryer basket. Air fry for 4 minutes. Flip the meatballs and spray them with more oil. Air fry for 4 minutes more, until an instant-read thermometer reads 160°F (71°C). Transfer the meatballs to a plate and allow them to rest. 6. While the meatballs are resting, heat the marinara in a saucepan on the stove over medium heat. 7. Place the zucchini noodles in the air fryer, and cook at 400°F (204°C) for 3 to 5 minutes. 8. To serve, place the zucchini noodles in serving bowls. Top with meatballs and warm marinara.

Buttery Pork Chops

Prep time: 5 minutes | Cook time: 12 minutes | Serves 4

4 (4-ounce / 113-g) boneless pork chops
½ teaspoon salt
¼ teaspoon ground black pepper
2 tablespoons salted butter, softened

1. Sprinkle pork chops on all sides with salt and pepper. Place chops into ungreased air fryer basket in a single layer. Adjust the temperature to 400°F (204°C) and air fry for 12 minutes. Pork chops will be golden and have an internal temperature of at least 145°F (63°C) when done. 2. Use tongs to remove cooked pork chops from air fryer and place onto a large plate. Top each chop with ½ tablespoon butter and let sit 2 minutes to melt. Serve warm.

Herb Pistachio Rack of Lamb

Prep time: 10 minutes | Cook time: 19 minutes | Serves 2

½ cup finely chopped pistachios
3 tablespoons panko bread crumbs
1 teaspoon chopped fresh rosemary
2 teaspoons chopped fresh oregano
Salt and freshly ground black pepper, to taste
1 tablespoon olive oil
1 rack of lamb, bones trimmed of fat and frenched
1 tablespoon Dijon mustard

1. Preheat the air fryer to 380°F (193°C). 2. Combine the pistachios, bread crumbs, rosemary, oregano, salt and pepper in a small bowl. (This is a good job for your food processor if you have one.) Drizzle in the olive oil and stir to combine. 3. Season the rack of lamb with salt and pepper on all sides and transfer it to the air fryer basket with the fat side facing up. Air fry the lamb for 12 minutes. Remove the lamb from the air fryer and brush the fat side of the lamb rack with the Dijon mustard. Coat the rack with the pistachio mixture, pressing the bread crumbs onto the lamb with your hands and rolling the bottom of the rack in any of the crumbs that fall off. 4. Return the rack of lamb to the air fryer and air fry for another 3 to 7 minutes or until an instant read thermometer reads 140°F (60°C) for medium. Add or subtract a couple of minutes for lamb that is more or less well cooked. (Your time will vary depending on how big the rack of lamb is.) 5. Let the lamb rest for at least 5 minutes. Then, slice into chops and serve.

Poblano Pepper Cheeseburgers

Prep time: 5 minutes | Cook time: 30 minutes | Serves 4

2 poblano chile peppers
1½ pounds (680 g) 85% lean ground beef
1 clove garlic, minced
1 teaspoon salt
½ teaspoon freshly ground black pepper
4 slices Cheddar cheese (about 3 ounces / 85 g)
4 large lettuce leaves

1. Preheat the air fryer to 400°F (204°C). 2. Arrange the poblano peppers in the basket of the air fryer. Pausing halfway through the cooking time to turn the peppers, air fry for 20 minutes, or until they are softened and beginning to char. Transfer the peppers to a large bowl and cover with a plate. When cool enough to handle, peel off the skin, remove the seeds and stems, and slice into strips. Set aside. 3. Meanwhile, in a large bowl, combine the ground beef with the garlic, salt, and pepper. Shape the beef into 4 patties. 4. Lower the heat on the air fryer to 360°F (182°C). Arrange the burgers in a single layer in the basket of the air fryer. Pausing halfway through the cooking time to turn the burgers, air fry for 10 minutes, or until a thermometer inserted into the thickest part registers 160°F (71°C). 5. Top the burgers with the cheese slices and continue baking for a minute or two, just until the cheese has melted. Serve the burgers on a lettuce leaf topped with the roasted poblano peppers.

Saucy Beef Fingers

Prep time: 30 minutes | Cook time: 14 minutes | Serves 4

1½ pounds (680 g) sirloin steak
¼ cup red wine
¼ cup fresh lime juice
1 teaspoon garlic powder
1 teaspoon shallot powder
1 teaspoon celery seeds
1 teaspoon mustard seeds
Coarse sea salt and ground black pepper, to taste
1 teaspoon red pepper flakes
2 eggs, lightly whisked
1 cup Parmesan cheese
1 teaspoon paprika

1. Place the steak, red wine, lime juice, garlic powder, shallot powder, celery seeds, mustard seeds, salt, black pepper, and red pepper in a large ceramic bowl; let it marinate for 3 hours. 2. Tenderize the cube steak by pounding with a mallet; cut into 1-inch strips. 3. In a shallow bowl, whisk the eggs. In another bowl, mix the Parmesan cheese and paprika. 4. Dip the beef pieces into the whisked eggs and coat on all sides. Now, dredge the beef pieces in the Parmesan mixture. 5. Cook at 400°F (204°C) for 14 minutes, flipping halfway through the cooking time. 6. Meanwhile, make the sauce by heating the reserved marinade in a saucepan over medium heat; let it simmer until thoroughly warmed. Serve the steak fingers with the sauce on the side. Enjoy!

Stuffed Bell Peppers with Sausage

Prep time: 15 minutes | Cook time: 28 to 30 minutes | Serves 6

Avocado oil spray
8 ounces (227 g) Italian sausage, casings removed
½ cup chopped mushrooms
¼ cup diced onion
1 teaspoon Italian seasoning
Sea salt and freshly ground black pepper, to taste
1 cup keto-friendly marinara sauce
3 bell peppers, halved and seeded
3 ounces (85 g) provolone cheese, shredded

1. Spray a large skillet with oil and place it over medium-high heat. Add the sausage and cook for 5 minutes, breaking up the meat with a wooden spoon. Add the mushrooms, onion, and Italian seasoning, and season with salt and pepper. Cook for 5 minutes more. Stir in the marinara sauce and cook until heated through. 2. Scoop the sausage filling into the bell pepper halves. 3. Set the air fryer to 350°F (177°C). Arrange the peppers in a single layer in the air fryer basket, working in batches if necessary. Air fry for 15 minutes. 4. Top the stuffed peppers with the cheese and air fry for 3 to 5 minutes more, until the cheese is melted and the peppers are tender.

Nuts Crusted Pork Rack

Prep time: 5 minutes | Cook time: 35 minutes | Serves 2

1 clove garlic, minced
2 tablespoons olive oil
1 pound (454 g) rack of pork
1 cup chopped macadamia nuts
1 tablespoon breadcrumbs
1 tablespoon rosemary, chopped
1 egg
Salt and ground black pepper, to taste

1. Preheat the air fryer to 350°F (177°C). 2. Combine the garlic and olive oil in a small bowl. Stir to mix well. 3. On a clean work surface, rub the pork rack with the garlic oil and sprinkle with salt and black pepper on both sides. 4. Combine the macadamia nuts, breadcrumbs, and rosemary in a shallow dish. Whisk the egg in a large bowl. 5. Dredge the pork in the egg, then roll the pork over the macadamia nut mixture to coat well. Shake the excess off. 6. Arrange the pork in the preheated air fryer and air fry for 30 minutes on both sides. Increase to 390°F (199°C) and fry for 5 more minutes or until the pork is well browned. 7. Serve immediately.

Spicy Sirloin Tip Steak

Prep time: 25 minutes | Cook time: 12 to 18 minutes | Serves 4

2 tablespoons salsa
1 tablespoon minced chipotle pepper
1 tablespoon apple cider vinegar
1 teaspoon ground cumin
⅛ teaspoon freshly ground black pepper
⅛ teaspoon red pepper flakes
12 ounces (340 g) sirloin tip steak, cut into 4 pieces and gently pounded to about ⅓ inch thick
Cooking oil spray

1. In a small bowl, thoroughly mix the salsa, chipotle pepper, vinegar, cumin, black pepper, and red pepper flakes. Rub this mixture into both sides of each steak piece. Let stand for 15 minutes at room temperature. 2. Insert the crisper plate into the basket and place the basket into the unit. Preheat the unit by selecting AIR FRY, setting the temperature to 390ºF (199ºC), and setting the time to 3 minutes. Select START/STOP to begin. 3. Once the unit is preheated, spray the crisper plate with cooking oil. Working in batches, place 2 steaks into the basket. 4. Select AIR FRY, set the temperature to 390ºF (199ºC), and set the time to 9 minutes. Select START/STOP to begin. 5. After about 6 minutes, check the steaks. If a food thermometer inserted into the meat registers at least 145ºF (63ºC), they are done. If not, resume cooking. 6. When the cooking is done, transfer the steaks to a clean plate and cover with aluminum foil to keep warm. Repeat steps 3, 4, and 5 with the remaining steaks. 7. Thinly slice the steaks against the grain and serve.

Sweet Potatoes with Glazed Ham

Prep time: 20 minutes | Cook time: 15 to 17 minutes | Serves 4

1 cup freshly squeezed orange juice
½ cup packed light brown sugar
1 tablespoon Dijon mustard
½ teaspoon salt
½ teaspoon freshly ground black pepper
3 sweet potatoes, cut into small wedges
2 ham steaks (8 ounces / 227 g each), halved
1 to 2 tablespoons oil

1. In a large bowl, whisk the orange juice, brown sugar, Dijon, salt, and pepper until blended. Toss the sweet potato wedges with the brown sugar mixture. 2. Preheat the air fryer to 400ºF (204ºC). Line the air fryer basket with parchment paper and spritz with oil. 3. Place the sweet potato wedges on the parchment. 4. Cook for 10 minutes. 5. Place ham steaks on top of the sweet potatoes and brush everything with more of the orange juice mixture. 6. Cook for 3 minutes. Flip the ham and cook or 2 to 4 minutes more until the sweet potatoes are soft and the glaze has thickened. Cut the ham steaks in half to serve.

Blackened Steak Nuggets

Prep time: 10 minutes | Cook time: 7 minutes | Serves 2

1 pound (454 g) rib eye steak, cut into 1-inch cubes
2 tablespoons salted butter, melted
½ teaspoon paprika
½ teaspoon salt
¼ teaspoon garlic powder
¼ teaspoon onion powder
¼ teaspoon ground black pepper
⅛ teaspoon cayenne pepper

1. Place steak into a large bowl and pour in butter. Toss to coat. Sprinkle with remaining ingredients. 2. Place bites into ungreased air fryer basket. Adjust the temperature to 400ºF (204ºC) and air fry for 7 minutes, shaking the basket three times during cooking. Steak will be crispy on the outside and browned when done and internal temperature is at least 150ºF (66ºC) for medium and 180ºF (82ºC) for well-done. Serve warm.

Pepper Steak

Prep time: 30 minutes | Cook time: 16 to 20 minutes | Serves 4

1 pound (454 g) cube steak, cut into 1-inch pieces
1 cup Italian dressing
1½ cups beef broth
1 tablespoon soy sauce
½ teaspoon salt
¼ teaspoon freshly ground black pepper
¼ cup cornstarch
1 cup thinly sliced bell pepper, any color
1 cup chopped celery
1 tablespoon minced garlic
1 to 2 tablespoons oil

1. In a large resealable bag, combine the beef and Italian dressing. Seal the bag and refrigerate to marinate for 8 hours. 2. In a small bowl, whisk the beef broth, soy sauce, salt, and pepper until blended. 3. In another small bowl, whisk ¼ cup water and the cornstarch until dissolved. Stir the cornstarch mixture into the beef broth mixture until blended. 4. Preheat the air fryer to 375ºF (191ºC). 5. Pour the broth mixture into a baking pan. Cook for 4 minutes. Stir and cook for 4 to 5 minutes more. Remove and set aside. 6. Increase the air fryer temperature to 400ºF (204ºC). Line the air fryer basket with parchment paper. 7. Remove the steak from the marinade and place it in a medium bowl. Discard the marinade. Stir in the bell pepper, celery, and garlic. 8. Place the steak and pepper mixture on the parchment. Spritz with oil. 9. Cook for 4 minutes. Shake the basket and cook for 4 to 7 minutes more, until the vegetables are tender and the meat reaches an internal temperature of 145ºF (63ºC). Serve with the gravy.

Cinnamon-Beef Kofta

Prep time: 10 minutes | Cook time: 13 minutes per batch | Makes 12 koftas

1½ pounds (680 g) lean ground beef
1 teaspoon onion powder
¾ teaspoon ground cinnamon
¾ teaspoon ground dried turmeric
1 teaspoon ground cumin
¾ teaspoon salt
¼ teaspoon cayenne
12 (3½- to 4-inch-long) cinnamon sticks
Cooking spray

1. Preheat the air fryer to 375°F (191°C). Spritz the air fryer basket with cooking spray. 2. Combine all the ingredients, except for the cinnamon sticks, in a large bowl. Toss to mix well. 3. Divide and shape the mixture into 12 balls, then wrap each ball around each cinnamon stick and leave a quarter of the length uncovered. 4. Arrange the beef-cinnamon sticks in the preheated air fryer and spritz with cooking spray. Work in batches to avoid overcrowding. 5. Air fry for 13 minutes or until the beef is browned. Flip the sticks halfway through. 6. Serve immediately.

Five-Spice Pork Belly

Prep time: 10 minutes | Cook time: 17 minutes | Serves 4

1 pound (454 g) unsalted pork belly
Sauce:
1 tablespoon coconut oil
1 (1-inch) piece fresh ginger, peeled and grated
2 cloves garlic, minced
½ cup beef or chicken broth
¼ to ½ cup Swerve confectioners'-style sweetener or equivalent
2 teaspoons Chinese five-spice powder
amount of liquid or powdered sweetener
3 tablespoons wheat-free tamari, or ½ cup coconut aminos
1 green onion, sliced, plus more for garnish

1. Spray the air fryer basket with avocado oil. Preheat the air fryer to 400°F (204°C). 2. Cut the pork belly into ½-inch-thick slices and season well on all sides with the five-spice powder. Place the slices in a single layer in the air fryer basket (if you're using a smaller air fryer, work in batches if necessary) and cook for 8 minutes, or until cooked to your liking, flipping halfway through. 3. While the pork belly cooks, make the sauce: Heat the coconut oil in a small saucepan over medium heat. Add the ginger and garlic and sauté for 1 minute, or until fragrant. Add the broth, sweetener, and tamari and simmer for 10 to 15 minutes, until thickened. Add the green onion and cook for another minute, until the green onion is softened. Taste and adjust the seasoning to your liking. 4. Transfer the pork belly to a large bowl. Pour the sauce over the pork belly and coat well. Place the pork belly slices on a serving platter and garnish with sliced green onions. 5. Best served fresh. Store leftovers in an airtight container in the fridge for up to 4 days. Reheat in a preheated 400°F (204°C) air fryer for 3 minutes, or until heated through.

Zucchini with Seasoned Ground Beef

Prep time: 5 minutes | Cook time: 12 minutes | Serves 4

1½ pounds (680 g) ground beef
1 pound (454 g) chopped zucchini
2 tablespoons extra-virgin olive oil
1 teaspoon dried oregano
1 teaspoon dried basil
1 teaspoon dried rosemary
2 tablespoons fresh chives, chopped

1. Preheat the air fryer to 400°F (204°C). 2. In a large bowl, combine all the ingredients, except for the chives, until well blended. 3. Place the beef and zucchini mixture in the baking pan. Air fry for 12 minutes, or until the beef is browned and the zucchini is tender. 4. Divide the beef and zucchini mixture among four serving dishes. Top with fresh chives and serve hot.

Air Fried Crispy Venison

Prep time: 10 minutes | Cook time: 20 minutes | Serves 4

2 eggs
¼ cup milk
1 cup whole wheat flour
½ teaspoon salt
¼ teaspoon ground black pepper
1 pound (454 g) venison backstrap, sliced
Cooking spray

1. Preheat the air fryer to 360°F (182°C) and spritz with cooking spray. 2. Whisk the eggs with milk in a large bowl. Combine the flour with salt and ground black pepper in a shallow dish. 3. Dredge the venison in the flour first, then into the egg mixture. Shake the excess off and roll the venison back over the flour to coat well. 4. Arrange half of the venison in the preheated air fryer and spritz with cooking spray. 5. Air fry for 10 minutes or until the internal temperature of the venison reaches at least 145°F (63°C) for medium rare. Flip the venison halfway through. Repeat with remaining venison. 6. Serve immediately.

Slow-Cooked BBQ Ribs

Prep time: 5 minutes | Cook time: 30 minutes | Serves 4

1 (2 pounds / 907 g) rack baby back ribs
1 teaspoon onion powder
1 teaspoon garlic powder
1 teaspoon light brown sugar
1 teaspoon dried oregano
Salt and freshly ground black pepper, to taste
Cooking oil spray
½ cup barbecue sauce

1. Use a sharp knife to remove the thin membrane from the back of the ribs. Cut the rack in half, or as needed, so the ribs fit in the air fryer basket. The best way to do this is to cut the ribs into 4- or 5-rib sections. 2. In a small bowl, stir together the onion powder, garlic powder, brown sugar, and oregano and season with salt and pepper. Rub the spice seasoning onto the front and back of the ribs. 3. Cover the ribs with plastic wrap or foil and let sit at room temperature for 30 minutes. 4. Insert the crisper plate into the basket and the basket into the unit. Preheat the unit by selecting AIR ROAST, setting the temperature to 360°F (182°C), and setting the time to 3 minutes. Select START/STOP to begin. 5. Once the unit is preheated, spray the crisper plate with cooking oil. Place the ribs into the basket. It is okay to stack them. 6. Select AIR ROAST, set the temperature to 360°F (182°C), and set the time to 30 minutes. Select START/STOP to begin. 7. After 15 minutes, flip the ribs. Resume cooking for 15 minutes, or until a food thermometer registers 190°F (88°C). 8. When the cooking is complete, transfer the ribs to a serving dish. Drizzle the ribs with the barbecue sauce and serve.

Chapter 6
Fish and Seafood

South Indian Fried Fish

Prep time: 20 minutes | Cook time: 8 minutes | Serves 4

2 tablespoons olive oil
2 tablespoons fresh lime or lemon juice
1 teaspoon minced fresh ginger
1 clove garlic, minced
1 teaspoon ground turmeric
½ teaspoon kosher salt
¼ to ½ teaspoon cayenne pepper
1 pound (454 g) tilapia fillets (2 to 3 fillets)
Olive oil spray
Lime or lemon wedges (optional)

1. In a large bowl, combine the oil, lime juice, ginger, garlic, turmeric, salt, and cayenne. Stir until well combined; set aside. 2. Cut each tilapia fillet into three or four equal-size pieces. Add the fish to the bowl and gently mix until all of the fish is coated in the marinade. Marinate for 10 to 15 minutes at room temperature. (Don't marinate any longer or the acid in the lime juice will "cook" the fish.) 3. Spray the air fryer basket with olive oil spray. Place the fish in the basket and spray the fish. Set the air fryer to 325°F (163°C) for 3 minutes to partially cook the fish. Set the air fryer to 400°F (204°C) for 5 minutes to finish cooking and crisp up the fish. (Thinner pieces of fish will cook faster so you may want to check at the 3-minute mark of the second cooking time and remove those that are cooked through, and then add them back toward the end of the second cooking time to crisp.) 4. Carefully remove the fish from the basket. Serve hot, with lemon wedges if desired.

Jalapeño-Lime Fish Tacos

Prep time: 25 minutes | Cook time: 7 to 10 minutes | Serves 4

Fish Tacos:
1 pound (454 g) fish fillets
¼ teaspoon cumin
¼ teaspoon coriander
⅛ teaspoon ground red pepper
1 tablespoon lime zest
¼ teaspoon smoked paprika
1 teaspoon oil
Cooking spray
6 to 8 corn or flour tortillas (6-inch size)

Jalapeño-Lime Sauce:
½ cup sour cream
1 tablespoon lime juice
¼ teaspoon grated lime zest
½ teaspoon minced jalapeño (flesh only)
¼ teaspoon cumin

Napa Cabbage Garnish:
1 cup shredded Napa cabbage
¼ cup slivered red or green bell pepper
¼ cup slivered onion

1. Slice the fish fillets into strips approximately ½-inch thick. 2. Put the strips into a sealable plastic bag along with the cumin, coriander, red pepper, lime zest, smoked paprika, and oil. Massage seasonings into the fish until evenly distributed. 3. Spray the air fryer basket with nonstick cooking spray and place seasoned fish inside. 4. Air fry at 390°F (199°C) for approximately 5 minutes. Shake basket to distribute fish. Cook an additional 2 to 5 minutes, until fish flakes easily. 5. While the fish is cooking, prepare the Jalapeño-Lime Sauce by mixing the sour cream, lime juice, lime zest, jalapeño, and cumin together to make a smooth sauce. Set aside. 6. Mix the cabbage, bell pepper, and onion together and set aside. 7. To warm refrigerated tortillas, wrap in damp paper towels and microwave for 30 to 60 seconds. 8. To serve, spoon some of fish into a warm tortilla. Add one or two tablespoons Napa Cabbage Garnish and drizzle with Jalapeño-Lime Sauce.

Cod Tacos with Mango Salsa

Prep time: 15 minutes | Cook time: 17 minutes | Serves 4

1 mango, peeled and diced
1 small jalapeño pepper, diced
½ red bell pepper, diced
½ red onion, minced
Pinch chopped fresh cilantro
Juice of ½ lime
¼ teaspoon salt
¼ teaspoon ground black pepper
½ cup Mexican beer
1 egg
¾ cup cornstarch
¾ cup all-purpose flour
½ teaspoon ground cumin
¼ teaspoon chili powder
1 pound (454 g) cod, cut into 4 pieces
Olive oil spray
4 corn tortillas, or flour tortillas, at room temperature

1. In a small bowl, stir together the mango, jalapeño, red bell pepper, red onion, cilantro, lime juice, salt, and pepper. Set aside. 2. In a medium bowl, whisk the beer and egg. 3. In another medium bowl, stir together the cornstarch, flour, cumin, and chili powder. 4. Insert the crisper plate into the basket and the basket into the unit. Preheat the unit by selecting AIR FRY, setting the temperature to 375°F (191°C), and setting the time to 3 minutes. Select START/STOP to begin. 5. Dip the fish pieces into the egg mixture and in the flour mixture to coat completely. 6. Once the unit is preheated, place a parchment paper liner into the basket. Place the fish on the liner in a single layer. 7. Select AIR FRY, set the temperature to 375°F (191°C), and set the time to 17 minutes. Select START/STOP to begin. 8. After about 9 minutes, spray the fish with olive oil. Reinsert the basket to resume cooking. 9. When the cooking is complete, the fish should be golden and crispy. Place the pieces in the tortillas, top with the mango salsa, and serve.

Breaded Shrimp Tacos

Prep time: 10 minutes | Cook time: 9 minutes | Makes 8 tacos

2 large eggs
1 teaspoon prepared yellow mustard
1 pound (454 g) small shrimp, peeled, deveined, and tails removed
½ cup finely shredded Gouda or Parmesan cheese
½ cup pork dust

For Serving:
8 large Boston lettuce leaves
¼ cup pico de gallo
¼ cup shredded purple cabbage
1 lemon, sliced
Guacamole (optional)

1. Preheat the air fryer to 400ºF (204ºC). 2. Crack the eggs into a large bowl, add the mustard, and whisk until well combined. Add the shrimp and stir well to coat. 3. In a medium-sized bowl, mix together the cheese and pork dust until well combined. 4. One at a time, roll the coated shrimp in the pork dust mixture and use your hands to press it onto each shrimp. Spray the coated shrimp with avocado oil and place them in the air fryer basket, leaving space between them. 5. Air fry the shrimp for 9 minutes, or until cooked through and no longer translucent, flipping after 4 minutes. 6. To serve, place a lettuce leaf on a serving plate, place several shrimp on top, and top with 1½ teaspoons each of pico de gallo and purple cabbage. Squeeze some lemon juice on top and serve with guacamole, if desired. 7. Store leftover shrimp in an airtight container in the refrigerator for up to 3 days. Reheat in a preheated 400ºF (204ºC) air fryer for 5 minutes, or until warmed through.

Classic Oyster Po'Boy Sandwich

Prep time: 20 minutes | Cook time: 5 minutes | Serves 4

¾ cup all-purpose flour
¼ cup yellow cornmeal
1 tablespoon Cajun seasoning
1 teaspoon salt
2 large eggs, beaten
1 teaspoon hot sauce
1 pound (454 g) pre-shucked oysters
1 (12-inch) French baguette, quartered and sliced horizontally
Tartar Sauce, as needed
2 cups shredded lettuce, divided
2 tomatoes, cut into slices
Cooking spray

1. In a shallow bowl, whisk the flour, cornmeal, Cajun seasoning, and salt until blended. In a second shallow bowl, whisk together the eggs and hot sauce. 2. One at a time, dip the oysters in the cornmeal mixture, the eggs, and again in the cornmeal, coating thoroughly. 3. Preheat the air fryer to 400ºF (204ºC). Line the air fryer basket with parchment paper. 4. Place the oysters on the parchment and spritz with oil. 5. Air fry for 2 minutes. Shake the basket, spritz the oysters with oil, and air fry for 3 minutes more until lightly browned and crispy. 6. Spread each sandwich half with Tartar Sauce. Assemble the po'boys by layering each sandwich with fried oysters, ½ cup shredded lettuce, and 2 tomato slices. 7. Serve immediately.

Savory Jalea

Prep time: 20 minutes | Cook time: 10 minutes | Serves 4

Salsa Criolla
½ red onion, thinly sliced
2 tomatoes, diced
1 serrano or jalapeño pepper, deseeded and diced
1 clove garlic, minced
¼ cup chopped fresh cilantro
Pinch of kosher salt
3 limes
Fried Seafood
1 pound (454 g) firm, white-fleshed fish such as cod (add an extra ½ pound /227 g fish if not using shrimp)
20 large or jumbo shrimp, shelled and deveined
¼ cup all-purpose flour
¼ cup cornstarch
1 teaspoon garlic powder
1 teaspoon kosher salt
¼ teaspoon cayenne pepper
2 cups panko bread crumbs
2 eggs, beaten with 2 tablespoons water
Vegetable oil, for spraying
Mayonnaise or tartar sauce, for serving (optional)

1. To make the Salsa Criolla, combine the red onion, tomatoes, pepper, garlic, cilantro, and salt in a medium bowl. Add the juice and zest of 2 of the limes. Refrigerate the salad while you make the fish. 2. To make the seafood, cut the fish fillets into strips approximately 2 inches long and 1 inch wide. Place the flour, cornstarch, garlic powder, salt, and cayenne pepper on a plate and whisk to combine. Place the panko on a separate plate. Dredge the fish strips in the seasoned flour mixture, shaking off any excess. Dip the strips in the egg mixture, coating them completely, then dredge in the panko, shaking off any excess. Place the fish strips on a plate or rack. Repeat with the shrimp, if using. 3. Spray the air fryer basket with oil, and preheat the air fryer to 400ºF (204ºC). Working in 2 or 3 batches, arrange the fish and shrimp in a single layer in the basket, taking care not to crowd the basket. Spray with oil. Air fry for 5 minutes, then flip and air fry for another 4 to 5 minutes until the outside is brown and crisp and the inside of the fish is opaque and flakes easily with a fork. Repeat with the remaining seafood. 4. Place the fried seafood on a platter. Use a slotted spoon to remove the salsa criolla from the bowl, leaving behind any liquid that has accumulated. Place the salsa criolla on top of the fried seafood. Serve immediately with the remaining lime, cut into wedges, and mayonnaise or tartar sauce as desired.

Steamed Tuna with Lemongrass

Prep time: 10 minutes | Cook time: 10 minutes | Serves 4

4 small tuna steaks
2 tablespoons low-sodium soy sauce
2 teaspoons sesame oil
2 teaspoons rice wine vinegar
1 teaspoon grated peeled fresh ginger
⅛ teaspoon freshly ground black pepper
1 stalk lemongrass, bent in half
3 tablespoons freshly squeezed lemon juice

1. Place the tuna steaks on a plate. 2. In a small bowl, whisk the soy sauce, sesame oil, vinegar, and ginger until combined. Pour this mixture over the tuna and gently rub it into both sides. Sprinkle the fish with the pepper. Let marinate for 10 minutes. 3. Insert the crisper plate into the basket and the basket into the unit. Preheat the unit by selecting BAKE, setting the temperature to 390°F (199°C), and setting the time to 3 minutes. Select START/STOP to begin. 4. Once the unit is preheated, place the lemongrass into the basket and top it with the tuna steaks. Drizzle the tuna with the lemon juice and 1 tablespoon of water. 5. Select BAKE, set the temperature to 390°F (199°C), and set the time to 10 minutes. Select START/STOP to begin. 6. When the cooking is complete, a food thermometer inserted into the tuna should register at least 145°F (63°C). Discard the lemongrass and serve the tuna.

Cod with Avocado

Prep time: 30 minutes | Cook time: 10 minutes | Serves 2

1 cup shredded cabbage
¼ cup full-fat sour cream
2 tablespoons full-fat mayonnaise
¼ cup chopped pickled jalapeños
2 (3-ounce / 85-g) cod fillets
1 teaspoon chili powder
1 teaspoon cumin
½ teaspoon paprika
¼ teaspoon garlic powder
1 medium avocado, peeled, pitted, and sliced
½ medium lime

1. In a large bowl, place cabbage, sour cream, mayonnaise, and jalapeños. Mix until fully coated. Let sit for 20 minutes in the refrigerator. 2. Sprinkle cod fillets with chili powder, cumin, paprika, and garlic powder. Place each fillet into the air fryer basket. 3. Adjust the temperature to 370°F (188°C) and set the timer for 10 minutes. 4. Flip the fillets halfway through the cooking time. When fully cooked, fish should have an internal temperature of at least 145°F (63°C). 5. To serve, divide slaw mixture into two serving bowls, break cod fillets into pieces and spread over the bowls, and top with avocado. Squeeze lime juice over each bowl. Serve immediately.

Crunchy Panko Fish Sticks

Prep time: 10 minutes | Cook time: 15 minutes | Serves 4

Tartar Sauce:
2 cups mayonnaise
2 tablespoons dill pickle relish
1 tablespoon dried minced onions

Fish Sticks:
Oil, for spraying
1 pound (454 g) tilapia fillets
½ cup all-purpose flour
2 cups panko bread crumbs
2 tablespoons Creole seasoning
2 teaspoons granulated garlic
1 teaspoon onion powder
½ teaspoon salt
¼ teaspoon freshly ground black pepper
1 large egg

Make the Tartar Sauce 1. In a small bowl, whisk together the mayonnaise, pickle relish, and onions. Cover with plastic wrap and refrigerate until ready to serve. You can make this sauce ahead of time; the flavors will intensify as it chills. Make the Fish Sticks 2. Preheat the air fryer to 350°F (177°C). Line the air fryer basket with parchment and spray lightly with oil. 3. Cut the fillets into equal-size sticks and place them in a zip-top plastic bag. 4. Add the flour to the bag, seal, and shake well until evenly coated. 5. In a shallow bowl, mix together the bread crumbs, Creole seasoning, garlic, onion powder, salt, and black pepper. 6. In a small bowl, whisk the egg. 7. Dip the fish sticks in the egg, then dredge in the bread crumb mixture until completely coated. 8. Place the fish sticks in the prepared basket. You may need to work in batches, depending on the size of your air fryer. Do not overcrowd. Spray lightly with oil. 9. Cook for 12 to 15 minutes, or until browned and cooked through. Serve with the tartar sauce.

Tilapia with Chili Seasoning

Prep time: 5 minutes | Cook time: 20 minutes | Serves 4

4 tilapia fillets, boneless
1 teaspoon chili flakes
1 teaspoon dried oregano
1 tablespoon avocado oil
1 teaspoon mustard

1. Rub the tilapia fillets with chili flakes, dried oregano, avocado oil, and mustard and put in the air fryer. 2. Cook it for 10 minutes per side at 360°F (182°C).

Crunchy Fried Fish Sticks

Prep time: 15 minutes | Cook time: 10 minutes | Serves 4

1 ounce (28 g) pork rinds, finely ground
¼ cup blanched finely ground almond flour
½ teaspoon Old Bay seasoning
1 tablespoon coconut oil
1 large egg
1 pound (454 g) cod fillet, cut into ¾-inch strips

1. Place ground pork rinds, almond flour, Old Bay seasoning, and coconut oil into a large bowl and mix together. In a medium bowl, whisk egg. 2. Dip each fish stick into the egg and then gently press into the flour mixture, coating as fully and evenly as possible. Place fish sticks into the air fryer basket. 3. Adjust the temperature to 400ºF (204ºC) and air fry for 10 minutes or until golden. 4. Serve immediately.

Crispy Battered Shrimp

Prep time: 15 minutes | Cook time: 5 minutes | Serves 4

½ cup self-rising flour
1 teaspoon paprika
1 teaspoon salt
½ teaspoon freshly ground black pepper
1 large egg, beaten
1 cup finely crushed panko bread crumbs
20 frozen large shrimp (about 1-pound / 907-g), peeled and deveined
Cooking spray

1. In a shallow bowl, whisk the flour, paprika, salt, and pepper until blended. Add the beaten egg to a second shallow bowl and the bread crumbs to a third. 2. One at a time, dip the shrimp into the flour, the egg, and the bread crumbs, coating thoroughly. 3. Preheat the air fryer to 400ºF (204ºC). Line the air fryer basket with parchment paper. 4. Place the shrimp on the parchment and spritz with oil. 5. Air fry for 2 minutes. Shake the basket, spritz the shrimp with oil, and air fry for 3 minutes more until lightly browned and crispy. Serve hot.

Shrimp Kebabs

Prep time: 15 minutes | Cook time: 6 minutes | Serves 4

Oil, for spraying
1 pound (454 g) medium raw shrimp, peeled and deveined
4 tablespoons unsalted butter, melted
1 tablespoon Old Bay seasoning
1 tablespoon packed light brown sugar
1 teaspoon granulated garlic
1 teaspoon onion powder
½ teaspoon freshly ground black pepper

1. Line the air fryer basket with parchment and spray lightly with oil. 2. Thread the shrimp onto the skewers and place them in the prepared basket. 3. In a small bowl, mix together the butter, Old Bay, brown sugar, garlic, onion powder, and black pepper. Brush the sauce on the shrimp. 4. Air fry at 400ºF (204ºC) for 5 to 6 minutes, or until pink and firm. Serve immediately.

Shrimp-Stuffed Empanadas

Prep time: 10 minutes | Cook time: 8 minutes | Serves 5

½ pound (227g) raw shrimp, peeled, deveined and chopped
¼ cup chopped red onion
1 scallion, chopped
2 garlic cloves, minced
2 tablespoons minced red bell pepper
2 tablespoons chopped fresh cilantro
½ tablespoon fresh lime juice
¼ teaspoon sweet paprika
⅛ teaspoon kosher salt
⅛ teaspoon crushed red pepper flakes (optional)
1 large egg, beaten
10 frozen Goya Empanada Discos, thawed
Cooking spray

1. In a medium bowl, combine the shrimp, red onion, scallion, garlic, bell pepper, cilantro, lime juice, paprika, salt, and pepper flakes (if using). 2. In a small bowl, beat the egg with 1 teaspoon water until smooth. 3. Place an empanada disc on a work surface and put 2 tablespoons of the shrimp mixture in the center. Brush the outer edges of the disc with the egg wash. Fold the disc over and gently press the edges to seal. Use a fork and press around the edges to crimp and seal completely. Brush the tops of the empanadas with the egg wash. 4. Preheat the air fryer to 380ºF (193ºC). 5. Spray the bottom of the air fryer basket with cooking spray to prevent sticking. Working in batches, arrange a single layer of the empanadas in the air fryer basket and air fry for about 8 minutes, flipping halfway, until golden brown and crispy. 6. Serve hot.

Almond Catfish

Prep time: 10 minutes | Cook time: 12 minutes | Serves 4

2 pounds (907 g) catfish fillet
½ cup almond flour
2 eggs, beaten
1 teaspoon salt
1 teaspoon avocado oil

1. Sprinkle the catfish fillet with salt and dip in the eggs. 2. Then coat the fish in the almond flour and put in the air fryer basket. Sprinkle the fish with avocado oil. 3. Cook the fish for 6 minutes per side at 380ºF (193ºC).

Zesty Lime Lobster Tails

Prep time: 10 minutes | Cook time: 6 minutes | Serves 4

4 lobster tails, peeled
2 tablespoons lime juice
½ teaspoon dried basil
½ teaspoon coconut oil, melted

1. Mix lobster tails with lime juice, dried basil, and coconut oil. 2. Put the lobster tails in the air fryer and cook at 380ºF (193ºC) for 6 minutes.

Tomato-Braised Snapper with Shallots

Prep time: 20 minutes | Cook time: 15 minutes | Serves 2

2 snapper fillets
1 shallot, peeled and sliced
2 garlic cloves, halved
1 bell pepper, sliced
1 small-sized serrano pepper, sliced
1 tomato, sliced
1 tablespoon olive oil
¼ teaspoon freshly ground black pepper
½ teaspoon paprika
Sea salt, to taste
2 bay leaves

1. Place two parchment sheets on a working surface. Place the fish in the center of one side of the parchment paper. 2. Top with the shallot, garlic, peppers, and tomato. Drizzle olive oil over the fish and vegetables. Season with black pepper, paprika, and salt. Add the bay leaves. 3. Fold over the other half of the parchment. Now, fold the paper around the edges tightly and create a half moon shape, sealing the fish inside. 4. Cook in the preheated air fryer at 390ºF (199ºC) for 15 minutes. Serve warm.

Garlic Shrimp with Swiss Chard

Prep time: 10 minutes | Cook time: 10 minutes | Serves 4

1 pound (454 g) shrimp, peeled and deveined
½ teaspoon smoked paprika
½ cup Swiss chard, chopped
2 tablespoons apple cider vinegar
1 tablespoon coconut oil
¼ cup heavy cream

1. Mix shrimps with smoked paprika and apple cider vinegar. 2. Put the shrimps in the air fryer and add coconut oil. 3. Cook the shrimps at 350ºF (177ºC) for 10 minutes. 4. Then mix cooked shrimps with remaining ingredients and carefully mix.

Smoky Shrimp and Chorizo Tapas

Prep time: 15 minutes | Cook time: 10 minutes | Serves 2 to 4

4 ounces (113 g) Spanish (cured) chorizo, halved horizontally and sliced crosswise
½ pound (227 g) raw medium shrimp, peeled and deveined
1 tablespoon extra-virgin olive oil
1 small shallot, halved and thinly sliced
1 garlic clove, minced
1 tablespoon finely chopped fresh oregano
½ teaspoon smoked Spanish paprika
¼ teaspoon kosher salt
¼ teaspoon black pepper
3 tablespoons fresh orange juice
1 tablespoon minced fresh parsley

1. Place the chorizo in a baking pan. Set the pan in the air fryer basket. Set the air fryer to 375ºF (191ºC) for 5 minutes, or until the chorizo has started to brown and render its fat. 2. Meanwhile, in a large bowl, combine the shrimp, olive oil, shallot, garlic, oregano, paprika, salt, and pepper. Toss until the shrimp is well coated. 3. Transfer the shrimp to the pan with the chorizo. Stir to combine. Place the pan in the air fryer basket. Cook for 10 minutes, stirring halfway through the cooking time. 4. Transfer the shrimp and chorizo to a serving dish. Drizzle with the orange juice and toss to combine. Sprinkle with the parsley.

Cajun and Lemon Pepper Cod

Prep time: 5 minutes | Cook time: 12 minutes | Makes 2 cod fillets

1 tablespoon Cajun seasoning
1 teaspoon salt
½ teaspoon lemon pepper
½ teaspoon freshly ground black pepper
2 (8 ounces / 227 g) cod fillets, cut to fit into the air fryer basket
Cooking spray
2 tablespoons unsalted butter, melted
1 lemon, cut into 4 wedges

1. Preheat the air fryer to 360ºF (182ºC). Spritz the air fryer basket with cooking spray. 2. Thoroughly combine the Cajun seasoning, salt, lemon pepper, and black pepper in a small bowl. Rub this mixture all over the cod fillets until completely coated. 3. Put the fillets in the air fryer basket and brush the melted butter over both sides of each fillet. 4. Bake in the preheated air fryer for 12 minutes, flipping the fillets halfway through, or until the fish flakes easily with a fork. 5. Remove the fillets from the basket and serve with fresh lemon wedges.

Steamed Cod with Garlic and Swiss Chard

Prep time: 5 minutes | Cook time: 12 minutes | Serves 4

1 teaspoon salt
½ teaspoon dried oregano
½ teaspoon dried thyme
½ teaspoon garlic powder
4 cod fillets
½ white onion, thinly sliced
2 cups Swiss chard, washed, stemmed, and torn into pieces
¼ cup olive oil
1 lemon, quartered

1. Preheat the air fryer to 380°F (193°C). 2. In a small bowl, whisk together the salt, oregano, thyme, and garlic powder. 3. Tear off four pieces of aluminum foil, with each sheet being large enough to envelop one cod fillet and a quarter of the vegetables. 4. Place a cod fillet in the middle of each sheet of foil, then sprinkle on all sides with the spice mixture. 5. In each foil packet, place a quarter of the onion slices and ½ cup Swiss chard, then drizzle 1 tablespoon olive oil and squeeze ¼ lemon over the contents of each foil packet. 6. Fold and seal the sides of the foil packets and then place them into the air fryer basket. Steam for 12 minutes. 7. Remove from the basket, and carefully open each packet to avoid a steam burn.

Wrapped in Bacon

Prep time: 15 minutes | Cook time: 10 minutes | Serves 4

24 ounces (680 g) halibut steaks (6 ounces / 170 g each fillet)
1 teaspoon avocado oil
1 teaspoon ground black pepper
4 ounces bacon, sliced

1. Sprinkle the halibut steaks with avocado oil and ground black pepper. 2. Then wrap the fish in the bacon slices and put in the air fryer. 3. Cook the fish at 390°F (199°C) for 5 minutes per side.

Fennel-Roasted Salmon with Carrots

Prep time: 15 minutes | Cook time: 15 minutes | Serves 4

1 fennel bulb, thinly sliced
2 large carrots, sliced
1 large onion, thinly sliced
2 teaspoons extra-virgin olive oil
½ cup sour cream
1 teaspoon dried tarragon leaves
4 (5-ounce / 142-g) salmon fillets
⅛ teaspoon salt
¼ teaspoon coarsely ground black pepper

1. Insert the crisper plate into the basket and the basket into the unit. Preheat the unit by selecting AIR ROAST, setting the temperature to 400°F (204°C), and setting the time to 3 minutes. Select START/STOP to begin. 2. In a medium bowl, toss together the fennel, carrots, and onion. Add the olive oil and toss again to coat the vegetables. Put the vegetables into a 6-inch round metal pan. 3. Once the unit is preheated, place the pan into the basket. 4. Select AIR ROAST, set the temperature to 400°F (204°C), and set the time to 15 minutes. Select START/STOP to begin. 5. After 5 minutes, the vegetables should be crisp-tender. Remove the pan and stir in the sour cream and tarragon. Top with the salmon fillets and sprinkle the fish with the salt and pepper. Reinsert the pan into the basket and resume cooking. 6. When the cooking is complete, the salmon should flake easily with a fork and a food thermometer should register at least 145°F (63°C). Serve the salmon on top of the vegetables.

Shrimp with Smoky Tomato Dressing

Prep time: 5 minutes | Cook time: 8 minutes | Serves 2

3 tablespoons mayonnaise
1 tablespoon ketchup
1 tablespoon minced garlic
1 teaspoon Sriracha
½ teaspoon smoked paprika
½ teaspoon kosher salt
1 pound (454 g) large raw shrimp (21 to 25 count), peeled (tails left on) and deveined
Vegetable oil spray
½ cup chopped scallions

1. In a large bowl, combine the mayonnaise, ketchup, garlic, Sriracha, paprika, and salt. Add the shrimp and toss to coat with the sauce. 2. Spray the air fryer basket with vegetable oil spray. Place the shrimp in the basket. Set the air fryer to 350°F (177°C) for 8 minutes, tossing and spraying the shrimp with vegetable oil spray halfway through the cooking time. 3. Sprinkle with the chopped scallions before serving.

Almond Pesto Salmon

Prep time: 5 minutes | Cook time: 12 minutes | Serves 2

¼ cup pesto
¼ cup sliced almonds, roughly chopped
2 (1½-inch-thick) salmon fillets (about 4 ounces / 113 g each)
2 tablespoons unsalted butter, melted

1. In a small bowl, mix pesto and almonds. Set aside. 2. Place fillets into a round baking dish. 3. Brush each fillet with butter and place half of the pesto mixture on the top of each fillet. Place dish into the air fryer basket. 4. Adjust the temperature to 390°F (199°C) and set the timer for 12 minutes. 5. Salmon will easily flake when fully cooked and reach an internal temperature of at least 145°F (63°C). Serve warm.

Marinated Swordfish Skewers

Prep time: 30 minutes | Cook time: 6 to 8 minutes | Serves 4

1 pound (454 g) filleted swordfish
¼ cup avocado oil
2 tablespoons freshly squeezed lemon juice
1 tablespoon minced fresh parsley
2 teaspoons Dijon mustard
Sea salt and freshly ground black pepper, to taste
3 ounces (85 g) cherry tomatoes

1. Cut the fish into 1½-inch chunks, picking out any remaining bones. 2. In a large bowl, whisk together the oil, lemon juice, parsley, and Dijon mustard. Season to taste with salt and pepper. Add the fish and toss to coat the pieces. Cover and marinate the fish chunks in the refrigerator for 30 minutes. 3. Remove the fish from the marinade. Thread the fish and cherry tomatoes on 4 skewers, alternating as you go. 4. Set the air fryer to 400°F (204°C). Place the skewers in the air fryer basket and air fry for 3 minutes. Flip the skewers and cook for 3 to 5 minutes longer, until the fish is cooked through and an instant-read thermometer reads 140°F (60°C).

Tortilla Shrimp Tacos

Prep time: 10 minutes | Cook time: 6 minutes | Serves 4

Spicy Mayo:
3 tablespoons mayonnaise
1 tablespoon Louisiana-style hot pepper sauce

Cilantro-Lime Slaw:
2 cups shredded green cabbage
½ small red onion, thinly sliced
1 small jalapeño, thinly sliced
2 tablespoons chopped fresh cilantro
Juice of 1 lime
¼ teaspoon kosher salt

Shrimp:
1 large egg, beaten
1 cup crushed tortilla chips
24 jumbo shrimp (about 1 pound / 454 g), peeled and deveined
⅛ teaspoon kosher salt
Cooking spray
8 corn tortillas, for serving

1. For the spicy mayo: In a small bowl, mix the mayonnaise and hot pepper sauce. 2. For the cilantro-lime slaw: In a large bowl, toss together the cabbage, onion, jalapeño, cilantro, lime juice, and salt to combine. Cover and refrigerate to chill. 3. For the shrimp: Place the egg in a shallow bowl and the crushed tortilla chips in another. Season the shrimp with the salt. Dip the shrimp in the egg, then in the crumbs, pressing gently to adhere. Place on a work surface and spray both sides with oil. 4. Preheat the air fryer to 360°F (182°C). 5. Working in batches, arrange a single layer of the shrimp in the air fryer basket. Air fry for 6 minutes, flipping halfway, until golden and cooked through in the center. 6. To serve, place 2 tortillas on each plate and top each with 3 shrimp. Top each taco with ¼ cup slaw, then drizzle with spicy mayo.

Dukkah-Crusted Halibut

Prep time: 15 minutes | Cook time: 17 minutes | Serves 2

Dukkah:
1 tablespoon coriander seeds
1 tablespoon sesame seeds
1½ teaspoons cumin seeds
⅓ cup roasted mixed nuts
¼ teaspoon kosher salt
¼ teaspoon black pepper

Fish:
2 (5 ounces / 142 g) halibut fillets
2 tablespoons mayonnaise
Vegetable oil spray
Lemon wedges, for serving

1. For the dukkah: Combine the coriander, sesame seeds, and cumin in a small baking pan. Place the pan in the air fryer basket. Set the air fryer to 400°F (204°C) for 5 minutes. Toward the end of the cooking time, you will hear the seeds popping. Transfer to a plate and let cool for 5 minutes. 2. Transfer the toasted seeds to a food processor or spice grinder and add the mixed nuts. Pulse until coarsely chopped. Add the salt and pepper and stir well. 3. For the fish: Spread each fillet with 1 tablespoon of the mayonnaise. Press a heaping tablespoon of the dukkah into the mayonnaise on each fillet, pressing lightly to adhere. 4. Spray the air fryer basket with vegetable oil spray. Place the fish in the basket. Set the air fryer to 400°F (204°C) for 12 minutes, or until the fish flakes easily with a fork. 5. Serve the fish with lemon wedges.

Crab Burgers with Paprika Seasoning

Prep time: 30 minutes | Cook time: 14 minutes | Serves 3

2 eggs, beaten
1 shallot, chopped
2 garlic cloves, crushed
1 tablespoon olive oil
1 teaspoon yellow mustard
1 teaspoon fresh cilantro, chopped
10 ounces (283 g) crab meat
1 teaspoon smoked paprika
½ teaspoon ground black pepper
Sea salt, to taste
¾ cup Parmesan cheese

1. In a mixing bowl, thoroughly combine the eggs, shallot, garlic, olive oil, mustard, cilantro, crab meat, paprika, black pepper, and salt. Mix until well combined. 2. Shape the mixture into 6 patties. Roll the crab patties over grated Parmesan cheese, coating well on all sides. Place in your refrigerator for 2 hours. 3. Spritz the crab patties with cooking oil on both sides. Cook in the preheated air fryer at 360°F (182°C) for 14 minutes. Serve on dinner rolls if desired. Bon appétit!

Louisiana-Style Crab Cakes

Prep time: 10 minutes | Cook time: 8 to 10 minutes | Serves 4

1¼ cups bread crumbs
2 teaspoons Creole Seasoning
1 teaspoon dry mustard
1 teaspoon salt
1 teaspoon freshly ground black pepper
1½ cups crab meat
2 large eggs, beaten
1 teaspoon butter, melted
⅓ cup minced onion
Cooking spray
Pecan Tartar Sauce, for serving

1. Preheat the air fryer to 350°F (177°C). Line the air fryer basket with parchment paper. 2. In a medium bowl, whisk the bread crumbs, Creole Seasoning, dry mustard, salt, and pepper until blended. Add the crab meat, eggs, butter, and onion. Stir until blended. Shape the crab mixture into 8 patties. 3. Place the crab cakes on the parchment and spritz with oil. 4. Air fry for 4 minutes. Flip the cakes, spritz them with oil, and air fry for 4 to 6 minutes more until the outsides are firm and a fork inserted into the center comes out clean. Serve with the Pecan Tartar Sauce.

Classic Fish Sticks with Tartar Sauce

Prep time: 10 minutes | Cook time: 12 to 15 minutes | Serves 4

1½ pounds (680 g) cod fillets, cut into 1-inch strips
1 teaspoon salt
½ teaspoon freshly ground black pepper
Tartar Sauce:
½ cup sour cream
½ cup mayonnaise
3 tablespoons chopped dill pickle
2 tablespoons capers,
2 eggs
¾ cup almond flour
¼ cup grated Parmesan cheese

drained and chopped
½ teaspoon dried dill
1 tablespoon dill pickle liquid (optional)

1. Preheat the air fryer to 400°F (204°C). 2. Season the cod with the salt and black pepper; set aside. 3. In a shallow bowl, lightly beat the eggs. In a second shallow bowl, combine the almond flour and Parmesan cheese. Stir until thoroughly combined. 4. Working with a few pieces at a time, dip the fish into the egg mixture followed by the flour mixture. Press lightly to ensure an even coating. 5. Working in batches if necessary, arrange the fish in a single layer in the air fryer basket and spray lightly with olive oil. Pausing halfway through the cooking time to turn the fish, air fry for 12 to 15 minutes, until the fish flakes easily with a fork. Let sit in the basket for a few minutes before serving with the tartar sauce. 6. To make the tartar sauce: In a small bowl, combine the sour cream, mayonnaise, pickle, capers, and dill. If you prefer a thinner sauce, stir in the pickle liquid.

Mustard-Breaded Fish Fillets

Prep time: 5 minutes | Cook time: 8 to 11 minutes | Serves 4

5 teaspoons low-sodium yellow mustard
1 tablespoon freshly squeezed lemon juice
4 (3½-ounce / 99-g) sole fillets
½ teaspoon dried thyme
½ teaspoon dried marjoram
⅛ teaspoon freshly ground black pepper
1 slice low-sodium whole-wheat bread, crumbled
2 teaspoons olive oil

1. In a small bowl, mix the mustard and lemon juice. Spread this evenly over the fillets. Place them in the air fryer basket. 2. In another small bowl, mix the thyme, marjoram, pepper, bread crumbs, and olive oil. Mix until combined. 3. Gently but firmly press the spice mixture onto the top of each fish fillet. 4. Bake at 320°F (160°C) for 8 to 11 minutes, or until the fish reaches an internal temperature of at least 145°F (63°C) on a meat thermometer and the topping is browned and crisp. Serve immediately.

Sweet and Tangy Glazed Salmon

Prep time: 5 minutes | Cook time: 10 minutes | Serves 4

4 (6-ounce / 170-g) fillets of salmon
Salt and freshly ground black pepper, to taste
Vegetable oil
¼ cup pure maple syrup
3 tablespoons balsamic vinegar
1 teaspoon Dijon mustard

1. Preheat the air fryer to 400°F (204°C). 2. Season the salmon well with salt and freshly ground black pepper. Spray or brush the bottom of the air fryer basket with vegetable oil and place the salmon fillets inside. Air fry the salmon for 5 minutes. 3. While the salmon is air frying, combine the maple syrup, balsamic vinegar and Dijon mustard in a small saucepan over medium heat and stir to blend well. Let the mixture simmer while the fish is cooking. It should start to thicken slightly, but keep your eye on it so it doesn't burn. 4. Brush the glaze on the salmon fillets and air fry for an additional 5 minutes. The salmon should feel firm to the touch when finished and the glaze should be nicely browned on top. Brush a little more glaze on top before removing and serving with rice and vegetables, or a nice green salad.

Shrimp Pasta with Basil and Mushrooms

Prep time: 10 minutes | Cook time: 10 minutes | Serves 6

1 pound (454 g) small shrimp, peeled and deveined	5 garlic cloves, minced
¼ cup plus 1 tablespoon olive oil, divided	8 ounces (227 g) baby bella mushrooms, sliced
¼ teaspoon garlic powder	½ cup Parmesan, plus more for serving (optional)
¼ teaspoon cayenne	1 teaspoon salt
1 pound (454 g) whole grain pasta	½ teaspoon black pepper
	½ cup fresh basil

1. Preheat the air fryer to 380°F (193°C). 2. In a small bowl, combine the shrimp, 1 tablespoon olive oil, garlic powder, and cayenne. Toss to coat the shrimp. 3. Place the shrimp into the air fryer basket and roast for 5 minutes. Remove the shrimp and set aside. 4. Cook the pasta according to package directions. Once done cooking, reserve ½ cup pasta water, then drain. 5. Meanwhile, in a large skillet, heat ¼ cup of olive oil over medium heat. Add the garlic and mushrooms and cook down for 5 minutes. 6. Pour the pasta, reserved pasta water, Parmesan, salt, pepper, and basil into the skillet with the vegetable-and-oil mixture, and stir to coat the pasta. 7. Toss in the shrimp and remove from heat, then let the mixture sit for 5 minutes before serving with additional Parmesan, if desired.

Pecan-Crusted Tilapia

Prep time: 10 minutes | Cook time: 10 minutes | Serves 4

1¼ cups pecans	tablespoons water
¾ cup panko bread crumbs	4 (6-ounce/ 170-g) tilapia fillets
½ cup all-purpose flour	Vegetable oil, for spraying
2 tablespoons Cajun seasoning	Lemon wedges, for serving
2 eggs, beaten with 2	

1. Grind the pecans in the food processor until they resemble coarse meal. Combine the ground pecans with the panko on a plate. On a second plate, combine the flour and Cajun seasoning. Dry the tilapia fillets using paper towels and dredge them in the flour mixture, shaking off any excess. Dip the fillets in the egg mixture and then dredge them in the pecan and panko mixture, pressing the coating onto the fillets. Place the breaded fillets on a plate or rack. 2. Preheat the air fryer to 375°F (191°C). Spray both sides of the breaded fillets with oil. Carefully transfer 2 of the fillets to the air fryer basket and air fry for 9 to 10 minutes, flipping once halfway through, until the flesh is opaque and flaky. Repeat with the remaining fillets. 3. Serve immediately with lemon wedges.

Creamy Leek Noodles with Parmesan Lobster Tails

Prep time: 5 minutes | Cook time: 7 minutes | Serves 4

4 (4 ounces / 113 g) lobster tails	¼ teaspoon ground black pepper
2 tablespoons salted butter, melted	¼ cup grated Parmesan cheese
1½ teaspoons Cajun seasoning, divided	½ ounce (14 g) plain pork rinds, finely crushed
¼ teaspoon salt	

1. Cut lobster tails open carefully with a pair of scissors and gently pull meat away from shells, resting meat on top of shells. 2. Brush lobster meat with butter and sprinkle with 1 teaspoon Cajun seasoning, ¼ teaspoon per tail. 3. In a small bowl, mix remaining Cajun seasoning, salt, pepper, Parmesan, and pork rinds. Gently press ¼ mixture onto meat on each lobster tail. 4. Carefully place tails into ungreased air fryer basket. Adjust the temperature to 400°F (204°C) and air fry for 7 minutes. Lobster tails will be crispy and golden on top and have an internal temperature of at least 145°F (63°C) when done. Serve warm.

Browned Shrimp Patties

Prep time: 15 minutes | Cook time: 10 to 12 minutes | Serves 4

½ pound (227 g) raw shrimp, shelled, deveined, and chopped finely	2 teaspoons Worcestershire sauce
2 cups cooked sushi rice	½ teaspoon salt
¼ cup chopped red bell pepper	½ teaspoon garlic powder
¼ cup chopped celery	½ teaspoon Old Bay seasoning
¼ cup chopped green onion	½ cup plain bread crumbs
	Cooking spray

1. Preheat the air fryer to 390°F (199°C). 2. Put all the ingredients except the bread crumbs and oil in a large bowl and stir to incorporate. 3. Scoop out the shrimp mixture and shape into 8 equal-sized patties with your hands, no more than ½-inch thick. Roll the patties in the bread crumbs on a plate and spray both sides with cooking spray. 4. Place the patties in the air fryer basket. You may need to work in batches to avoid overcrowding. 5. Air fry for 10 to 12 minutes, flipping the patties halfway through, or until the outside is crispy brown. 6. Divide the patties among four plates and serve warm.

Baked Fish with Cheese Topping

Prep time: 30 minutes | Cook time: 17 minutes | Serves 4

1 tablespoon avocado oil
1 pound (454 g) hake fillets
1 teaspoon garlic powder
Sea salt and ground white pepper, to taste
2 tablespoons shallots, chopped
1 bell pepper, seeded and chopped
½ cup Cottage cheese
½ cup sour cream
1 egg, well whisked
1 teaspoon yellow mustard
1 tablespoon lime juice
½ cup Swiss cheese, shredded

1. Brush the bottom and sides of a casserole dish with avocado oil. Add the hake fillets to the casserole dish and sprinkle with garlic powder, salt, and pepper. 2. Add the chopped shallots and bell peppers. 3. In a mixing bowl, thoroughly combine the Cottage cheese, sour cream, egg, mustard, and lime juice. Pour the mixture over fish and spread evenly. 4. Cook in the preheated air fryer at 370°F (188°C) for 10 minutes. 5. Top with the Swiss cheese and cook an additional 7 minutes. Let it rest for 10 minutes before slicing and serving. Bon appétit!

Tuna Skewers with Fresh Fruits

Prep time: 15 minutes | Cook time: 8 to 12 minutes | Serves 4

1 pound (454 g) tuna steaks, cut into 1-inch cubes
½ cup canned pineapple chunks, drained, juice reserved
½ cup large red grapes
1 tablespoon honey
2 teaspoons grated fresh ginger
1 teaspoon olive oil
Pinch cayenne pepper

1. Thread the tuna, pineapple, and grapes on 8 bamboo or 4 metal skewers that fit in the air fryer. 2. In a small bowl, whisk the honey, 1 tablespoon of reserved pineapple juice, the ginger, olive oil, and cayenne. Brush this mixture over the kebabs. Let them stand for 10 minutes. 3. Air fry the kebabs at 370°F (188°C) for 8 to 12 minutes, or until the tuna reaches an internal temperature of at least 145°F (63°C) on a meat thermometer, and the fruit is tender and glazed, brushing once with the remaining sauce. Discard any remaining marinade. Serve immediately.

Cod

Prep time: 10 minutes | Cook time: 24 minutes | Serves 4

1 small leek, sliced into long thin noodles (about 2 cups)
½ cup heavy cream
2 cloves garlic, minced
Coating:
¼ cup grated Parmesan cheese
2 tablespoons mayonnaise
2 tablespoons unsalted butter, softened
1 teaspoon fine sea salt, divided
4 (4-ounce / 113-g) cod fillets (about 1 inch thick)
½ teaspoon ground black pepper
1 tablespoon chopped fresh thyme, or ½ teaspoon dried thyme leaves, plus more for garnish

1. Preheat the air fryer to 350°F (177°C). 2. Place the leek noodles in a casserole dish or a pan that will fit in your air fryer. 3. In a small bowl, stir together the cream, garlic, and ½ teaspoon of the salt. Pour the mixture over the leeks and cook in the air fryer for 10 minutes, or until the leeks are very tender. 4. Pat the fish dry and season with the remaining ½ teaspoon of salt and the pepper. When the leeks are ready, open the air fryer and place the fish fillets on top of the leeks. Air fry for 8 to 10 minutes, until the fish flakes easily with a fork (the thicker the fillets, the longer this will take). 5. While the fish cooks, make the coating: In a small bowl, combine the Parmesan, mayo, butter, and thyme. 6. When the fish is ready, remove it from the air fryer and increase the heat to 425°F (218°C) (or as high as your air fryer can go). Spread the fillets with a ½-inch-thick to ¾-inch-thick layer of the coating. 7. Place the fish back in the air fryer and air fry for 3 to 4 minutes, until the coating browns. 8. Garnish with fresh or dried thyme, if desired. Store leftovers in an airtight container in the refrigerator for up to 3 days. Reheat in a casserole dish in a preheated 350°F (177°C) air fryer for 6 minutes, or until heated through.

Chapter 7
Snacks and Appetizers

Veggie Salmon Nachos

Prep time: 10 minutes | Cook time: 9 to 12 minutes | Serves 6

2 ounces (57 g) baked no-salt corn tortilla chips
1 (5 ounces / 142 g) baked salmon fillet, flaked
½ cup canned low-sodium black beans, rinsed and drained
1 red bell pepper, chopped
½ cup grated carrot
1 jalapeño pepper, minced
⅓ cup shredded low-sodium low-fat Swiss cheese
1 tomato, chopped

1. Preheat the air fryer to 360ºF (182ºC). 2. In a baking pan, layer the tortilla chips. Top with the salmon, black beans, red bell pepper, carrot, jalapeño, and Swiss cheese. 3. Bake in the air fryer for 9 to 12 minutes, or until the cheese is melted and starts to brown. 4. Top with the tomato and serve.

Savory Egg Rolls with Pork and Cabbage

Prep time: 15 minutes | Cook time: 12 minutes | Makes 12 egg rolls

Cooking oil spray
2 garlic cloves, minced
12 ounces (340 g) ground pork
1 teaspoon sesame oil
¼ cup soy sauce
2 teaspoons grated peeled fresh ginger
2 cups shredded green cabbage
4 scallions, green parts (white parts optional), chopped
24 egg roll wrappers

1. Spray a skillet with the cooking oil and place it over medium-high heat. Add the garlic and cook for 1 minute until fragrant. 2. Add the ground pork to the skillet. Using a spoon, break the pork into smaller chunks. 3. In a small bowl, whisk the sesame oil, soy sauce, and ginger until combined. Add the sauce to the skillet. Stir to combine and continue cooking for about 5 minutes until the pork is browned and thoroughly cooked. 4. Stir in the cabbage and scallions. Transfer the pork mixture to a large bowl. 5. Lay the egg roll wrappers on a flat surface. Dip a basting brush in water and glaze each egg roll wrapper along the edges with the wet brush. This will soften the dough and make it easier to roll. 6. Stack 2 egg roll wrappers (it works best if you double-wrap the egg rolls). Scoop 1 to 2 tablespoons of the pork mixture into the center of each wrapper stack. 7. Roll one long side of the wrappers up over the filling. Press firmly on the area with the filling, tucking it in lightly to secure it in place. Fold in the left and right sides. Continue rolling to close. Use the basting brush to wet the seam and seal the egg roll. Repeat with the remaining ingredients. 8. Insert the crisper plate into the basket and the basket into the unit. Preheat the unit by selecting AIR FRY, setting the temperature to 400ºF (204ºC), and setting the time to 3 minutes. Select START/STOP to begin. 9. Once the unit is preheated, spray the crisper plate with cooking oil. Place the egg rolls into the basket. It is okay to stack them. Spray them with cooking oil. 10. Select AIR FRY, set the temperature to 400ºF (204ºC), and set the time to 12 minutes. Insert the basket into the unit. Select START/STOP to begin. 11. After 8 minutes, use tongs to flip the egg rolls. Reinsert the basket to resume cooking. 12. When the cooking is complete, serve the egg rolls hot.

Buffalo Bites

Prep time: 15 minutes | Cook time: 11 to 12 minutes per batch | Makes 16 meatballs

1½ cups cooked jasmine or sushi rice
¼ teaspoon salt
1 pound (454 g) ground chicken
8 tablespoons buffalo wing sauce
2 ounces (57 g) Gruyère cheese, cut into 16 cubes
1 tablespoon maple syrup

1. Mix 4 tablespoons buffalo wing sauce into all the ground chicken. 2. Shape chicken into a log and divide into 16 equal portions. 3. With slightly damp hands, mold each chicken portion around a cube of cheese and shape into a firm ball. When you have shaped 8 meatballs, place them in air fryer basket. 4. Air fry at 390ºF (199ºC) for approximately 5 minutes. Shake basket, reduce temperature to 360ºF (182ºC), and cook for 5 to 6 minutes longer. 5. While the first batch is cooking, shape remaining chicken and cheese into 8 more meatballs. 6. Repeat step 4 to cook second batch of meatballs. 7. In a medium bowl, mix the remaining 4 tablespoons of buffalo wing sauce with the maple syrup. Add all the cooked meatballs and toss to coat. 8. Place meatballs back into air fryer basket and air fry at 390ºF (199ºC) for 2 to 3 minutes to set the glaze. Skewer each with a toothpick and serve.

Fiery Spicy Chicken Bites

Prep time: 10 minutes | Cook time: 10 to 12 minutes | Makes 30 bites

8 ounces boneless and skinless chicken thighs, cut into 30 pieces
¼ teaspoon kosher salt
2 tablespoons hot sauce
Cooking spray

1. Preheat the air fryer to 390ºF (199ºC). 2. Spray the air fryer basket with cooking spray and season the chicken bites with the kosher salt, then place in the basket and air fry for 10 to 12 minutes or until crispy. 3. While the chicken bites cook, pour the hot sauce into a large bowl. 4. Remove the bites and add to the sauce bowl, tossing to coat. Serve warm.

Hot Pepperoni Pizza Cheese Dip

Prep time: 10 minutes | Cook time: 10 minutes | Serves 6

6 ounces (170 g) cream cheese, softened
¾ cup shredded Italian cheese blend
¼ cup sour cream
1½ teaspoons dried Italian seasoning
¼ teaspoon garlic salt
¼ teaspoon onion powder
¾ cup pizza sauce
½ cup sliced miniature pepperoni
¼ cup sliced black olives
1 tablespoon thinly sliced green onion
Cut-up raw vegetables, toasted baguette slices, pita chips, or tortilla chips, for serving

1. In a small bowl, combine the cream cheese, ¼ cup of the shredded cheese, the sour cream, Italian seasoning, garlic salt, and onion powder. Stir until smooth and the ingredients are well blended. 2. Spread the mixture in a baking pan. Top with the pizza sauce, spreading to the edges. Sprinkle with the remaining ½ cup shredded cheese. Arrange the pepperoni slices on top of the cheese. Top with the black olives and green onion. 3. Place the pan in the air fryer basket. Set the air fryer to 350°F (177°C) for 10 minutes, or until the pepperoni is beginning to brown on the edges and the cheese is bubbly and lightly browned. 4. Let stand for 5 minutes before serving with vegetables, toasted baguette slices, pita chips, or tortilla chips.

Five-Ingredient Falafel with Garlic-Yogurt Sauce

Prep time: 5 minutes | Cook time: 15 minutes | Serves 4

Falafel:
1 (15-ounce / 425-g) can chickpeas, drained and rinsed
½ cup fresh parsley
2 garlic cloves, minced
Garlic-Yogurt Sauce:
1 cup nonfat plain Greek yogurt
1 garlic clove, minced
½ tablespoon ground cumin
1 tablespoon whole wheat flour
Salt
1 tablespoon chopped fresh dill
2 tablespoons lemon juice

Make the Falafel: 1. Preheat the air fryer to 360°F (182°C). 2. Put the chickpeas into a food processor. Pulse until mostly chopped, then add the parsley, garlic, and cumin and pulse for another 1 to 2 minutes, or until the ingredients are combined and turning into a dough. 3. Add the flour. Pulse a few more times until combined. The dough will have texture, but the chickpeas should be pulsed into small bits. 4. Using clean hands, roll the dough into 8 balls of equal size, then pat the balls down a bit so they are about ½-thick disks. 5. Spray the basket of the air fryer with olive oil cooking spray, then place the falafel patties in the basket in a single layer, making sure they don't touch each other. 6. Fry in the air fryer for 15 minutes. Make the garlic-yogurt sauce 7. In a small bowl, combine the yogurt, garlic, dill, and lemon juice. 8. Once the falafel are done cooking and nicely browned on all sides, remove them from the air fryer and season with salt. 9. Serve hot with a side of dipping sauce.

Cheddar Cheese Wafers

Prep time: 30 minutes | Cook time: 5 to 6 minutes per batch | Makes 4 dozen

4 ounces (113 g) sharp Cheddar cheese, grated
¼ cup butter
½ cup flour
¼ teaspoon salt
½ cup crisp rice cereal
Oil for misting or cooking spray

1. Cream the butter and grated cheese together. You can do it by hand, but using a stand mixer is faster and easier. 2. Sift flour and salt together. Add it to the cheese mixture and mix until well blended. 3. Stir in cereal. 4. Place dough on wax paper and shape into a long roll about 1 inch in diameter. Wrap well with the wax paper and chill for at least 4 hours. 5. When ready to cook, preheat the air fryer to 360°F (182°C). 6. Cut cheese roll into ¼-inch slices. 7. Spray the air fryer basket with oil or cooking spray and place slices in a single layer, close but not touching. 8. Cook for 5 to 6 minutes or until golden brown. When done, place them on paper towels to cool. 9. Repeat previous step to cook remaining cheese bites.

Sweet Bacon Tater Tots

Prep time: 5 minutes | Cook time: 7 minutes | Serves 4

24 frozen tater tots
6 slices cooked bacon
2 tablespoons maple syrup
1 cup shredded Cheddar cheese

1. Preheat the air fryer to 400°F (204°C). 2. Put the tater tots in the air fryer basket. Air fry for 10 minutes, shaking the basket halfway through the cooking time. 3. Meanwhile, cut the bacon into 1-inch pieces. 4. Remove the tater tots from the air fryer basket and put into a baking pan. Top with the bacon and drizzle with the maple syrup. Air fry for 5 minutes, or until the tots and bacon are crisp. 5. Top with the cheese and air fry for 2 minutes, or until the cheese is melted. 6. Serve hot.

Spiced Roasted Cashews

Prep time: 5 minutes | Cook time: 10 minutes | Serves 4

2 cups raw cashews	¼ teaspoon chili powder
2 tablespoons olive oil	⅛ teaspoon garlic powder
¼ teaspoon salt	⅛ teaspoon smoked paprika

1. Preheat the air fryer to 360°F(182°C). 2. In a large bowl, toss all of the ingredients together. 3. Pour the cashews into the air fryer basket and roast them for 5 minutes. Shake the basket, then cook for 5 minutes more. 4. Serve immediately.

Crispy Cream Cheese-Filled Wontons

Prep time: 15 minutes | Cook time: 6 minutes | Makes 20 wontons

Oil, for spraying	4 ounces (113 g) cream cheese
20 wonton wrappers	

1. Line the air fryer basket with parchment and spray lightly with oil. 2. Pour some water in a small bowl. 3. Lay out a wonton wrapper and place 1 teaspoon of cream cheese in the center. 4. Dip your finger in the water and moisten the edge of the wonton wrapper. Fold over the opposite corners to make a triangle and press the edges together. 5. Pinch the corners of the triangle together to form a classic wonton shape. Place the wonton in the prepared basket. Repeat with the remaining wrappers and cream cheese. You may need to work in batches, depending on the size of your air fryer. 6. Air fry at 400°F (204°C) for 6 minutes, or until golden brown around the edges.

Tortellini with Spicy Dipping Sauce

Prep time: 5 minutes | Cook time: 20 minutes | Serves 4

¾ cup mayonnaise	1½ cups bread crumbs
2 tablespoons mustard	2 tablespoons olive oil
1 egg	2 cups frozen cheese tortellini
½ cup flour	
½ teaspoon dried oregano	

1. Preheat the air fryer to 380°F (193°C). 2. In a small bowl, combine the mayonnaise and mustard and mix well. Set aside. 3. In a shallow bowl, beat the egg. In a separate bowl, combine the flour and oregano. In another bowl, combine the bread crumbs and olive oil, and mix well. 4. Drop the tortellini, a few at a time, into the egg, then into the flour, then into the egg again, and then into the bread crumbs to coat. Put into the air fryer basket, cooking in batches. 5. Air fry for about 10 minutes, shaking halfway through the cooking time, or until the tortellini are crisp and golden brown on the outside. Serve with the mayonnaise mixture.

Grilled Ham and Cheese on Raisin Bread

Prep time: 5 minutes | Cook time: 10 minutes | Serves 1

2 slices raisin bread	ham (about 3 ounces / 85 g)
2 tablespoons butter, softened	4 slices Muenster cheese (about 3 ounces / 85 g)
2 teaspoons honey mustard	2 toothpicks
3 slices thinly sliced honey	

1. Preheat the air fryer to 370°F (188°C). 2. Spread the softened butter on one side of both slices of raisin bread and place the bread, buttered side down on the counter. Spread the honey mustard on the other side of each slice of bread. Layer 2 slices of cheese, the ham and the remaining 2 slices of cheese on one slice of bread and top with the other slice of bread. Remember to leave the buttered side of the bread on the outside. 3. Transfer the sandwich to the air fryer basket and secure the sandwich with toothpicks. 4. Air fry for 5 minutes. Flip the sandwich over, remove the toothpicks and air fry for another 5 minutes. Cut the sandwich in half and enjoy!

Cheese-Stuffed Sausage Balls

Prep time: 10 minutes | Cook time: 10 to 11 minutes | Serves 8

12 ounces (340 g) mild ground sausage	Cheddar cheese
1½ cups baking mix	3 ounces (85 g) cream cheese, at room temperature
1 cup shredded mild	1 to 2 tablespoons olive oil

1. Preheat the air fryer to 325°F (163°C). Line the air fryer basket with parchment paper. 2. Mix together the ground sausage, baking mix, Cheddar cheese, and cream cheese in a large bowl and stir to incorporate. 3. Divide the sausage mixture into 16 equal portions and roll them into 1-inch balls with your hands. 4. Arrange the sausage balls on the parchment, leaving space between each ball. You may need to work in batches to avoid overcrowding. 5. Brush the sausage balls with the olive oil. Bake for 10 to 11 minutes, shaking the basket halfway through, or until the balls are firm and lightly browned on both sides. 6. Remove from the basket to a plate and repeat with the remaining balls. 7. Serve warm.

String Bean Fries

Prep time: 15 minutes | Cook time: 5 to 6 minutes | Serves 4

½ pound (227 g) fresh string beans
2 eggs
4 teaspoons water
½ cup white flour
½ cup bread crumbs
¼ teaspoon salt
¼ teaspoon ground black pepper
¼ teaspoon dry mustard (optional)
Oil for misting or cooking spray

1. Preheat the air fryer to 360°F (182°C). 2. Trim stem ends from string beans, wash, and pat dry. 3. In a shallow dish, beat eggs and water together until well blended. 4. Place flour in a second shallow dish. 5. In a third shallow dish, stir together the bread crumbs, salt, pepper, and dry mustard if using. 6. Dip each string bean in egg mixture, flour, egg mixture again, then bread crumbs. 7. When you finish coating all the string beans, open air fryer and place them in basket. 8. Cook for 3 minutes. 9. Stop and mist string beans with oil or cooking spray. 10. Cook for 2 to 3 more minutes or until string beans are crispy and nicely browned.

Golden Onion Rings

Prep time: 15 minutes | Cook time: 14 minutes per batch | Serves 4

1 large white onion, peeled and cut into ½ to ¾-inch-thick slices (about 2 cups)
½ cup 2% milk
1 cup whole-wheat pastry flour, or all-purpose flour
2 tablespoons cornstarch
¾ teaspoon sea salt, divided
½ teaspoon freshly ground black pepper, divided
¾ teaspoon granulated garlic, divided
1½ cups whole-grain bread crumbs, or gluten-free bread crumbs
Cooking oil spray (coconut, sunflower, or safflower)
Ketchup, for serving (optional)

1. Carefully separate the onion slices into rings—a gentle touch is important here. 2. Place the milk in a shallow bowl and set aside. 3. Make the first breading: In a medium bowl, stir together the flour, cornstarch, ¼ teaspoon of salt, ¼ teaspoon of pepper, and ¼ teaspoon of granulated garlic. Set aside. 4. Make the second breading: In a separate medium bowl, stir together the bread crumbs with the remaining ½ teaspoon of salt, the remaining ½ teaspoon of garlic, and the remaining ½ teaspoon of pepper. Set aside. 5. Insert the crisper plate into the basket and the basket into the unit. Preheat the unit by selecting AIR FRY, setting the temperature to 390°F (199°C), and setting the time to 3 minutes. Select START/STOP to begin. 6. Once the unit is preheated, spray the crisper plate and the basket with cooking oil. 7. To make the onion rings, dip one ring into the milk and into the first breading mixture. Dip the ring into the milk again and back into the first breading mixture, coating thoroughly. Dip the ring into the milk one last time and then into the second breading mixture, coating thoroughly. Gently lay the onion ring in the basket. Repeat with additional rings and, as you place them into the basket, do not overlap them too much. Once all the onion rings are in the basket, generously spray the tops with cooking oil. 8. Select AIR FRY, set the temperature to 390°F (199°C), and set the time to 14 minutes. Insert the basket into the unit. Select START/STOP to begin. 9. After 4 minutes, open the unit and spray the rings generously with cooking oil. Close the unit to resume cooking. After 3 minutes, remove the basket and spray the onion rings again. Remove the rings, turn them over, and place them back into the basket. Generously spray them again with oil. Reinsert the basket to resume cooking. After 4 minutes, generously spray the rings with oil one last time. Resume cooking for the remaining 3 minutes, or until the onion rings are very crunchy and brown. 10. When the cooking is complete, serve the hot rings with ketchup, or other sauce of choice.

Fried Green Tomatoes with Horseradish Cream

Prep time: 18 minutes | Cook time: 10 to 15 minutes | Serves 4

2 eggs
¼ cup buttermilk
½ cup bread crumbs
½ cup cornmeal
¼ teaspoon salt
Horseradish Sauce:
¼ cup sour cream
¼ cup mayonnaise
2 teaspoons prepared horseradish
1½ pounds (680 g) firm green tomatoes, cut into ¼-inch slices
Cooking spray
½ teaspoon lemon juice
½ teaspoon Worcestershire sauce
⅛ teaspoon black pepper

1. Preheat air fryer to 390°F (199°C). Spritz the air fryer basket with cooking spray. 2. In a small bowl, whisk together all the ingredients for the horseradish sauce until smooth. Set aside. 3. In a shallow dish, beat the eggs and buttermilk. 4. In a separate shallow dish, thoroughly combine the bread crumbs, cornmeal, and salt. 5. Dredge the tomato slices, one at a time, in the egg mixture, then roll in the bread crumb mixture until evenly coated. 6. Working in batches, place the tomato slices in the air fryer basket in a single layer. Spray them with cooking spray. 7. Air fry for 10 to 15 minutes, flipping the slices halfway through, or until the tomato slices are nicely browned and crisp. 8. Remove from the basket to a platter and repeat with the remaining tomato slices. 9. Serve drizzled with the prepared horseradish sauce.

Lemon Shrimp with Garlic Olive Oil

Prep time: 5 minutes | Cook time: 6 minutes | Serves 4

1 pound (454 g) medium shrimp, cleaned and deveined
¼ cup plus 2 tablespoons olive oil, divided
Juice of ½ lemon
3 garlic cloves, minced and divided
½ teaspoon salt
¼ teaspoon red pepper flakes
Lemon wedges, for serving (optional)
Marinara sauce, for dipping (optional)

1. Preheat the air fryer to 380°F(193°C). 2. In a large bowl, combine the shrimp with 2 tablespoons of the olive oil, as well as the lemon juice, ⅓ of the minced garlic, salt, and red pepper flakes. Toss to coat the shrimp well. 3. In a small ramekin, combine the remaining ¼ cup of olive oil and the remaining minced garlic. 4. Tear off a 12-by-12-inch sheet of aluminum foil. Pour the shrimp into the center of the foil, then fold the sides up and crimp the edges so that it forms an aluminum foil bowl that is open on top. Place this packet into the air fryer basket. 5. Roast the shrimp for 4 minutes, then open the air fryer and place the ramekin with oil and garlic in the basket beside the shrimp packet. Cook for 2 more minutes. 6. Transfer the shrimp on a serving plate or platter with the ramekin of garlic olive oil on the side for dipping. You may also serve with lemon wedges and marinara sauce, if desired.

Shrimp-Filled Cajun Pirogues

Prep time: 15 minutes | Cook time: 4 to 5 minutes | Serves 8

12 ounces (340 g) small, peeled, and deveined raw shrimp
3 ounces (85 g) cream cheese, room temperature
2 tablespoons plain yogurt
1 teaspoon lemon juice
1 teaspoon dried dill weed, crushed
Salt, to taste
4 small hothouse cucumbers, each approximately 6 inches long

1. Pour 4 tablespoons water in bottom of air fryer drawer. 2. Place shrimp in air fryer basket in single layer and air fry at 390°F (199°C) for 4 to 5 minutes, just until done. Watch carefully because shrimp cooks quickly, and overcooking makes it tough. 3. Chop shrimp into small pieces, no larger than ½ inch. Refrigerate while mixing the remaining ingredients. 4. With a fork, mash and whip the cream cheese until smooth. 5. Stir in the yogurt and beat until smooth. Stir in lemon juice, dill weed, and chopped shrimp. 6. Taste for seasoning. If needed, add ¼ to ½ teaspoon salt to suit your taste. 7. Store in refrigerator until serving time. 8. When ready to serve, wash and dry cucumbers and split them lengthwise. Scoop out the seeds and turn cucumbers upside down on paper towels to drain for 10 minutes. 9. Just before filling, wipe centers of cucumbers dry. Spoon the shrimp mixture into the pirogues and cut in half crosswise. Serve immediately.

Greens Chips with Curried Yogurt Sauce

Prep time: 10 minutes | Cook time: 5 to 6 minutes | Serves 4

1 cup low-fat Greek yogurt
1 tablespoon freshly squeezed lemon juice
1 tablespoon curry powder
½ bunch curly kale, stemmed, ribs removed and discarded, leaves cut into 2- to 3-inch pieces
½ bunch chard, stemmed, ribs removed and discarded, leaves cut into 2- to 3-inch pieces
1½ teaspoons olive oil

1. In a small bowl, stir together the yogurt, lemon juice, and curry powder. Set aside. 2. In a large bowl, toss the kale and chard with the olive oil, working the oil into the leaves with your hands. This helps break up the fibers in the leaves so the chips are tender. 3. Air fry the greens in batches at 390°F (199°C) for 5 to 6 minutes, until crisp, shaking the basket once during cooking. Serve with the yogurt sauce.

Stuffed Fried Mushrooms

Prep time: 20 minutes | Cook time: 10 to 11 minutes | Serves 10

½ cup panko bread crumbs
½ teaspoon freshly ground black pepper
½ teaspoon onion powder
½ teaspoon cayenne pepper
1 (8-ounce / 227-g) package cream cheese, at room temperature
20 cremini or button mushrooms, stemmed
1 to 2 tablespoons oil

1. In a medium bowl, whisk the bread crumbs, black pepper, onion powder, and cayenne until blended. 2. Add the cream cheese and mix until well blended. Fill each mushroom top with 1 teaspoon of the cream cheese mixture 3. Preheat the air fryer to 360°F (182°C). Line the air fryer basket with a piece of parchment paper. 4. Place the mushrooms on the parchment and spritz with oil. 5. Cook for 5 minutes. Shake the basket and cook for 5 to 6 minutes more until the filling is firm and the mushrooms are soft.

Spicy Tortilla Chips

Prep time: 5 minutes | Cook time: 8 to 12 minutes | Serves 4

½ teaspoon ground cumin
½ teaspoon paprika
½ teaspoon chili powder
½ teaspoon salt
Pinch cayenne pepper
8 (6-inch) corn tortillas, each cut into 6 wedges
Cooking spray

1. Preheat the air fryer to 375ºF (191ºC). Lightly spritz the air fryer basket with cooking spray. 2. Stir together the cumin, paprika, chili powder, salt, and pepper in a small bowl. 3. Working in batches, arrange the tortilla wedges in the air fryer basket in a single layer. Lightly mist them with cooking spray. Sprinkle some seasoning mixture on top of the tortilla wedges. 4. Air fry for 4 to 6 minutes, shaking the basket halfway through, or until the chips are lightly browned and crunchy. 5. Repeat with the remaining tortilla wedges and seasoning mixture. 6. Let the tortilla chips cool for 5 minutes and serve.

Crispy Garlic and Cheese Croutons

Prep time: 3 minutes | Cook time: 12 minutes | Serves 4

Oil, for spraying
4 cups cubed French bread
1 tablespoon grated Parmesan cheese
3 tablespoons olive oil
1 tablespoon granulated garlic
½ teaspoon unsalted salt

1. Line the air fryer basket with parchment and spray lightly with oil. 2. In a large bowl, mix together the bread, Parmesan cheese, olive oil, garlic, and salt, tossing with your hands to evenly distribute the seasonings. Transfer the coated bread cubes to the prepared basket. 3. Air fry at 350ºF (177ºC) for 10 to 12 minutes, stirring once after 5 minutes, or until crisp and golden brown.

Crispy Seasoned Roasted Chickpeas

Prep time: 5 minutes | Cook time: 15 minutes | Makes about 1 cup

1 (15-ounce / 425-g) can chickpeas, drained
2 teaspoons curry powder
¼ teaspoon salt
1 tablespoon olive oil

1. Drain chickpeas thoroughly and spread in a single layer on paper towels. Cover with another paper towel and press gently to remove extra moisture. Don't press too hard or you'll crush the chickpeas. 2. Mix curry powder and salt together. 3. Place chickpeas in a medium bowl and sprinkle with seasonings. Stir well to coat. 4. Add olive oil and stir again to distribute oil. 5. Air fry at 390ºF (199ºC) for 15 minutes, stopping to shake basket about halfway through cooking time. 6. Cool completely and store in airtight container.

Stuffed Figs with Goat Cheese and Honey

Prep time: 5 minutes | Cook time: 10 minutes | Serves 4

8 fresh figs
2 ounces (57 g) goat cheese
¼ teaspoon ground cinnamon
1 tablespoon honey, plus more for serving
1 tablespoon olive oil

1. Preheat the air fryer to 360ºF (182ºC). 2. Cut the stem off of each fig. 3. Cut an X into the top of each fig, cutting halfway down the fig. Leave the base intact. 4. In a small bowl, mix together the goat cheese, cinnamon, and honey. 5. Spoon the goat cheese mixture into the cavity of each fig. 6. Place the figs in a single layer in the air fryer basket. Drizzle the olive oil over top of the figs and roast for 10 minutes. 7. Serve with an additional drizzle of honey.

Herb-Drizzled Shishito Peppers

Prep time: 10 minutes | Cook time: 6 minutes | Serves 2 to 4

6 ounces (170 g) shishito peppers
1 tablespoon vegetable oil
Kosher salt and freshly ground black pepper, to taste
½ cup mayonnaise
2 tablespoons finely chopped fresh basil leaves
2 tablespoons finely chopped fresh flat-leaf parsley
1 tablespoon finely chopped fresh tarragon
1 tablespoon finely chopped fresh chives
Finely grated zest of ½ lemon
1 tablespoon fresh lemon juice
Flaky sea salt, for serving

1. Preheat the air fryer to 400ºF (204ºC). 2. In a bowl, toss together the shishitos and oil to evenly coat and season with kosher salt and black pepper. Transfer to the air fryer and air fry for 6 minutes, shaking the basket halfway through, or until the shishitos are blistered and lightly charred. 3. Meanwhile, in a small bowl, whisk together the mayonnaise, basil, parsley, tarragon, chives, lemon zest, and lemon juice. 4. Pile the peppers on a plate, sprinkle with flaky sea salt, and serve hot with the dressing.

Cheese-Stuffed Blooming Onion

Prep time: 10 minutes | Cook time: 15 minutes | Serves 2

1 large yellow onion (14 ounces / 397 g)	cheese
1 tablespoon olive oil	3 tablespoons mayonnaise
Kosher salt and freshly ground black pepper, to taste	1 tablespoon fresh lemon juice
	1 tablespoon chopped fresh flat-leaf parsley
¼ cup plus 2 tablespoons panko bread crumbs	2 teaspoons whole-grain Dijon mustard
¼ cup grated Parmesan	1 garlic clove, minced

1. Place the onion on a cutting board and trim the top off and peel off the outer skin. Turn the onion upside down and use a paring knife, cut vertical slits halfway through the onion at ½-inch intervals around the onion, keeping the root intact. When you turn the onion right side up, it should open up like the petals of a flower. Drizzle the cut sides of the onion with the olive oil and season with salt and pepper. Place petal-side up in the air fryer and air fry at 350°F (177°C) for 10 minutes. 2. Meanwhile, in a bowl, stir together the panko, Parmesan, mayonnaise, lemon juice, parsley, mustard, and garlic until incorporated into a smooth paste. 3. Remove the onion from the fryer and stuff the paste all over and in between the onion "petals." Return the onion to the air fryer and air fry at 375°F (191°C) until the onion is tender in the center and the bread crumb mixture is golden brown, about 5 minutes. Remove the onion from the air fryer, transfer to a plate, and serve hot.

Cheesy Italian Arancini

Prep time: 20 minutes | Cook time: 10 minutes | Makes 8 rice balls

1½ cups cooked sticky rice	(small enough to stuff into olives)
½ teaspoon Italian seasoning blend	2 eggs
¾ teaspoon salt, divided	⅓ cup Italian bread crumbs
8 black olives, pitted	¾ cup panko bread crumbs
1 ounce (28 g) Mozzarella cheese, cut into tiny pieces	Cooking spray

1. Preheat air fryer to 390°F (199°C). 2. Stuff each black olive with a piece of Mozzarella cheese. Set aside. 3. In a bowl, combine the cooked sticky rice, Italian seasoning blend, and ½ teaspoon of salt and stir to mix well. Form the rice mixture into a log with your hands and divide it into 8 equal portions. Mold each portion around a black olive and roll into a ball. 4. Transfer to the freezer to chill for 10 to 15 minutes until firm. 5. In a shallow dish, place the Italian bread crumbs. In a separate shallow dish, whisk the eggs. In a third shallow dish, combine the panko bread crumbs and remaining salt. 6. One by one, roll the rice balls in the Italian bread crumbs, then dip in the whisked eggs, finally coat them with the panko bread crumbs. 7. Arrange the rice balls in the air fryer basket and spritz both sides with cooking spray. 8. Air fry for 10 minutes until the rice balls are golden brown. Flip the balls halfway through the cooking time. 9. Serve warm.

Roasted Mushrooms with Garlic

Prep time: 3 minutes | Cook time: 22 to 27 minutes | Serves 4

16 garlic cloves, peeled	⅛ teaspoon freshly ground black pepper
2 teaspoons olive oil, divided	1 tablespoon white wine or low-sodium vegetable broth
16 button mushrooms	
½ teaspoon dried marjoram	

1. In a baking pan, mix the garlic with 1 teaspoon of olive oil. Roast in the air fryer at 350°F (177°C) for 12 minutes. 2. Add the mushrooms, marjoram, and pepper. Stir to coat. Drizzle with the remaining 1 teaspoon of olive oil and the white wine. 3. Return to the air fryer and roast for 10 to 15 minutes more, or until the mushrooms and garlic cloves are tender. Serve.

Cheese-Stuffed Jalapeños

Prep time: 12 minutes | Cook time: 6 to 8 minutes | Serves 10

8 ounces (227 g) cream cheese, at room temperature	minced
	1 teaspoon chili powder
1 cup panko bread crumbs, divided	10 jalapeño peppers, halved and seeded
2 tablespoons fresh parsley,	Cooking oil spray

1. In a small bowl, whisk the cream cheese, ½ cup of panko, the parsley, and chili powder until combined. Stuff the cheese mixture into the jalapeño halves. 2. Sprinkle the tops of the stuffed jalapeños with the remaining ½ cup of panko and press it lightly into the filling. 3. Insert the crisper plate into the basket and the basket into the unit. Preheat the unit by selecting AIR FRY, setting the temperature to 375°F (191°C), and setting the time to 3 minutes. Select START/STOP to begin. 4. Once the unit is preheated, spray the crisper plate with cooking oil. Place the poppers into the basket. 5. Select AIR FRY, set the temperature to 375°F (191°C), and set the time to 8 minutes. Select START/STOP to begin. 6. After 6 minutes, check the poppers. If they are softened and the cheese is melted, they are done. If not, resume cooking. 7. When the cooking is complete, serve warm.

Spiced Nuts

Prep time: 5 minutes | Cook time: 25 minutes | Makes 3 cups

1 egg white, lightly beaten	¼ teaspoon ground allspice
¼ cup sugar	Pinch ground cayenne pepper
1 teaspoon salt	1 cup pecan halves
½ teaspoon ground cinnamon	1 cup cashews
¼ teaspoon ground cloves	1 cup almonds

1. Combine the egg white with the sugar and spices in a bowl. 2. Preheat the air fryer to 300ºF (149ºC). 3. Spray or brush the air fryer basket with vegetable oil. Toss the nuts together in the spiced egg white and transfer the nuts to the air fryer basket. 4. Air fry for 25 minutes, stirring the nuts in the basket a few times during the cooking process. Taste the nuts (carefully because they will be very hot) to see if they are crunchy and nicely toasted. Air fry for a few more minutes if necessary. 5. Serve warm or cool to room temperature and store in an airtight container for up to two weeks.

Shrimp Egg Rolls

Prep time: 15 minutes | Cook time: 10 minutes per batch | Serves 4

1 tablespoon vegetable oil	¼ cup hoisin sauce
½ head green or savoy cabbage, finely shredded	Freshly ground black pepper, to taste
1 cup shredded carrots	1 pound (454 g) cooked shrimp, diced
1 cup canned bean sprouts, drained	¼ cup scallions
1 tablespoon soy sauce	8 egg roll wrappers
½ teaspoon sugar	Vegetable oil
1 teaspoon sesame oil	Duck sauce

1. Preheat a large sauté pan over medium-high heat. Add the oil and cook the cabbage, carrots and bean sprouts until they start to wilt, about 3 minutes. Add the soy sauce, sugar, sesame oil, hoisin sauce and black pepper. Sauté for a few more minutes. Stir in the shrimp and scallions and cook until the vegetables are just tender. Transfer the mixture to a colander in a bowl to cool. Press or squeeze out any excess water from the filling so that you don't end up with soggy egg rolls. 2. Make the egg rolls: Place the egg roll wrappers on a flat surface with one of the points facing towards you so they look like diamonds. Dividing the filling evenly between the eight wrappers, spoon the mixture onto the center of the egg roll wrappers. Spread the filling across the center of the wrappers from the left corner to the right corner, but leave 2 inches from each corner empty. Brush the empty sides of the wrapper with a little water. Fold the bottom corner of the wrapper tightly up over the filling, trying to avoid making any air pockets. Fold the left corner in toward the center and then the right corner toward the center. It should now look like an envelope. Tightly roll the egg roll from the bottom to the top open corner. Press to seal the egg roll together, brushing with a little extra water if need be. Repeat this technique with all 8 egg rolls. 3. Preheat the air fryer to 370ºF (188ºC). 4. Spray or brush all sides of the egg rolls with vegetable oil. Air fry four egg rolls at a time for 10 minutes, turning them over halfway through the cooking time. 5. Serve hot with duck sauce or your favorite dipping sauce.

Crispy Mexican-Style Tortilla Chips

Prep time: 5 minutes | Cook time: 5 minutes | Serves 4

Olive oil	½ teaspoon paprika
½ teaspoon salt	Pinch cayenne pepper
½ teaspoon ground cumin	8 (6-inch) corn tortillas, each cut into 6 wedges
½ teaspoon chili powder	

1. Spray fryer basket lightly with olive oil. 2. In a small bowl, combine the salt, cumin, chili powder, paprika, and cayenne pepper. 3. Place the tortilla wedges in the air fryer basket in a single layer. Spray the tortillas lightly with oil and sprinkle with some of the seasoning mixture. You will need to cook the tortillas in batches. 4. Air fry at 375ºF (191ºC) for 2 to 3 minutes. Shake the basket and cook until the chips are light brown and crispy, an additional 2 to 3 minutes. Watch the chips closely so they do not burn.

Ranch-Flavored Oyster Crackers

Prep time: 3 minutes | Cook time: 12 minutes | Serves 6

Oil, for spraying	½ teaspoon granulated garlic
¼ cup olive oil	½ teaspoon salt
2 teaspoons dry ranch seasoning	1 (9 ounces / 255 g) bag oyster crackers
1 teaspoon chili powder	
½ teaspoon dried dill	

1. Preheat the air fryer to 325ºF (163ºC). Line the air fryer basket with parchment and spray lightly with oil. 2. In a large bowl, mix together the olive oil, ranch seasoning, chili powder, dill, garlic, and salt. Add the crackers and toss until evenly coated. 3. Place the mixture in the prepared basket. 4. Cook for 10 to 12 minutes, shaking or stirring every 3 to 4 minutes, or until crisp and golden brown.

Asiago Shishito Peppers

Prep time: 5 minutes | Cook time: 10 minutes | Serves 4

Oil, for spraying
6 ounces (170 g) shishito peppers
1 tablespoon olive oil
½ teaspoon salt
½ teaspoon lemon pepper
⅓ cup grated Asiago cheese, divided

1. Line the air fryer basket with parchment and spray lightly with oil. 2. Rinse the shishitos and pat dry with paper towels. 3. In a large bowl, mix together the shishitos, olive oil, salt, and lemon pepper. Place the shishitos in the prepared basket. 4. Roast at 350°F (177°C) for 10 minutes, or until blistered but not burned. 5. Sprinkle with half of the cheese and cook for 1 more minute. 6. Transfer to a serving plate. Immediately sprinkle with the remaining cheese and serve.

Cheesy Mushroom Pastry Tarts

Prep time: 15 minutes | Cook time: 38 minutes | Makes 15 tarts

2 tablespoons extra-virgin olive oil, divided
1 small white onion, sliced
8 ounces (227 g) shiitake mushrooms, sliced
¼ teaspoon sea salt
¼ teaspoon freshly ground black pepper
¼ cup dry white wine
1 sheet frozen puff pastry, thawed
1 cup shredded Gruyère cheese
Cooking oil spray
1 tablespoon thinly sliced fresh chives

1. Insert the crisper plate into the basket and the basket into the unit. Preheat the unit by selecting BAKE, setting the temperature to 300°F (149°C), and setting the time to 3 minutes. Select START/STOP to begin. 2. In a heatproof bowl that fits into the basket, stir together 1 tablespoon of olive oil, the onion, and the mushrooms. 3. Once the unit is preheated, place the bowl into the basket. 4. Select BAKE, set the temperature to 300°F (149°C), and set the time to 7 minutes. Select START/STOP to begin. 5. After about 2½ minutes, stir the vegetables. Resume cooking. After another 2½ minutes, the vegetables should be browned and tender. Season with the salt and pepper and add the wine. Resume cooking until the liquid evaporates, about 2 minutes. 6. When the cooking is complete, place the bowl on a heatproof surface. 7. Increase the air fryer temperature to 390°F (199°C) and set the time to 3 minutes. Select START/STOP to begin. 8. Unfold the puff pastry and cut it into 15 (3-by-3-inch) squares. Using a fork, pierce the dough and brush both sides with the remaining 1 tablespoon of olive oil. 9. Evenly distribute half the cheese among the puff pastry squares, leaving a ½-inch border around the edges. Divide the mushroom-onion mixture among the pastry squares and top with the remaining cheese. 10. Once the unit is preheated, spray the crisper plate with cooking oil. Working in batches, place 5 tarts into the basket; do not stack or overlap. 11. Select BAKE, set the temperature to 390°F (199°C), and set the time to 8 minutes. Select START/STOP to begin. 12. After 6 minutes, check the tarts; if not yet golden brown, resume cooking for about 2 minutes more. 13. When the cooking is complete, remove the tarts and transfer to a wire rack to cool. Repeat steps 10, 11, and 12 with the remaining tarts. 14. Serve garnished with the chives.

Mediterranean Style Greek Tacos

Prep time: 10 minutes | Cook time: 3 minutes | Makes 8 small tacos

8 small flour tortillas (4-inch diameter)
8 tablespoons hummus
4 tablespoons crumbled feta cheese
4 tablespoons chopped kalamata or other olives (optional)
Olive oil for misting

1. Place 1 tablespoon of hummus or tapenade in the center of each tortilla. Top with 1 teaspoon of feta crumbles and 1 teaspoon of chopped olives, if using. 2. Using your finger or a small spoon, moisten the edges of the tortilla all around with water. 3. Fold tortilla over to make a half-moon shape. Press center gently. Then press the edges firmly to seal in the filling. 4. Mist both sides with olive oil. 5. Place in air fryer basket very close but try not to overlap. 6. Air fry at 390°F (199°C) for 3 minutes, just until lightly browned and crispy.

Garlic-Infused Edamame

Prep time: 5 minutes | Cook time: 10 minutes | Serves 4

Olive oil
1 (16-ounce / 454-g) bag frozen edamame in pods
½ teaspoon salt
½ teaspoon garlic salt
¼ teaspoon freshly ground black pepper
½ teaspoon red pepper flakes (optional)

1. Spray the air fryer basket lightly with olive oil. 2. In a medium bowl, add the frozen edamame and lightly spray with olive oil. Toss to coat. 3. In a small bowl, mix together the salt, garlic salt, black pepper, and red pepper flakes (if using). Add the mixture to the edamame and toss until evenly coated. 4. Place half the edamame in the air fryer basket. Do not overfill the basket. 5. Air fry at 375°F (191°C) for 5 minutes. Shake the basket and cook until the edamame is starting to brown and get crispy, 3 to 5 more minutes. 6. Repeat with the remaining edamame and serve immediately.

70 | Chapter 7 Snacks and Appetizers

Cheesy Parmesan-Crusted Fries

Prep time: 10 minutes | Cook time: 25 minutes | Serves 2 to 3

2 to 3 large russet potatoes, peeled and cut into ½-inch sticks
2 teaspoons vegetable or canola oil
¾ cup grated Parmesan cheese
½ teaspoon salt
Freshly ground black pepper, to taste
1 teaspoon fresh chopped parsley

1. Bring a large saucepan of salted water to a boil on the stovetop while you peel and cut the potatoes. Blanch the potatoes in the boiling salted water for 4 minutes while you preheat the air fryer to 400°F (204°C). Strain the potatoes and rinse them with cold water. Dry them well with a clean kitchen towel. 2. Toss the dried potato sticks gently with the oil and place them in the air fryer basket. Air fry for 25 minutes, shaking the basket a few times while the fries cook to help them brown evenly. 3. Combine the Parmesan cheese, salt and pepper. With 2 minutes left on the air fryer cooking time, sprinkle the fries with the Parmesan cheese mixture. Toss the fries to coat them evenly with the cheese mixture and continue to air fry for the final 2 minutes, until the cheese has melted and just starts to brown. Sprinkle the finished fries with chopped parsley, a little more grated Parmesan cheese if you like, and serve.

Rumaki

Prep time: 30 minutes | Cook time: 10 to 12 minutes per batch | Makes about 24 rumaki

10 ounces (283 g) raw chicken livers
1 can sliced water chestnuts, drained
¼ cup low-sodium teriyaki sauce
12 slices turkey bacon

1. Cut livers into 1½-inch pieces, trimming out tough veins as you slice. 2. Place livers, water chestnuts, and teriyaki sauce in small container with lid. If needed, add another tablespoon of teriyaki sauce to make sure livers are covered. Refrigerate for 1 hour. 3. When ready to cook, cut bacon slices in half crosswise. 4. Wrap 1 piece of liver and 1 slice of water chestnut in each bacon strip. Secure with toothpick. 5. When you have wrapped half of the livers, place them in the air fryer basket in a single layer. 6. Air fry at 390°F (199°C) for 10 to 12 minutes, until liver is done and bacon is crispy. 7. While first batch cooks, wrap the remaining livers. Repeat step 6 to cook your second batch.

Crispy Egg Roll Pizza Sticks

Prep time: 10 minutes | Cook time: 5 minutes | Serves 4

Olive oil
8 pieces reduced-fat string cheese
8 egg roll wrappers
24 slices turkey pepperoni
Marinara sauce, for dipping (optional)

1. Spray the air fryer basket lightly with olive oil. Fill a small bowl with water. 2. Place each egg roll wrapper diagonally on a work surface. It should look like a diamond. 3. Place 3 slices of turkey pepperoni in a vertical line down the center of the wrapper. 4. Place 1 Mozzarella cheese stick on top of the turkey pepperoni. 5. Fold the top and bottom corners of the egg roll wrapper over the cheese stick. 6. Fold the left corner over the cheese stick and roll the cheese stick up to resemble a spring roll. Dip a finger in the water and seal the edge of the roll 7. Repeat with the rest of the pizza sticks. 8. Place them in the air fryer basket in a single layer, making sure to leave a little space between each one. Lightly spray the pizza sticks with oil. You may need to cook these in batches. 9. Air fry at 375°F (191°C) until the pizza sticks are lightly browned and crispy, about 5 minutes. 10. These are best served hot while the cheese is melted. Accompany with a small bowl of marinara sauce, if desired.

Chapter 8
Vegetables and Sides

Fire-Roasted Tomato Salsa

Prep time: 15 minutes | Cook time: 30 minutes | Makes 2 cups

2 large San Marzano tomatoes, cored and cut into large chunks
½ medium white onion, peeled and large-diced
½ medium jalapeño, seeded and large-diced
2 cloves garlic, peeled and diced
½ teaspoon salt
1 tablespoon coconut oil
¼ cup fresh lime juice

1. Place tomatoes, onion, and jalapeño into an ungreased round nonstick baking dish. Add garlic, then sprinkle with salt and drizzle with coconut oil. 2. Place dish into air fryer basket. Adjust the temperature to 300ºF (149ºC) and bake for 30 minutes. Vegetables will be dark brown around the edges and tender when done. 3. Pour mixture into a food processor or blender. Add lime juice. Process on low speed 30 seconds until only a few chunks remain. 4. Transfer salsa to a sealable container and refrigerate at least 1 hour. Serve chilled.

Roasted Radishes with Sea Salt

Prep time: 5 minutes | Cook time: 18 minutes | Serves 4

1 pound (454 g) radishes, ends trimmed if needed
2 tablespoons olive oil
½ teaspoon sea salt

1. Preheat the air fryer to 360°F(182°C). 2. In a large bowl, combine the radishes with olive oil and sea salt. 3. Pour the radishes into the air fryer and roast for 10 minutes. Stir or turn the radishes over and roast for 8 minutes more, then serve.

Sausage-Filled Baked Mushrooms

Prep time: 10 minutes | Cook time: 8 minutes | Serves 2

6 large portobello mushroom caps
½ pound (227 g) Italian sausage
¼ cup chopped onion
2 tablespoons blanched finely ground almond flour
¼ cup grated Parmesan cheese
1 teaspoon minced fresh garlic

1. Use a spoon to hollow out each mushroom cap, reserving scrapings. 2. In a medium skillet over medium heat, brown the sausage about 10 minutes or until fully cooked and no pink remains. Drain and then add reserved mushroom scrapings, onion, almond flour, Parmesan, and garlic. Gently fold ingredients together and continue cooking an additional minute, then remove from heat. 3. Evenly spoon the mixture into mushroom caps and place the caps into a 6-inch round pan. Place pan into the air fryer basket. 4. Adjust the temperature to 375ºF (191ºC) and set the timer for 8 minutes. 5. When finished cooking, the tops will be browned and bubbling. Serve warm.

Simple Greek-Style Ratatouille

Prep time: 15 minutes | Cook time: 40 minutes | Serves 6

2 russet potatoes, cubed
½ cup Roma tomatoes, cubed
1 eggplant, cubed
1 zucchini, cubed
1 red onion, chopped
1 red bell pepper, chopped
2 garlic cloves, minced
1 teaspoon dried mint
1 teaspoon dried parsley
1 teaspoon dried oregano
½ teaspoon salt
½ teaspoon black pepper
¼ teaspoon red pepper flakes
⅓ cup olive oil
1 (8-ounce / 227-g) can tomato paste
¼ cup vegetable broth
¼ cup water

1. Preheat the air fryer to 320°F(160°C). 2. In a large bowl, combine the potatoes, tomatoes, eggplant, zucchini, onion, bell pepper, garlic, mint, parsley, oregano, salt, black pepper, and red pepper flakes. 3. In a small bowl, mix together the olive oil, tomato paste, broth, and water. 4. Pour the oil-and-tomato-paste mixture over the vegetables and toss until everything is coated. 5. Pour the coated vegetables into the air fryer basket in an even layer and roast for 20 minutes. After 20 minutes, stir well and spread out again. Roast for an additional 10 minutes, then repeat the process and cook for another 10 minutes.

Roasted Grape Tomatoes and Asparagus

Prep time: 5 minutes | Cook time: 12 minutes | Serves 6

2 cups grape tomatoes
1 bunch asparagus, trimmed
2 tablespoons olive oil
3 garlic cloves, minced
½ teaspoon kosher salt

1. Preheat the air fryer to 380°F(193°C). 2. In a large bowl, combine all of the ingredients, tossing until the vegetables are well coated with oil. 3. Pour the vegetable mixture into the air fryer basket and spread into a single layer, then roast for 12 minutes.

Corn on the Cob

Prep time: 5 minutes | Cook time: 12 to 15 minutes | Serves 4

2 large ears fresh corn
Olive oil for misting
Salt, to taste (optional)

1. Shuck corn, remove silks, and wash. 2. Cut or break each ear in half crosswise. 3. Spray corn with olive oil. 4. Air fry at 390°F (199°C) for 12 to 15 minutes or until browned as much as you like. 5. Serve plain or with coarsely ground salt.

Garlic and Thyme Tomatoes

Prep time: 10 minutes | Cook time: 15 minutes | Serves 2 to 4

4 Roma tomatoes
1 tablespoon olive oil
Salt and freshly ground
black pepper, to taste
1 clove garlic, minced
½ teaspoon dried thyme

1. Preheat the air fryer to 390°F (199°C). 2. Cut the tomatoes in half and scoop out the seeds and any pithy parts with your fingers. Place the tomatoes in a bowl and toss with the olive oil, salt, pepper, garlic and thyme. 3. Transfer the tomatoes to the air fryer, cut side up. Air fry for 15 minutes. The edges should just start to brown. Let the tomatoes cool to an edible temperature for a few minutes and then use in pastas, on top of crostini, or as an accompaniment to any poultry, meat or fish.

Herbed Parmesan Focaccia

Prep time: 10 minutes | Cook time: 10 minutes | Serves 6

1 cup shredded Mozzarella cheese
1 ounce (28 g) full-fat cream cheese
1 cup blanched finely ground almond flour
¼ cup ground golden flaxseed
¼ cup grated Parmesan cheese
½ teaspoon baking soda
2 large eggs
½ teaspoon garlic powder
¼ teaspoon dried basil
¼ teaspoon dried rosemary
2 tablespoons salted butter, melted and divided

1. Place Mozzarella, cream cheese, and almond flour into a large microwave-safe bowl and microwave for 1 minute. Add the flaxseed, Parmesan, and baking soda and stir until smooth ball forms. If the mixture cools too much, it will be hard to mix. Return to microwave for 10 to 15 seconds to rewarm if necessary. 2. Stir in eggs. You may need to use your hands to get them fully incorporated. Just keep stirring and they will absorb into the dough. 3. Sprinkle dough with garlic powder, basil, and rosemary and knead into dough. Grease a baking pan with 1 tablespoon melted butter. Press the dough evenly into the pan. Place pan into the air fryer basket. 4. Adjust the temperature to 400°F (204°C) and bake for 10 minutes. 5. At 7 minutes, cover with foil if bread begins to get too dark. 6. Remove and let cool at least 30 minutes. Drizzle with remaining butter and serve.

Broccoli with Sesame Dressing

Prep time: 5 minutes | Cook time: 10 minutes | Serves 4

6 cups broccoli florets, cut into bite-size pieces
1 tablespoon olive oil
¼ teaspoon salt
2 tablespoons sesame seeds
2 tablespoons rice vinegar
2 tablespoons coconut aminos
2 tablespoons sesame oil
½ teaspoon Swerve
¼ teaspoon red pepper flakes (optional)

1. Preheat the air fryer to 400°F (204°C). 2. In a large bowl, toss the broccoli with the olive oil and salt until thoroughly coated. 3. Transfer the broccoli to the air fryer basket. Pausing halfway through the cooking time to shake the basket, air fry for 10 minutes until the stems are tender and the edges are beginning to crisp. 4. Meanwhile, in the same large bowl, whisk together the sesame seeds, vinegar, coconut aminos, sesame oil, Swerve, and red pepper flakes (if using). 5. Transfer the broccoli to the bowl and toss until thoroughly coated with the seasonings. Serve warm or at room temperature.

Sweet and Crispy Roasted Pearl Onions

Prep time: 5 minutes | Cook time: 18 minutes | Serves 3

1 (14½ ounces / 411 g) package frozen pearl onions (do not thaw)
2 tablespoons extra-virgin olive oil
2 tablespoons balsamic vinegar
2 teaspoons finely chopped fresh rosemary
½ teaspoon kosher salt
¼ teaspoon black pepper

1. In a medium bowl, combine the onions, olive oil, vinegar, rosemary, salt, and pepper until well coated. 2. Transfer the onions to the air fryer basket. Set the air fryer to 400°F (204°C) for 18 minutes, or until the onions are tender and lightly charred, stirring once or twice during the cooking time.

Lime-Infused Cauliflower

Prep time: 10 minutes | Cook time: 7 minutes | Serves 4

2 cups chopped cauliflower florets
2 tablespoons coconut oil, melted
2 teaspoons chili powder
½ teaspoon garlic powder
1 medium lime
2 tablespoons chopped cilantro

1. In a large bowl, toss cauliflower with coconut oil. Sprinkle with chili powder and garlic powder. Place seasoned cauliflower into the air fryer basket. 2. Adjust the temperature to 350°F (177°C) and set the timer for 7 minutes. 3. Cauliflower will be tender and begin to turn golden at the edges. Place into a serving bowl. 4. Cut the lime into quarters and squeeze juice over cauliflower. Garnish with cilantro.

Buttery Garlic Fried Cabbage

Prep time: 5 minutes | Cook time: 9 minutes | Serves 2

Oil, for spraying
½ head cabbage, cut into bite-size pieces
2 tablespoons unsalted butter, melted
1 teaspoon granulated garlic
½ teaspoon coarse sea salt
¼ teaspoon freshly ground black pepper

1. Line the air fryer basket with parchment and spray lightly with oil. 2. In a large bowl, mix together the cabbage, butter, garlic, salt, and black pepper until evenly coated. 3. Transfer the cabbage to the prepared basket and spray lightly with oil. 4. Air fry at 375°F (191°C) for 5 minutes, toss, and cook for another 3 to 4 minutes, or until lightly crispy.

Asian-Inspired Roasted Broccoli

Prep time: 10 minutes | Cook time: 15 minutes | Serves 4

Broccoli:
Oil, for spraying
1 pound (454 g) broccoli florets
Sauce:
2 tablespoons soy sauce
2 teaspoons honey
2 teaspoons peanut oil
1 tablespoon minced garlic
½ teaspoon salt
2 teaspoons Sriracha
1 teaspoon rice vinegar

Make the Broccoli 1. Line the air fryer basket with parchment and spray lightly with oil. 2. In a large bowl, toss together the broccoli, peanut oil, garlic, and salt until evenly coated. 3. Spread out the broccoli in an even layer in the prepared basket. 4. Air fry at 400°F (204°C) for 15 minutes, stirring halfway through. Make the Sauce 5. Meanwhile, in a small microwave-safe bowl, combine the soy sauce, honey, Sriracha, and rice vinegar and microwave on high for about 15 seconds. Stir to combine. 6. Transfer the broccoli to a serving bowl and add the sauce. Gently toss until evenly coated and serve immediately.

Fresh Fig and Chickpea Arugula Salad

Prep time: 15 minutes | Cook time: 20 minutes | Serves 4

8 fresh figs, halved
1½ cups cooked chickpeas
1 teaspoon crushed roasted cumin seeds
4 tablespoons balsamic vinegar
2 tablespoons extra-virgin olive oil, plus more for greasing
Salt and ground black pepper, to taste
3 cups arugula rocket, washed and dried

1. Preheat the air fryer to 375°F (191°C). 2. Cover the air fryer basket with aluminum foil and grease lightly with oil. Put the figs in the air fryer basket and air fry for 10 minutes. 3. In a bowl, combine the chickpeas and cumin seeds. 4. Remove the air fried figs from the air fryer and replace with the chickpeas. Air fry for 10 minutes. Leave to cool. 5. In the meantime, prepare the dressing. Mix the balsamic vinegar, olive oil, salt and pepper. 6. In a salad bowl, combine the arugula rocket with the cooled figs and chickpeas. 7. Toss with the sauce and serve.

Herb-Roasted Parmesan Butternut Squash

Prep time: 15 minutes | Cook time: 20 minutes | Serves 4

2½ cups butternut squash, cubed into 1-inch pieces (approximately 1 medium)
2 tablespoons olive oil
¼ teaspoon salt
¼ teaspoon garlic powder
¼ teaspoon black pepper
1 tablespoon fresh thyme
¼ cup grated Parmesan

1. Preheat the air fryer to 360°F (182°C). 2. In a large bowl, combine the cubed squash with the olive oil, salt, garlic powder, pepper, and thyme until the squash is well coated. 3. Pour this mixture into the air fryer basket, and roast for 10 minutes. Stir and roast another 8 to 10 minutes more. 4. Remove the squash from the air fryer and toss with freshly grated Parmesan before serving.

Roasted Sweet Potatoes

Prep time: 10 minutes | Cook time: 25 minutes | Serves 4

Cooking oil spray
2 sweet potatoes, peeled and cut into 1-inch cubes
1 tablespoon extra-virgin olive oil
Pinch salt
Freshly ground black pepper, to taste
½ teaspoon dried thyme
½ teaspoon dried marjoram
¼ cup grated Parmesan cheese

1. Insert the crisper plate into the basket and the basket into the unit. Preheat the unit by selecting AIR ROAST, setting the temperature to 330°F (166°C), and setting the time to 3 minutes. Select START/STOP to begin. 2. Once the unit is preheated, spray the crisper plate with cooking oil. Put the sweet potato cubes into the basket and drizzle with olive oil. Toss gently to coat. Sprinkle with the salt, pepper, thyme, and marjoram and toss again. 3. Select AIR ROAST, set the temperature to 330°F (166°C), and set the time to 25 minutes. Select START/STOP to begin. 4. After 10 minutes, remove the basket and shake the potatoes. Reinsert the basket to resume cooking. After another 10 minutes, remove the basket and shake the potatoes one more time. Sprinkle evenly with the Parmesan cheese. Reinsert the basket to resume cooking. 5. When the cooking is complete, the potatoes should be tender. Serve immediately.

Broccoli with Lemon Juice

Prep time: 10 minutes | Cook time: 9 to 14 minutes per batch | Serves 4

1 large head broccoli, rinsed and patted dry
2 teaspoons extra-virgin olive oil
1 tablespoon freshly squeezed lemon juice
Olive oil spray

1. Cut off the broccoli florets and separate them. You can use the stems, too; peel the stems and cut them into 1-inch chunks. 2. Insert the crisper plate into the basket and the basket into the unit. Preheat the unit by selecting AIR ROAST, setting the temperature to 390°F (199°C), and setting the time to 3 minutes. Select START/STOP to begin. 3. In a large bowl, toss together the broccoli, olive oil, and lemon juice until coated. 4. Once the unit is preheated, spray the crisper plate with olive oil. Working in batches, place half the broccoli into the basket. 5. Select AIR ROAST, set the temperature to 390°F (199°C), and set the time to 14 minutes. Select START/STOP to begin. 6. After 5 minutes, remove the basket and shake the broccoli. Reinsert the basket to resume cooking. Check the broccoli after 5 minutes. If it is crisp-tender and slightly brown around the edges, it is done. If not, resume cooking. 7. When the cooking is complete, transfer the broccoli to a serving bowl. Repeat steps 5 and 6 with the remaining broccoli. Serve immediately.

Stuffed Red Peppers with Herbed Ricotta and Tomatoes

Prep time: 10 minutes | Cook time: 20 minutes | Serves 4

2 red bell peppers
1 cup cooked brown rice
2 Roma tomatoes, diced
1 garlic clove, minced
¼ teaspoon salt
¼ teaspoon black pepper
4 ounces (113 g) ricotta
3 tablespoons fresh basil, chopped
3 tablespoons fresh oregano, chopped
¼ cup shredded Parmesan, for topping

1. Preheat the air fryer to 360°F (182°C). 2. Cut the bell peppers in half and remove the seeds and stem. 3. In a medium bowl, combine the brown rice, tomatoes, garlic, salt, and pepper. 4. Distribute the rice filling evenly among the four bell pepper halves. 5. In a small bowl, combine the ricotta, basil, and oregano. Put the herbed cheese over the top of the rice mixture in each bell pepper. 6. Place the bell peppers into the air fryer and roast for 20 minutes. 7. Remove and serve with shredded Parmesan on top.

Garlic-Lemon Roasted Mushrooms

Prep time: 10 minutes | Cook time: 10 to 15 minutes | Serves 6

12 ounces (340 g) sliced mushrooms
1 tablespoon avocado oil
Sea salt and freshly ground black pepper, to taste
3 tablespoons unsalted butter
1 teaspoon minced garlic
1 teaspoon freshly squeezed lemon juice
½ teaspoon red pepper flakes
2 tablespoons chopped fresh parsley

1. Place the mushrooms in a medium bowl and toss with the oil. Season to taste with salt and pepper. 2. Place the mushrooms in a single layer in the air fryer basket. Set your air fryer to 375°F (191°C) and roast for 10 to 15 minutes, until the mushrooms are tender. 3. While the mushrooms cook, melt the butter in a small pot or skillet over medium-low heat. Stir in the garlic and cook for 30 seconds. Remove the pot from the heat and stir in the lemon juice and red pepper flakes. 4. Toss the mushrooms with the lemon-garlic butter and garnish with the parsley before serving.

Golden Potato Croquettes

Prep time: 15 minutes | Cook time: 15 minutes | Serves 10

¼ cup nutritional yeast
2 cups boiled potatoes, mashed
1 flax egg
1 tablespoon flour
2 tablespoons chopped chives
Salt and ground black pepper, to taste
2 tablespoons vegetable oil
¼ cup bread crumbs

1. Preheat the air fryer to 400°F (204°C). 2. In a bowl, combine the nutritional yeast, potatoes, flax egg, flour, and chives. Sprinkle with salt and pepper as desired. 3. In a separate bowl, mix the vegetable oil and bread crumbs to achieve a crumbly consistency. 4. Shape the potato mixture into small balls and dip each one into the bread crumb mixture. 5. Put the croquettes inside the air fryer and air fry for 15 minutes, ensuring the croquettes turn golden brown. 6. Serve immediately.

Chiles Rellenos with Red Chile Sauce

Prep time: 20 minutes | Cook time: 20 minutes | Serves 2

Peppers:
2 poblano peppers, rinsed and dried
⅔ cup thawed frozen or drained canned corn kernels
1 scallion, sliced
2 tablespoons chopped fresh cilantro
½ teaspoon kosher salt
¼ teaspoon black pepper
⅔ cup grated Monterey Jack cheese

Sauce:
3 tablespoons extra-virgin olive oil
½ cup finely chopped yellow onion
2 teaspoons minced garlic
1 (6-ounce / 170-g) can tomato paste
2 tablespoons ancho chile powder
1 teaspoon dried oregano
1 teaspoon ground cumin
½ teaspoon kosher salt
2 cups chicken broth
2 tablespoons fresh lemon juice
Mexican crema or sour cream, for serving

1. For the peppers: Place the peppers in the air fryer basket. Set the air fryer to 400°F (204°C) for 10 minutes, turning the peppers halfway through the cooking time, until their skins are charred. Transfer the peppers to a resealable plastic bag, seal, and set aside to steam for 5 minutes. Peel the peppers and discard the skins. Cut a slit down the center of each pepper, starting at the stem and continuing to the tip. Remove the seeds, being careful not to tear the chile. 2. In a medium bowl, combine the corn, scallion, cilantro, salt, black pepper, and cheese; set aside. 3. Meanwhile, for the sauce: In a large skillet, heat the olive oil over medium-high heat. Add the onion and cook, stirring, until tender, about 5 minutes. Add the garlic and cook, stirring, for 30 seconds. Stir in the tomato paste, chile powder, oregano, and cumin, and salt. Cook, stirring, for 1 minute. Whisk in the broth and lemon juice. Bring to a simmer and cook, stirring occasionally, while the stuffed peppers finish cooking. 4. Cut a slit down the center of each poblano pepper, starting at the stem and continuing to the tip. Remove the seeds, being careful not to tear the chile. 5. Carefully stuff each pepper with half the corn mixture. Place the stuffed peppers in a baking pan. Place the pan in the air fryer basket. Set the air fryer to 400°F (204°C) for 10 minutes, or until the cheese has melted. 6. Transfer the stuffed peppers to a serving platter and drizzle with the sauce and some crema.

Spiced Butternut Squash

Prep time: 10 minutes | Cook time: 15 minutes | Serves 4

4 cups 1-inch-cubed butternut squash
2 tablespoons vegetable oil
1 to 2 tablespoons brown sugar
1 teaspoon Chinese five-spice powder

1. In a medium bowl, combine the squash, oil, sugar, and five-spice powder. Toss to coat. 2. Place the squash in the air fryer basket. Set the air fryer to 400°F (204°C) for 15 minutes or until tender.

Fresh Broccoli Salad with Dressing

Prep time: 5 minutes | Cook time: 7 minutes | Serves 4

2 cups fresh broccoli florets, chopped
1 tablespoon olive oil
¼ teaspoon salt
⅛ teaspoon ground black pepper
¼ cup lemon juice, divided
¼ cup shredded Parmesan cheese
¼ cup sliced roasted almonds

1. In a large bowl, toss broccoli and olive oil together. Sprinkle with salt and pepper, then drizzle with 2 tablespoons lemon juice. 2. Place broccoli into ungreased air fryer basket. Adjust the temperature to 350°F (177°C) and set the timer for 7 minutes, shaking the basket halfway through cooking. Broccoli will be golden on the edges when done. 3. Place broccoli into a large serving bowl and drizzle with remaining lemon juice. Sprinkle with Parmesan and almonds. Serve warm.

Blackened Zucchini with Kimchi-Herb Sauce

Prep time: 10 minutes | Cook time: 15 minutes | Serves 2

2 medium zucchini, ends trimmed (about 6 ounces / 170 g each)
2 tablespoons olive oil
½ cup kimchi, finely chopped
¼ cup finely chopped fresh cilantro
¼ cup finely chopped fresh flat-leaf parsley, plus more for garnish
2 tablespoons rice vinegar
2 teaspoons Asian chili-garlic sauce
1 teaspoon grated fresh ginger
Kosher salt and freshly ground black pepper, to taste

1. Brush the zucchini with half of the olive oil, place in the air fryer, and air fry at 400°F (204°C), turning halfway through, until lightly charred on the outside and tender, about 15 minutes. 2. Meanwhile, in a small bowl, combine the remaining 1 tablespoon olive oil, the kimchi, cilantro, parsley, vinegar, chili-garlic sauce, and ginger. 3. Once the zucchini is finished cooking, transfer it to a colander and let it cool for 5 minutes. Using your fingers, pinch and break the zucchini into bite-size pieces, letting them fall back into the colander. Season the zucchini with salt and pepper, toss to combine, then let sit a further 5 minutes to allow some of its liquid to drain. Pile the zucchini atop the kimchi sauce on a plate and sprinkle with more parsley to serve.

Chermoula-Roasted Beets

Prep time: 15 minutes | Cook time: 25 minutes | Serves 4

Chermoula:
1 cup packed fresh cilantro leaves
½ cup packed fresh parsley leaves
6 cloves garlic, peeled
2 teaspoons smoked paprika
2 teaspoons ground cumin
1 teaspoon ground coriander
½ to 1 teaspoon cayenne pepper
Pinch crushed saffron (optional)
½ cup extra-virgin olive oil
Kosher salt, to taste

Beets:
3 medium beets, trimmed, peeled, and cut into 1-inch chunks
2 tablespoons chopped fresh cilantro
2 tablespoons chopped fresh parsley

1. For the chermoula: In a food processor, combine the cilantro, parsley, garlic, paprika, cumin, coriander, and cayenne. Pulse until coarsely chopped. Add the saffron, if using, and process until combined. With the food processor running, slowly add the olive oil in a steady stream; process until the sauce is uniform. Season to taste with salt. 2. For the beets: In a large bowl, drizzle the beets with ½ cup of the chermoula, or enough to coat. Arrange the beets in the air fryer basket. Set the air fryer to 375°F (191°C) for 25 to minutes, or until the beets are tender. 3. Transfer the beets to a serving platter. Sprinkle with chopped cilantro and parsley and serve.

Rich and Creamy Spinach

Prep time: 10 minutes | Cook time: 15 minutes | Serves 4

Vegetable oil spray
1 (10-ounce / 283-g) package frozen spinach, thawed and squeezed dry
½ cup chopped onion
2 cloves garlic, minced
4 ounces (113 g) cream cheese, diced
½ teaspoon ground nutmeg
1 teaspoon kosher salt
1 teaspoon black pepper
½ cup grated Parmesan cheese

1. Spray a baking pan with vegetable oil spray. 2. In a medium bowl, combine the spinach, onion, garlic, cream cheese, nutmeg, salt, and pepper. Transfer to the prepared pan. 3. Place the pan in the air fryer basket. Set the air fryer to 350°F (177°C) for 10 minutes. Open and stir to thoroughly combine the cream cheese and spinach. 4. Sprinkle the Parmesan cheese on top. Set the air fryer to 400°F (204°C) for 5 minutes, or until the cheese has melted and browned.

Cheese-Walnut Stuffed Mushrooms

Prep time: 5 minutes | Cook time: 10 minutes | Serves 4

4 large portobello mushrooms
1 tablespoon canola oil
½ cup shredded Mozzarella cheese
⅓ cup minced walnuts
2 tablespoons chopped fresh parsley
Cooking spray

1. Preheat the air fryer to 350°F (177°C). Spritz the air fryer basket with cooking spray. 2. On a clean work surface, remove the mushroom stems. Scoop out the gills with a spoon and discard. Coat the mushrooms with canola oil. Top each mushroom evenly with the shredded Mozzarella cheese, followed by the minced walnuts. 3. Arrange the mushrooms in the air fryer and roast for 10 minutes until golden brown. 4. Transfer the mushrooms to a plate and sprinkle the parsley on top for garnish before serving.

Asparagus Fries

Prep time: 15 minutes | Cook time: 5 to 7 minutes per batch | Serves 4

12 ounces (340 g) fresh asparagus spears with tough ends trimmed off
2 egg whites
¼ cup water
¾ cup panko bread crumbs
¼ cup grated Parmesan cheese, plus 2 tablespoons
¼ teaspoon salt
Oil for misting or cooking spray

1. Preheat the air fryer to 390°F (199°C). 2. In a shallow dish, beat egg whites and water until slightly foamy. 3. In another shallow dish, combine panko, Parmesan, and salt. 4. Dip asparagus spears in egg, then roll in crumbs. Spray with oil or cooking spray. 5. Place a layer of asparagus in air fryer basket, leaving just a little space in between each spear. Stack another layer on top, crosswise. Air fry at 390°F (199°C) for 5 to 7 minutes, until crispy and golden brown. 6. Repeat to cook remaining asparagus.

Bacon and Cheddar-Topped Broccoli

Prep time: 10 minutes | Cook time: 10 minutes | Serves 2

3 cups fresh broccoli florets
1 tablespoon coconut oil
½ cup shredded sharp Cheddar cheese
¼ cup full-fat sour cream
4 slices sugar-free bacon, cooked and crumbled
1 scallion, sliced on the bias

1. Place broccoli into the air fryer basket and drizzle it with coconut oil. 2. Adjust the temperature to 350°F (177°C) and set the timer for 10 minutes. 3. Toss the basket two or three times during cooking to avoid burned spots. 4. When broccoli begins to crisp at ends, remove from fryer. Top with shredded cheese, sour cream, and crumbled bacon and garnish with scallion slices.

Sweet and Spiced Curried Fruit

Prep time: 10 minutes | Cook time: 20 minutes | Serves 6 to 8

1 cup cubed fresh pineapple
1 cup cubed fresh pear (firm, not overly ripe)
8 ounces (227 g) frozen peaches, thawed
1 (15-ounce / 425-g) can dark, sweet, pitted cherries with juice
2 tablespoons brown sugar
1 teaspoon curry powder

1. Combine all ingredients in large bowl. Stir gently to mix in the sugar and curry. 2. Pour into a baking pan and bake at 360°F (182°C) for 10 minutes. 3. Stir fruit and cook 10 more minutes. 4. Serve hot.

Shishito Pepper Roast

Prep time: 4 minutes | Cook time: 9 minutes | Serves 4

Cooking oil spray (sunflower, safflower, or refined coconut)
1 pound (454 g) shishito, Anaheim, or bell peppers, rinsed
1 tablespoon soy sauce
2 teaspoons freshly squeezed lime juice
2 large garlic cloves, pressed

1. Insert the crisper plate into the basket and the basket into the unit. Preheat the unit by selecting AIR ROAST, setting the temperature to 390°F (199°C), and setting the time to 3 minutes. Select START/STOP to begin. 2. Once the unit is preheated, spray the crisper plate and the basket with cooking oil. Place the peppers into the basket and spray them with oil. 3. Select AIR ROAST, set the temperature to 390°F (199°C), and set the time to 9 minutes. Select START/STOP to begin. 4. After 3 minutes, remove the basket and shake the peppers. Spray the peppers with more oil. Reinsert the basket to resume cooking. Repeat this step again after 3 minutes. 5. While the peppers roast, in a medium bowl, whisk the soy sauce, lime juice, and garlic until combined. Set aside. 6. When the cooking is complete, several of the peppers should have lots of nice browned spots on them. If using Anaheim or bell peppers, cut a slit in the side of each pepper and remove the seeds, which can be bitter. 7. Place the roasted peppers in the bowl with the sauce. Toss to coat the peppers evenly and serve.

Pepperoni Mushroom Pizza with Marinara Sauce

Prep time: 5 minutes | Cook time: 18 minutes | Serves 4

4 large portobello mushrooms, stems removed
4 teaspoons olive oil
1 cup marinara sauce
1 cup shredded Mozzarella cheese
10 slices sugar-free pepperoni

1. Preheat the air fryer to 375°F (191°C). 2. Brush each mushroom cap with the olive oil, one teaspoon for each cap. 3. Put on a baking sheet and bake, stem-side down, for 8 minutes. 4. Take out of the air fryer and divide the marinara sauce, Mozzarella cheese and pepperoni evenly among the caps. 5. Air fry for another 10 minutes until browned. 6. Serve hot.

Crispy Artichoke Hearts in Lemon Juice

Prep time: 10 minutes | Cook time: 15 minutes | Serves 2

1 (15-ounce / 425-g) can artichoke hearts in water, drained
1 egg
1 tablespoon water
¼ cup whole wheat bread crumbs
¼ teaspoon salt
¼ teaspoon paprika
½ lemon

1. Preheat the air fryer to 380°F(193°C). 2. In a medium shallow bowl, beat together the egg and water until frothy. 3. In a separate medium shallow bowl, mix together the bread crumbs, salt, and paprika. 4. Dip each artichoke heart into the egg mixture, then into the bread crumb mixture, coating the outside with the crumbs. Place the artichokes hearts in a single layer of the air fryer basket. 5. Fry the artichoke hearts for 15 minutes. 6. Remove the artichokes from the air fryer, and squeeze fresh lemon juice over the top before serving.

Easy Rosemary Green Beans

Prep time: 5 minutes | Cook time: 5 minutes | Serves 1

1 tablespoon butter, melted
2 tablespoons rosemary
½ teaspoon salt
3 cloves garlic, minced
¾ cup chopped green beans

1. Preheat the air fryer to 390°F (199°C). 2. Combine the melted butter with the rosemary, salt, and minced garlic. Toss in the green beans, coating them well. 3. Air fry for 5 minutes. 4. Serve immediately.

Crispy Golden Pickles

Prep time: 10 minutes | Cook time: 15 minutes | Serves 4

14 dill pickles, sliced
¼ cup flour
⅛ teaspoon baking powder
Pinch of salt
2 tablespoons cornstarch
plus 3 tablespoons water
6 tablespoons panko bread crumbs
½ teaspoon paprika
Cooking spray

1. Preheat the air fryer to 400°F (204°C). 2. Drain any excess moisture out of the dill pickles on a paper towel. 3. In a bowl, combine the flour, baking powder and salt. 4. Throw in the cornstarch and water mixture and combine well with a whisk. 5. Put the panko bread crumbs in a shallow dish along with the paprika. Mix thoroughly. 6. Dip the pickles in the flour batter, before coating in the bread crumbs. Spritz all the pickles with the cooking spray. 7. Transfer to the air fryer basket and air fry for 15 minutes, or until golden brown. 8. Serve immediately.

Mexican Street Corn Cups

Prep time: 5 minutes | Cook time: 10 minutes | Serves 4

4 cups frozen corn kernels (do not thaw)
Vegetable oil spray
2 tablespoons butter
¼ cup sour cream
¼ cup mayonnaise
¼ cup grated Parmesan cheese (or feta, cotija, or queso fresco)
2 tablespoons fresh lemon or lime juice
1 teaspoon chili powder
Chopped fresh green onion (optional)
Chopped fresh cilantro (optional)

1. Place the corn in the bottom of the air fryer basket and spray with vegetable oil spray. Set the air fryer to 350°F (177°C) for 10 minutes. 2. Transfer the corn to a serving bowl. Add the butter and stir until melted. Add the sour cream, mayonnaise, cheese, lemon juice, and chili powder; stir until well combined. Serve immediately with green onion and cilantro (if using).

Sesame Carrots and Sugar Snap Peas

Prep time: 10 minutes | Cook time: 16 minutes | Serves 4

1 pound (454 g) carrots, peeled sliced on the bias (½-inch slices)
1 teaspoon olive oil
Salt and freshly ground black pepper, to taste
⅓ cup honey
1 tablespoon sesame oil
1 tablespoon soy sauce
½ teaspoon minced fresh ginger
4 ounces (113 g) sugar snap peas (about 1 cup)
1½ teaspoons sesame seeds

1. Preheat the air fryer to 360°F (182°C). 2. Toss the carrots with the olive oil, season with salt and pepper and air fry for 10 minutes, shaking the basket once or twice during the cooking process. 3. Combine the honey, sesame oil, soy sauce and minced ginger in a large bowl. Add the sugar snap peas and the air-fried carrots to the honey mixture, toss to coat and return everything to the air fryer basket. 4. Turn up the temperature to 400°F (204°C) and air fry for an additional 6 minutes, shaking the basket once during the cooking process. 5. Transfer the carrots and sugar snap peas to a serving bowl. Pour the sauce from the bottom of the cooker over the vegetables and sprinkle sesame seeds over top. Serve immediately.

Lemon-Thyme Asparagus

Prep time: 5 minutes | Cook time: 4 to 8 minutes | Serves 4

1 pound (454 g) asparagus, woody ends trimmed off
1 tablespoon avocado oil
½ teaspoon dried thyme or ½ tablespoon chopped fresh thyme
Sea salt and freshly ground black pepper, to taste
2 ounces (57 g) goat cheese, crumbled
Zest and juice of 1 lemon
Flaky sea salt, for serving (optional)

1. In a medium bowl, toss together the asparagus, avocado oil, and thyme, and season with sea salt and pepper. 2. Place the asparagus in the air fryer basket in a single layer. Set the air fryer to 400°F (204°C) and air fry for 4 to 8 minutes, to your desired doneness. 3. Transfer to a serving platter. Top with the goat cheese, lemon zest, and lemon juice. If desired, season with a pinch of flaky salt.

Tamarind Sweet Potatoes

Prep time: 5 minutes | Cook time: 20 to 25 minutes | Serves 4

5 garnet sweet potatoes, peeled and diced
1½ tablespoons fresh lime juice
1 tablespoon butter, melted
2 teaspoons tamarind paste
1½ teaspoon ground allspice
⅓ teaspoon white pepper
½ teaspoon turmeric powder
A few drops liquid stevia

1. Preheat the air fryer to 400°F (204°C). 2. In a large mixing bowl, combine all the ingredients and toss until the sweet potatoes are evenly coated. 3. Place the sweet potatoes in the air fryer basket and air fry for 20 t0 25 minutes, or until the potatoes are crispy on the outside and soft on the inside. Shake the basket twice during cooking. 4. Let the potatoes cool for 5 minutes before serving.Rustic

Rustic Flatbread

Prep time: 5 minutes | Cook time: 7 minutes | Serves 2

1 cup shredded Mozzarella cheese
¼ cup blanched finely ground almond flour
1 ounce (28 g) full-fat cream cheese, softened

1. In a large microwave-safe bowl, melt Mozzarella in the microwave for 30 seconds. Stir in almond flour until smooth and then add cream cheese. Continue mixing until dough forms, gently kneading it with wet hands if necessary. 2. Divide the dough into two pieces and roll out to ¼-inch thickness between two pieces of parchment. Cut another piece of parchment to fit your air fryer basket. 3. Place a piece of flatbread onto your parchment and into the air fryer, working in two batches if needed. 4. Adjust the temperature to 320°F (160°C) and air fry for 7 minutes. 5. Halfway through the cooking time flip the flatbread. Serve warm.

Chapter 9
Vegetarian Mains

Stuffed Mushroom Caps with Spinach and Artichokes

Prep time: 10 minutes | Cook time: 10 to 14 minutes | Serves 4

2 tablespoons olive oil
4 large portobello mushrooms, stems removed and gills scraped out
½ teaspoon salt
¼ teaspoon freshly ground pepper
4 ounces (113 g) goat cheese, crumbled
½ cup chopped marinated artichoke hearts
1 cup frozen spinach, thawed and squeezed dry
½ cup grated Parmesan cheese
2 tablespoons chopped fresh parsley

1. Preheat the air fryer to 400°F (204°C). 2. Rub the olive oil over the portobello mushrooms until thoroughly coated. Sprinkle both sides with the salt and black pepper. Place top-side down on a clean work surface. 3. In a small bowl, combine the goat cheese, artichoke hearts, and spinach. Mash with the back of a fork until thoroughly combined. Divide the cheese mixture among the mushrooms and sprinkle with the Parmesan cheese. 4. Air fry for 10 to 14 minutes until the mushrooms are tender and the cheese has begun to brown. Top with the fresh parsley just before serving.

Cauliflower Steak with Gremolata

Prep time: 15 minutes | Cook time: 25 minutes | Serves 4

2 tablespoons olive oil
1 tablespoon Italian seasoning
1 large head cauliflower, outer leaves removed and
Gremolata:
1 bunch Italian parsley (about 1 cup packed)
2 cloves garlic
Zest of 1 small lemon, plus
sliced lengthwise through the core into thick "steaks"
Salt and freshly ground black pepper, to taste
¼ cup Parmesan cheese

1 to 2 teaspoons lemon juice
½ cup olive oil
Salt and pepper, to taste

1. Preheat the air fryer to 400°F (204°C). 2. In a small bowl, combine the olive oil and Italian seasoning. Brush both sides of each cauliflower "steak" generously with the oil. Season to taste with salt and black pepper. 3. Working in batches if necessary, arrange the cauliflower in a single layer in the air fryer basket. Pausing halfway through the cooking time to turn the "steaks," air fry for 15 to 20 minutes until the cauliflower is tender and the edges begin to brown. Sprinkle with the Parmesan and air fry for 5 minutes longer. 4. To make the gremolata: In a food processor fitted with a metal blade, combine the parsley, garlic, and lemon zest and juice. With the motor running, add the olive oil in a steady stream until the mixture forms a bright green sauce. Season to taste with salt and black pepper. Serve the cauliflower steaks with the gremolata spooned over the top.

Eggplant Parmesan

Prep time: 15 minutes | Cook time: 17 minutes | Serves 4

1 medium eggplant, ends trimmed, sliced into ½-inch rounds
¼ teaspoon salt
2 tablespoons coconut oil
½ cup grated Parmesan cheese
1 ounce (28 g) 100% cheese crisps, finely crushed
½ cup low-carb marinara sauce
½ cup shredded Mozzarella cheese

1. Sprinkle eggplant rounds with salt on both sides and wrap in a kitchen towel for 30 minutes. Press to remove excess water, then drizzle rounds with coconut oil on both sides. 2. In a medium bowl, mix Parmesan and cheese crisps. Press each eggplant slice into mixture to coat both sides. 3. Place rounds into ungreased air fryer basket. Adjust the temperature to 350°F (177°C) and air fry for 15 minutes, turning rounds halfway through cooking. They will be crispy around the edges when done. 4. Spoon marinara over rounds and sprinkle with Mozzarella. Continue cooking an additional 2 minutes at 350°F (177°C) until cheese is melted. Serve warm.

Artichokes with Parmesan Topping

Prep time: 10 minutes | Cook time: 10 minutes | Serves 4

2 medium artichokes, trimmed and quartered, center removed
2 tablespoons coconut oil
1 large egg, beaten
½ cup grated vegetarian
Parmesan cheese
¼ cup blanched finely ground almond flour
½ teaspoon crushed red pepper flakes

1. In a large bowl, toss artichokes in coconut oil and then dip each piece into the egg. 2. Mix the Parmesan and almond flour in a large bowl. Add artichoke pieces and toss to cover as completely as possible, sprinkle with pepper flakes. Place into the air fryer basket. 3. Adjust the temperature to 400°F (204°C) and air fry for 10 minutes. 4. Toss the basket two times during cooking. Serve warm.

Super Vegetable Burger

Prep time: 15 minutes | Cook time: 12 minutes | Serves 8

½ pound (227 g) cauliflower, steamed and diced, rinsed and drained
2 teaspoons coconut oil, melted
2 teaspoons minced garlic
¼ cup desiccated coconut
½ cup oats
3 tablespoons flour
1 tablespoon flaxseeds
plus 3 tablespoons water, divided
1 teaspoon mustard powder
2 teaspoons thyme
2 teaspoons parsley
2 teaspoons chives
Salt and ground black pepper, to taste
1 cup bread crumbs

1. Preheat the air fryer to 390ºF (199ºC). 2. Combine the cauliflower with all the ingredients, except for the bread crumbs, incorporating everything well. 3. Using the hands, shape 8 equal-sized amounts of the mixture into burger patties. Coat the patties in bread crumbs before putting them in the air fryer basket in a single layer. 4. Air fry for 12 minutes or until crispy. 5. Serve hot.

Rolled White Zucchini with Garlic Flavor

Prep time: 20 minutes | Cook time: 20 minutes | Serves 4

2 medium zucchini
2 tablespoons unsalted butter
¼ white onion, peeled and diced
½ teaspoon finely minced roasted garlic
¼ cup heavy cream
2 tablespoons vegetable broth
⅛ teaspoon xanthan gum
½ cup full-fat ricotta cheese
¼ teaspoon salt
½ teaspoon garlic powder
¼ teaspoon dried oregano
2 cups spinach, chopped
½ cup sliced baby portobello mushrooms
¾ cup shredded Mozzarella cheese, divided

1. Using a mandoline or sharp knife, slice zucchini into long strips lengthwise. Place strips between paper towels to absorb moisture. Set aside. 2. In a medium saucepan over medium heat, melt butter. Add onion and sauté until fragrant. Add garlic and sauté 30 seconds. 3. Pour in heavy cream, broth, and xanthan gum. Turn off heat and whisk mixture until it begins to thicken, about 3 minutes. 4. In a medium bowl, add ricotta, salt, garlic powder, and oregano and mix well. Fold in spinach, mushrooms, and ½ cup Mozzarella. 5. Pour half of the sauce into a round baking pan. To assemble the rolls, place two strips of zucchini on a work surface. Spoon 2 tablespoons of ricotta mixture onto the slices and roll up. Place seam side down on top of sauce. Repeat with remaining ingredients. 6. Pour remaining sauce over the rolls and sprinkle with remaining Mozzarella. Cover with foil and place into the air fryer basket. 7. Adjust the temperature to 350ºF (177ºC) and bake for 20 minutes. 8. In the last 5 minutes, remove the foil to brown the cheese. Serve immediately.

Spinach and Cheese Baked Dish

Prep time: 15 minutes | Cook time: 15 minutes | Serves 4

1 tablespoon salted butter, melted
¼ cup diced yellow onion
8 ounces (227 g) full-fat cream cheese, softened
⅓ cup full-fat mayonnaise
⅓ cup full-fat sour cream
¼ cup chopped pickled jalapeños
2 cups fresh spinach, chopped
2 cups cauliflower florets, chopped
1 cup artichoke hearts, chopped

1. In a large bowl, mix butter, onion, cream cheese, mayonnaise, and sour cream. Fold in jalapeños, spinach, cauliflower, and artichokes. 2. Pour the mixture into a round baking dish. Cover with foil and place into the air fryer basket. 3. Adjust the temperature to 370ºF (188ºC) and set the timer for 15 minutes. In the last 2 minutes of cooking, remove the foil to brown the top. Serve warm.

Fresh and Vibrant Summer Rolls

Prep time: 15 minutes | Cook time: 15 minutes | Serves 4

1 cup shiitake mushroom, sliced thinly
1 celery stalk, chopped
1 medium carrot, shredded
½ teaspoon finely chopped ginger
1 teaspoon sugar
1 tablespoon soy sauce
1 teaspoon nutritional yeast
8 spring roll sheets
1 teaspoon corn starch
2 tablespoons water

1. In a bowl, combine the ginger, soy sauce, nutritional yeast, carrots, celery, mushroom, and sugar. 2. Mix the cornstarch and water to create an adhesive for the spring rolls. 3. Scoop a tablespoonful of the vegetable mixture into the middle of the spring roll sheets. Brush the edges of the sheets with the cornstarch adhesive and enclose around the filling to make spring rolls. 4. Preheat the air fryer to 400ºF (204ºC). When warm, place the rolls inside and air fry for 15 minutes or until crisp. 5. Serve hot.

Sweet Pepper Nachos

Prep time: 10 minutes | Cook time: 5 minutes | Serves 2

6 mini sweet peppers, seeded and sliced in half
¾ cup shredded Colby jack cheese
¼ cup sliced pickled jalapeños
½ medium avocado, peeled, pitted, and diced
2 tablespoons sour cream

1. Place peppers into an ungreased round nonstick baking dish. Sprinkle with Colby and top with jalapeños. 2. Place dish into air fryer basket. Adjust the temperature to 350ºF (177ºC) and bake for 5 minutes. Cheese will be melted and bubbly when done. 3. Remove dish from air fryer and top with avocado. Drizzle with sour cream. Serve warm.

Cauliflower Rice-FilledPeppers

Prep time: 10 minutes | Cook time: 15 minutes | Serves 4

2 cups uncooked cauliflower rice
¾ cup drained canned petite diced tomatoes
2 tablespoons olive oil
1 cup shredded Mozzarella cheese
¼ teaspoon salt
¼ teaspoon ground black pepper
4 medium green bell peppers, tops removed, seeded

1. In a large bowl, mix all ingredients except bell peppers. Scoop mixture evenly into peppers. 2. Place peppers into ungreased air fryer basket. Adjust the temperature to 350ºF (177ºC) and air fry for 15 minutes. Peppers will be tender and cheese will be melted when done. Serve warm.

Mushroom and Pepper Pizza Squares

Prep time: 10 minutes | Cook time: 10 minutes | Serves 10

1 pizza dough, cut into squares
1 cup chopped oyster mushrooms
1 shallot, chopped
¼ red bell pepper, chopped
2 tablespoons parsley
Salt and ground black pepper, to taste

1. Preheat the air fryer to 400ºF (204ºC). 2. In a bowl, combine the oyster mushrooms, shallot, bell pepper and parsley. Sprinkle some salt and pepper as desired. 3. Spread this mixture on top of the pizza squares. 4. Bake in the air fryer for 10 minutes. 5. Serve warm.

Baked Cabbage Wedges with Cheese

Prep time: 5 minutes | Cook time: 20 minutes | Serves 4

4 tablespoons melted butter
1 head cabbage, cut into wedges
1 cup shredded Parmesan cheese
Salt and black pepper, to taste
½ cup shredded Mozzarella cheese

1. Preheat the air fryer to 380ºF (193ºC). 2. Brush the melted butter over the cut sides of cabbage wedges and sprinkle both sides with the Parmesan cheese. Season with salt and pepper to taste. 3. Place the cabbage wedges in the air fryer basket and air fry for 20 minutes, flipping the cabbage halfway through, or until the cabbage wedges are lightly browned. 4. Transfer the cabbage wedges to a plate and serve with the Mozzarella cheese sprinkled on top.

Crispy Eggplant and Zucchini Bites

Prep time: 30 minutes | Cook time: 30 minutes | Serves 8

2 teaspoons fresh mint leaves, chopped
1½ teaspoons red pepper chili flakes
2 tablespoons melted butter
1 pound (454 g) eggplant, peeled and cubed
1 pound (454 g) zucchini, peeled and cubed
3 tablespoons olive oil

1. Toss all the above ingredients in a large-sized mixing dish. 2. Roast the eggplant and zucchini bites for 30 minutes at 325ºF (163ºC) in your air fryer, turning once or twice. 3. Serve with a homemade dipping sauce.

Cheesy Spinach Pie Without a Crust

Prep time: 10 minutes | Cook time: 20 minutes | Serves 4

6 large eggs
¼ cup heavy whipping cream
1 cup frozen chopped spinach, drained
1 cup shredded sharp Cheddar cheese
¼ cup diced yellow onion

1. In a medium bowl, whisk eggs and add cream. Add remaining ingredients to bowl. 2. Pour into a round baking dish. Place into the air fryer basket. 3. Adjust the temperature to 320ºF (160ºC) and bake for 20 minutes. 4. Eggs will be firm and slightly browned when cooked. Serve immediately.

Air Fryer Veggies with Halloumi

Prep time: 5 minutes | Cook time: 14 minutes | Serves 2

2 zucchinis, cut into even chunks
1 large eggplant, peeled, cut into chunks
1 large carrot, cut into chunks
6 ounces (170 g) halloumi cheese, cubed
2 teaspoons olive oil
Salt and black pepper, to taste
1 teaspoon dried mixed herbs

1. Preheat the air fryer to 340ºF (171ºC). 2. Combine the zucchinis, eggplant, carrot, cheese, olive oil, salt, and pepper in a large bowl and toss to coat well. 3. Spread the mixture evenly in the air fryer basket and air fry for 14 minutes until crispy and golden, shaking the basket once during cooking. Serve topped with mixed herbs.

Crispy Roasted Cabbage Steaks

Prep time: 5 minutes | Cook time: 10 minutes | Serves 4

1 small head green cabbage, cored and cut into ½-inch-thick slices
¼ teaspoon salt
¼ teaspoon ground black pepper
2 tablespoons olive oil
1 clove garlic, peeled and finely minced
½ teaspoon dried thyme
½ teaspoon dried parsley

1. Sprinkle each side of cabbage with salt and pepper, then place into ungreased air fryer basket, working in batches if needed. 2. Drizzle each side of cabbage with olive oil, then sprinkle with remaining ingredients on both sides. Adjust the temperature to 350ºF (177ºC) and air fry for 10 minutes, turning "steaks" halfway through cooking. 3.Cabbage will be browned at the edges and tender when done. Serve warm.

Whole Roasted Cauliflower with Lemon Drizzle

Prep time: 5 minutes | Cook time: 15 minutes | Serves 4

1 medium head cauliflower
2 tablespoons salted butter, melted
1 medium lemon
½ teaspoon garlic powder
1 teaspoon dried parsley

1. Remove the leaves from the head of cauliflower and brush it with melted butter. Cut the lemon in half and zest one half onto the cauliflower. Squeeze the juice of the zested lemon half and pour it over the cauliflower. 2. Sprinkle with garlic powder and parsley. Place cauliflower head into the air fryer basket. 3. Adjust the temperature to 350ºF (177ºC) and air fry for 15 minutes. 4. Check cauliflower every 5 minutes to avoid overcooking. It should be fork tender. 5. To serve, squeeze juice from other lemon half over cauliflower. Serve immediately.

Russet Potato Gratin

Prep time: 10 minutes | Cook time: 35 minutes | Serves 6

½ cup milk
7 medium russet potatoes, peeled
Salt, to taste
1 teaspoon black pepper
½ cup heavy whipping cream
½ cup grated semi-mature cheese
½ teaspoon nutmeg

1. Preheat the air fryer to 390ºF (199ºC). 2. Cut the potatoes into wafer-thin slices. 3. In a bowl, combine the milk and cream and sprinkle with salt, pepper, and nutmeg. 4. Use the milk mixture to coat the slices of potatoes. Put in a baking dish. Top the potatoes with the rest of the milk mixture. 5. Put the baking dish into the air fryer basket and bake for 25 minutes. 6. Pour the cheese over the potatoes. 7. Bake for an additional 10 minutes, ensuring the top is nicely browned before serving.

Basmati Risotto

Prep time: 10 minutes | Cook time: 30 minutes | Serves 2

1 onion, diced
1 small carrot, diced
2 cups vegetable broth, boiling
½ cup grated Cheddar cheese
1 clove garlic, minced
¾ cup long-grain basmati rice
1 tablespoon olive oil
1 tablespoon unsalted butter

1. Preheat the air fryer to 390ºF (199ºC). 2. Grease a baking tin with oil and stir in the butter, garlic, carrot, and onion. 3. Put the tin in the air fryer and bake for 4 minutes. 4. Pour in the rice and bake for a further 4 minutes, stirring three times throughout the baking time. 5. Turn the temperature down to 320ºF (160ºC). 6. Add the vegetable broth and give the dish a gentle stir. Bake for 22 minutes, leaving the air fryer uncovered. 7. Pour in the cheese, stir once more and serve.

Herb-Seasoned Air-Fried Veggies

Prep time: 10 minutes | Cook time: 6 minutes | Serves 4

1 large zucchini, sliced
1 cup cherry tomatoes, halved
1 parsnip, sliced
1 green pepper, sliced
1 carrot, sliced
1 teaspoon mixed herbs
1 teaspoon mustard
1 teaspoon garlic purée
6 tablespoons olive oil
Salt and ground black pepper, to taste

1. Preheat the air fryer to 400°F (204°C). 2. Combine all the ingredients in a bowl, making sure to coat the vegetables well. 3. Transfer to the air fryer and air fry for 6 minutes, ensuring the vegetables are tender and browned. 4. Serve immediately.

Chapter 10
Desserts

Rustic Blackberry Cobbler

Prep time: 15 minutes | Cook time: 25 to 30 minutes | Serves 6

3 cups fresh or frozen blackberries
1¾ cups sugar, divided
1 teaspoon vanilla extract
8 tablespoons (1 stick) butter, melted
1 cup self-rising flour
1 to 2 tablespoons oil

1. In a medium bowl, stir together the blackberries, 1 cup of sugar, and vanilla. 2. In another medium bowl, stir together the melted butter, remaining ¾ cup of sugar, and flour until a dough forms. 3. Spritz a baking pan with oil. Add the blackberry mixture. Crumble the flour mixture over the fruit. Cover the pan with aluminum foil. 4. Preheat the air fryer to 350°F (177°C). 5. Place the covered pan in the air fryer basket. Cook for 20 to 25 minutes until the filling is thickened. 6. Uncover the pan and cook for 5 minutes more, depending on how juicy and browned you like your cobbler. Let sit for 5 minutes before serving.

Lemon Poppy Seed Macaroons

Prep time: 10 minutes | Cook time: 14 minutes | Makes 1 dozen cookies

2 large egg whites, room temperature
⅓ cup Swerve confectioners'-style sweetener or equivalent amount of powdered sweetener
2 tablespoons grated lemon zest, plus more for garnish if desired
2 teaspoons poppy seeds
1 teaspoon lemon extract
¼ teaspoon fine sea salt
2 cups unsweetened shredded coconut

Lemon Icing:
¼ cup Swerve confectioners'-style sweetener or equivalent amount of powdered sweetener
1 tablespoon lemon juice

1. Preheat the air fryer to 325°F (163°C). Line a pie pan or a casserole dish that will fit inside your air fryer with parchment paper. 2. Place the egg whites in a medium-sized bowl and use a hand mixer on high to beat the whites until stiff peaks form. Add the sweetener, lemon zest, poppy seeds, lemon extract, and salt. Mix on low until combined. Gently fold in the coconut with a rubber spatula. 3. Use a 1-inch cookie scoop to place the cookies on the parchment, spacing them about ¼ inch apart. Place the pan in the air fryer and bake for 12 to 14 minutes, until the cookies are golden and a toothpick inserted into the center comes out clean. 4. While the cookies bake, make the lemon icing: Place the sweetener in a small bowl. Add the lemon juice and stir well. If the icing is too thin, add a little more sweetener. If the icing is too thick, add a little more lemon juice. 5. Remove the cookies from the air fryer and allow to cool for about 10 minutes, then drizzle with the icing. Garnish with lemon zest, if desired. Store leftovers in an airtight container in the fridge for up to 5 days or in the freezer for up to a month.

Brown Sugar-Infused Banana Loaf

Prep time: 20 minutes | Cook time: 22 to 24 minutes | Serves 4

1 cup packed light brown sugar
1 large egg, beaten
2 tablespoons butter, melted
½ cup milk, whole or 2%
2 cups all-purpose flour
1½ teaspoons baking powder
1 teaspoon ground cinnamon
½ teaspoon salt
1 banana, mashed
1 to 2 tablespoons oil
¼ cup confectioners' sugar (optional)

1. In a large bowl, stir together the brown sugar, egg, melted butter, and milk. 2. In a medium bowl, whisk the flour, baking powder, cinnamon, and salt until blended. Add the flour mixture to the sugar mixture and stir just to blend. 3. Add the mashed banana and stir to combine. 4. Preheat the air fryer to 350°F (177°C). Spritz 2 mini loaf pans with oil. 5. Evenly divide the batter between the prepared pans and place them in the air fryer basket. 6. Cook for 22 to 24 minutes, or until a knife inserted into the middle of the loaves comes out clean. 7. Dust the warm loaves with confectioners' sugar (if using).

Golden Fried Oreo Cookies

Prep time: 7 minutes | Cook time: 6 minutes per batch | Makes 12 cookies

Oil for misting or nonstick spray
1 cup complete pancake and waffle mix
1 teaspoon vanilla extract
½ cup water, plus 2 tablespoons
12 Oreos or other chocolate sandwich cookies
1 tablespoon confectioners' sugar

1. Spray baking pan with oil or nonstick spray and place in basket. 2. Preheat the air fryer to 390°F (199°C). 3. In a medium bowl, mix together the pancake mix, vanilla, and water. 4. Dip 4 cookies in batter and place in baking pan. 5. Cook for 6 minutes, until browned. 6. Repeat steps 4 and 5 for the remaining cookies. 7. Sift sugar over warm cookies.

Simple Apple Turnovers

Prep time: 10 minutes | Cook time: 10 minutes | Serves 4

1 apple, peeled, quartered, and thinly sliced
½ teaspoons pumpkin pie spice
Juice of ½ lemon
1 tablespoon granulated sugar
Pinch of kosher salt
6 sheets phyllo dough

1. Preheat the air fryer to 330°F (166°C). 2. In a medium bowl, combine the apple, pumpkin pie spice, lemon juice, granulated sugar, and kosher salt. 3. Cut the phyllo dough sheets into 4 equal pieces and place individual tablespoons of apple filling in the center of each piece, then fold in both sides and roll from front to back. 4. Spray the air fryer basket with nonstick cooking spray, then place the turnovers in the basket and bake for 10 minutes or until golden brown. 5. Remove the turnovers from the air fryer and allow to cool on a wire rack for 10 minutes before serving.

Molten Chocolate Almond Cakes

Prep time: 5 minutes | Cook time: 13 minutes | Serves 3

Butter and flour for the ramekins
4 ounces (113 g) bittersweet chocolate, chopped
½ cup (1 stick) unsalted butter
2 eggs
2 egg yolks
¼ cup sugar
½ teaspoon pure vanilla extract, or almond extract
1 tablespoon all-purpose flour
3 tablespoons ground almonds
8 to 12 semisweet chocolate discs (or 4 chunks of chocolate)
Cocoa powder or powdered sugar, for dusting
Toasted almonds, coarsely chopped

1. Butter and flour three (6 ounces / 170-g) ramekins. (Butter the ramekins and then coat the butter with flour by shaking it around in the ramekin and dumping out any excess.) 2. Melt the chocolate and butter together, either in the microwave or in a double boiler. In a separate bowl, beat the eggs, egg yolks and sugar together until light and smooth. Add the vanilla extract. Whisk the chocolate mixture into the egg mixture. Stir in the flour and ground almonds. 3. Preheat the air fryer to 330°F (166°C). 4. Transfer the batter carefully to the buttered ramekins, filling halfway. Place two or three chocolate discs in the center of the batter and then fill the ramekins to ½-inch below the top with the remaining batter. Place the ramekins into the air fryer basket and air fry at 330°F (166°C) for 13 minutes. The sides of the cake should be set, but the centers should be slightly soft. Remove the ramekins from the air fryer and let the cakes sit for 5 minutes. (If you'd like the cake a little less molten, air fry for 14 minutes and let the cakes sit for 4 minutes.) 5. Run a butter knife around the edge of the ramekins and invert the cakes onto a plate. Lift the ramekin off the plate slowly and carefully so that the cake doesn't break. Dust with cocoa powder or powdered sugar and serve with a scoop of ice cream and some coarsely chopped toasted almonds.

Fudgy Brownies with Pecans

Prep time: 10 minutes | Cook time: 20 minutes | Serves 6

½ cup blanched finely ground almond flour
½ cup powdered erythritol
2 tablespoons unsweetened cocoa powder
½ teaspoon baking powder
¼ cup unsalted butter, softened
1 large egg
¼ cup chopped pecans
¼ cup low-carb, sugar-free chocolate chips

1. In a large bowl, mix almond flour, erythritol, cocoa powder, and baking powder. Stir in butter and egg. 2. Fold in pecans and chocolate chips. Scoop mixture into a round baking pan. Place pan into the air fryer basket. 3. Adjust the temperature to 300°F (149°C) and bake for 20 minutes. 4. When fully cooked a toothpick inserted in center will come out clean. Allow 20 minutes to fully cool and firm up.

Grilled Peaches

Prep time: 5 minutes | Cook time: 10 minutes | Serves 4

Oil, for spraying
¼ cup graham cracker crumbs
¼ cup packed light brown sugar
8 tablespoons (1 stick)
unsalted butter, cubed
¼ teaspoon cinnamon
2 peaches, pitted and cut into quarters
4 scoops vanilla ice cream

1. Line the air fryer basket with parchment and spray lightly with oil. 2. In a small bowl, mix together the graham cracker crumbs, brown sugar, butter, and cinnamon with a fork until crumbly. 3. Place the peach wedges in the prepared basket, skin-side up. You may need to work in batches, depending on the size of your air fryer. 4. Air fry at 350°F (177°C) for 5 minutes, flip, and sprinkle with a spoonful of the graham cracker mixture. Cook for another 5 minutes, or until tender and caramelized. 5. Top with a scoop of vanilla ice cream and any remaining crumble mixture. Serve immediately.

Vanilla and Cardamon Walnuts Tart

Prep time: 5 minutes | Cook time: 13 minutes | Serves 6

1 cup coconut milk
½ cup walnuts, ground
½ cup Swerve
½ cup almond flour
½ stick butter, at room temperature
2 eggs
1 teaspoon vanilla essence
¼ teaspoon ground cardamom
¼ teaspoon ground cloves
Cooking spray

1. Preheat the air fryer to 360ºF (182ºC). Coat a baking pan with cooking spray. 2. Combine all the ingredients except the oil in a large bowl and stir until well blended. Spoon the batter mixture into the baking pan. 3. Bake in the preheated air fryer for approximately 13 minutes. Check the tart for doneness: If a toothpick inserted into the center of the tart comes out clean, it's done. 4. Remove from the air fryer and place on a wire rack to cool. Serve immediately.

Maple Bacon Moonshine Bread Pudding

Prep time: 20 minutes | Cook time: 15 minutes | Serves 6

1 cup whole milk
1 (4.6-ounce / 130-g) package cook-and-serve vanilla pudding and pie filling
¼ cup granulated sugar
2 large eggs, beaten
1 tablespoon butter, melted
1 teaspoon ground cinnamon
1 teaspoon vanilla extract
4 cups loosely packed cubed French bread
¼ cup packed light brown sugar
½ cup chopped toasted pecans
¾ cup maple bacon moonshine, plus 3 tablespoons
1 to 2 tablespoons oil

1. In a large bowl, whisk the milk, pudding mix, granulated sugar, eggs, melted butter, cinnamon, and vanilla until blended. Add the bread cubes and let soak for 10 minutes. 2. In a small bowl, stir together the brown sugar, pecans, and ¾ cup moonshine. Stir the pecan mixture into the bread mixture. 3. Preheat the air fryer to 355ºF (179ºC). Spritz a baking pan with oil. 4. Transfer the bread mixture to the prepared pan. 5. Bake for 10 minutes. The bottom of the pudding will still be mushy. Stir. Bake for 5 minutes more and stir again. The pudding will be soft, but not runny, and a knife inserted into the middle will have soft crumbs attached. 6. Drizzle the remaining 3 tablespoons of maple bacon moonshine over the pudding.

Egg-Free Farina Cake

Prep time: 30 minutes | Cook time: 25 minutes | Serves 6

Vegetable oil
2 cups hot water
1 cup chopped dried fruit, such as apricots, golden raisins, figs, and/or dates
1 cup farina (or very fine semolina)
1 cup milk
1 cup sugar
¼ cup ghee, butter, or coconut oil, melted
2 tablespoons plain Greek yogurt or sour cream
1 teaspoon ground cardamom
1 teaspoon baking powder
½ teaspoon baking soda
Whipped cream, for serving

1. Grease a baking pan with vegetable oil. 2. In a small bowl, combine the hot water and dried fruit; set aside for 20 minutes to plump the fruit. 3. Meanwhile, in a large bowl, whisk together the farina, milk, sugar, ghee, yogurt, and cardamom. Let stand for 20 minutes to allow the farina to soften and absorb some of the liquid. 4. Drain the dried fruit and gently stir it into the batter. Add the baking powder and baking soda and stir until thoroughly combined. 5. Pour the batter into the prepared pan. Set the pan in the air fryer basket. Set the air fryer to 325ºF (163ºC) for 25 minutes, or until a toothpick inserted into the center of the cake comes out clean. 6. Let the cake cool in the pan on a wire rack for 10 minutes. Remove the cake from the pan and let cool on the rack for 20 minutes before slicing. 7. Slice and serve topped with whipped cream.

Mixed Berry Crumble Dessert

Prep time: 10 minutes | Cook time: 15 minutes | Serves 4

For the Filling:
2 cups mixed berries
2 tablespoons sugar
1 tablespoon cornstarch
1 tablespoon fresh lemon juice
For the Topping
¼ cup all-purpose flour
¼ cup rolled oats
1 tablespoon sugar
2 tablespoons cold unsalted butter, cut into small cubes
Whipped cream or ice cream (optional)

1. Preheat the air fryer to 400ºF (204ºC). 2. For the filling: In a round baking pan, gently mix the berries, sugar, cornstarch, and lemon juice until thoroughly combined. 3. For the topping: In a small bowl, combine the flour, oats, and sugar. Stir the butter into the flour mixture until the mixture has the consistency of bread crumbs. 4. Sprinkle the topping over the berries. 5. Put the pan in the air fryer basket and air fry for 15 minutes. Let cool for 5 minutes on a wire rack. 6. Serve topped with whipped cream or ice cream, if desired.

Rich Bourbon-Infused Bread Pudding

Prep time: 10 minutes | Cook time: 20 minutes | Serves 4

- 3 slices whole grain bread, cubed
- 1 large egg
- 1 cup whole milk
- 2 tablespoons bourbon
- ½ teaspoons vanilla extract
- ¼ cup maple syrup, divided
- ½ teaspoons ground cinnamon
- 2 teaspoons sparkling sugar

1. Preheat the air fryer to 270°F (132°C). 2. Spray a baking pan with nonstick cooking spray, then place the bread cubes in the pan. 3. In a medium bowl, whisk together the egg, milk, bourbon, vanilla extract, 3 tablespoons of maple syrup, and cinnamon. Pour the egg mixture over the bread and press down with a spatula to coat all the bread, then sprinkle the sparkling sugar on top and bake for 20 minutes. 4. Remove the pudding from the air fryer and allow to cool in the pan on a wire rack for 10 minutes. Drizzle the remaining 1 tablespoon of maple syrup on top. Slice and serve warm.

Citrus Ginger Skillet Cookie with Anise

Prep time: 20 minutes | Cook time: 15 minutes | Serves 2 to 4

Cookie:
- Vegetable oil
- 1 cup plus 2 tablespoons all-purpose flour
- 1 tablespoon grated orange zest
- 1 teaspoon ground ginger
- 1 teaspoon aniseeds, crushed
- ¼ teaspoon kosher salt
- 4 tablespoons (½ stick) unsalted butter, at room temperature
- ½ cup granulated sugar, plus more for sprinkling
- 3 tablespoons dark molasses
- 1 large egg

Icing:
- ½ cup confectioners' sugar
- 2 to 3 teaspoons milk

1. For the cookie: Generously grease a baking pan with vegetable oil. 2. In a medium bowl, whisk together the flour, orange zest, ginger, aniseeds, and salt. 3. In a medium bowl using a hand mixer, beat the butter and sugar on medium-high speed until well combined, about 2 minutes. Add the molasses and egg and beat until light in color, about 2 minutes. Add the flour mixture and mix on low until just combined. Use a rubber spatula to scrape the dough into the prepared pan, spreading it to the edges and smoothing the top. Sprinkle with sugar. 4. Place the pan in the basket. Set the air fryer to 325°F (163°C) for 15 minutes, or until sides are browned but the center is still quite soft. 5. Let cool in the pan on a wire rack for 15 minutes. Turn the cookie out of the pan onto the rack. 6. For the icing: Whisk together the sugar and 2 teaspoons of milk. Add 1 teaspoon milk if needed for the desired consistency. Spread, or drizzle onto the cookie.

Baked Crumble with Rhubarb and Strawberries

Prep time: 10 minutes | Cook time: 55 minutes | Serves 4

- Unsalted butter, at room temperature
- 1 cup almond flour
- ½ cup sugar
- 3 large eggs
- ¼ cup heavy cream
- ¼ cup full-fat ricotta cheese
- ¼ cup coconut oil, melted
- 2 tablespoons poppy seeds
- 1 teaspoon baking powder
- 1 teaspoon pure lemon extract
- Grated zest and juice of 1 lemon, plus more zest for garnish

1. Generously butter a baking pan. Line the bottom of the pan with parchment paper cut to fit. 2. In a large bowl, combine the almond flour, sugar, eggs, cream, ricotta, coconut oil, poppy seeds, baking powder, lemon extract, lemon zest, and lemon juice. Beat with a hand mixer on medium speed until well blended and fluffy. 3. Pour the batter into the prepared pan. Cover the pan tightly with aluminum foil. Set the pan in the air fryer basket. Set the air fryer to 325°F (163°C) for 45 minutes. Remove the foil and cook for 10 to 15 minutes more, until a knife (do not use a toothpick) inserted into the center of the cake comes out clean. 4. Let the cake cool in the pan on a wire rack for 10 minutes. Remove the cake from pan and let it cool on the rack for 15 minutes before slicing. 5. Top with additional lemon zest, slice and serve.

Kentucky Chocolate Nut Pie

Prep time: 20 minutes | Cook time: 25 minutes | Serves 8

- 2 large eggs, beaten
- ⅓ cup butter, melted
- 1 cup sugar
- ½ cup all-purpose flour
- 1½ cups coarsely chopped pecans
- 1 cup milk chocolate chips
- 2 tablespoons bourbon
- 1 (9-inch) unbaked piecrust

1. In a large bowl, stir together the eggs and melted butter. Add the sugar and flour and stir until combined. Stir in the pecans, chocolate chips, and bourbon until well mixed. 2. Using a fork, prick holes in the bottom and sides of the pie crust. Pour the pie filling into the crust. 3. Preheat the air fryer to 350°F (177°C). 4. Cook for 25 minutes, or until a knife inserted into the middle of the pie comes out clean. Let set for 5 minutes before serving.

Honeyed Roasted Apples with Walnuts

Prep time: 5 minutes | Cook time: 12 to 15 minutes | Serves 4

2 Granny Smith apples
¼ cup certified gluten-free rolled oats
2 tablespoons honey
½ teaspoon ground cinnamon
2 tablespoons chopped walnuts
Pinch salt
1 tablespoon olive oil

1. Preheat the air fryer to 380°F(193°C). 2. Core the apples and slice them in half. 3. In a medium bowl, mix together the oats, honey, cinnamon, walnuts, salt, and olive oil. 4. Scoop a quarter of the oat mixture onto the top of each half apple. 5. Place the apples in the air fryer basket, and roast for 12 to 15 minutes, or until the apples are fork-tender.

Graham Cracker Cheesecake

Prep time: 10 minutes | Cook time: 20 minutes | Serves 8

1 cup graham cracker crumbs
3 tablespoons butter, at room temperature
1½ (8-ounce / 227-g) packages cream cheese, at room temperature
⅓ cup sugar
2 eggs, beaten
1 tablespoon all-purpose flour
1 teaspoon vanilla extract
¼ cup chocolate syrup

1. In a small bowl, stir together the graham cracker crumbs and butter. Press the crust into the bottom of a 6-by-2-inch round baking pan and freeze to set while you prepare the filling. 2. In a medium bowl, stir together the cream cheese and sugar until mixed well. 3. One at a time, beat in the eggs. Add the flour and vanilla and stir to combine. 4. Transfer ⅔ cup of filling to a small bowl and stir in the chocolate syrup until combined. 5. Insert the crisper plate into the basket and the basket into the unit. Preheat the unit by selecting BAKE, setting the temperature to 325°F (163°C), and setting the time to 3 minutes. Select START/STOP to begin. 6. Pour the vanilla filling into the pan with the crust. Drop the chocolate filling over the vanilla filling by the spoonful. With a clean butter knife stir the fillings in a zigzag pattern to marbleize them. Do not let the knife touch the crust. 7. Once the unit is preheated, place the pan into the basket. 8. Select BAKE, set the temperature to 325°F (163°C), and set the time to 20 minutes. Select START/STOP to begin. 9. When the cooking is done, the cheesecake should be just set. Cool on a wire rack for 1 hour. Refrigerate the cheesecake until firm before slicing.

Rich Vanilla Butter Pound Cake

Prep time: 10 minutes | Cook time: 25 minutes | Serves 6

1 cup blanched finely ground almond flour
¼ cup salted butter, melted
½ cup granular erythritol
1 teaspoon vanilla extract
1 teaspoon baking powder
½ cup full-fat sour cream
1 ounce (28 g) full-fat cream cheese, softened
2 large eggs

1. In a large bowl, mix almond flour, butter, and erythritol. 2. Add in vanilla, baking powder, sour cream, and cream cheese and mix until well combined. Add eggs and mix. 3. Pour batter into a round baking pan. Place pan into the air fryer basket. 4. Adjust the temperature to 300°F (149°C) and bake for 25 minutes. 5. When the cake is done, a toothpick inserted in center will come out clean. The center should not feel wet. Allow it to cool completely, or the cake will crumble when moved.

Rhubarb and Strawberry Crumble

Prep time: 10 minutes | Cook time: 12 to 17 minutes | Serves 6

1½ cups sliced fresh strawberries
¾ cup sliced rhubarb
⅓ cup granulated sugar
⅔ cup quick-cooking oatmeal
½ cup whole-wheat pastry flour, or all-purpose flour
¼ cup packed light brown sugar
½ teaspoon ground cinnamon
3 tablespoons unsalted butter, melted

1. Insert the crisper plate into the basket and the basket into the unit. Preheat the unit by selecting BAKE, setting the temperature to 375°F (191°C), and setting the time to 3 minutes. Select START/STOP to begin. 2. In a 6-by-2-inch round metal baking pan, combine the strawberries, rhubarb, and granulated sugar. 3. In a medium bowl, stir together the oatmeal, flour, brown sugar, and cinnamon. Stir the melted butter into this mixture until crumbly. Sprinkle the crumble mixture over the fruit. 4. Once the unit is preheated, place the pan into the basket. 5. Select BAKE, set the temperature to 375°F (191°C), and set the time to 17 minutes. Select START/STOP to begin. 6. After about 12 minutes, check the crumble. If the fruit is bubbling and the topping is golden brown, it is done. If not, resume cooking. 7. When the cooking is complete, serve warm.

Appendix 1
Basic Kitchen Conversions & Equivalents

DRY MEASUREMENTS CONVERSION CHART

3 teaspoons = 1 tablespoon = 1/16 cup

6 teaspoons = 2 tablespoons = 1/8 cup

12 teaspoons = 4 tablespoons = 1/4 cup

24 teaspoons = 8 tablespoons = 1/2 cup

36 teaspoons = 12 tablespoons = 3/4 cup

48 teaspoons = 16 tablespoons = 1 cup

METRIC TO US COOKING CONVERSIONS

OVEN TEMPERATURES

120 °C = 250 °F

160 °C = 320 °F

180 °C = 350 °F

205 °C = 400 °F

220 °C = 425 °F

LIQUID MEASUREMENTS CONVERSION CHART

8 fluid ounces = 1 cup = 1/2 pint = 1/4 quart

16 fluid ounces = 2 cups = 1 pint = 1/2 quart

32 fluid ounces = 4 cups = 2 pints = 1 quart = 1/4 gallon

128 fluid ounces = 16 cups = 8 pints = 4 quarts = 1 gallon

BAKING IN GRAMS

1 cup flour = 140 grams

1 cup sugar = 150 grams

1 cup powdered sugar = 160 grams

1 cup heavy cream = 235 grams

VOLUME

1 milliliter = 1/5 tsp

5 ml = 1 tsp

15 ml = 1 tbsp

240 ml = 1 cup or 8 fluid ounces

1 liter = 34 fluid ounces

WEIGHT

1 gram = 0.035 ounces

100 grams = 3.5 ounces

500 grams = 1.1 pounds

1 kilogram = 35 ounces

Appendix 2

Index

A

Air Fried Beef Satay with Peanut Dipping Sauce ·········· 39
Air Fried Crispy Venison ·············· 48
Air-Fried Edamame Bites ·············· 22
Air Fryer Veggies with Halloumi ·············· 86
Almond Catfish ·············· 54
Almond-Crusted Chicken ·············· 28
Almond Pesto Salmon ·············· 56
Apple Cinnamon Rolls ·············· 6
Artichokes with Parmesan Topping ·············· 83
Asiago Shishito Peppers ·············· 70
Asian-Inspired Roasted Broccoli ·············· 75
Asian-Style Spareribs ·············· 18
Asparagus Fries ·············· 79
Avocado and Chicken Cobb Salad ·············· 30
Avocado Bacon and Egg Breakfast ·············· 12
Avocado Toast with Poached Eggs ·············· 8

B

Bacon and Cheddar-Topped Broccoli ·············· 79
Bacon, Cheese, and Avocado Melt ·············· 11
Bacon Wrapped Pork with Apple Gravy ·············· 44
Bacon-Wrapped Sausages ·············· 16
Bacon-Wrapped Stuffed Chicken Breasts ·············· 29
Baked Cabbage Wedges with Cheese ·············· 85
Baked Crumble with Rhubarb and Strawberries ·········· 92
Baked Fish with Cheese Topping ·············· 60
Baked Halloumi with Fresh Salsa ·············· 23
Banana-Walnut Whole Wheat Bread ·············· 7
Basil Chicken Pizzas ·············· 27
Basmati Risotto ·············· 86
Bean and Beef Meatball Taco Pizza ·············· 43
BitesPeach-Cherry Glazed Chicken ·············· 35
Blackened Steak Nuggets ·············· 47
Blackened Zucchini with Kimchi-Herb Sauce ·············· 78
Bone-in Pork Chops ·············· 41
Breaded Shrimp Tacos ·············· 52
Breakfast Pizza ·············· 6

Breakfast Sandwiches ·············· 4
Broccoli Pork Teriyaki Stir-Fry ·············· 42
Broccoli with Lemon Juice ·············· 76
Broccoli with Sesame Dressing ·············· 74
Browned Shrimp Patties ·············· 59
Brown Rice and Pepper Fritters ·············· 25
Brown Sugar-Infused Banana Loaf ·············· 89
Buffalo Bites ·············· 62
Bunless Breakfast Turkey Burgers ·············· 9
Buttermilk Breaded Chicken ·············· 29
Butternut Squash and Ricotta Frittata ·············· 12
Buttery Garlic Fried Cabbage ·············· 75
Buttery Pork Chops ·············· 45

C

Cajun and Lemon Pepper Cod ·············· 55
Canadian Bacon Muffin Sandwiches ·············· 9
Cauliflower Rice-FilledPeppers ·············· 85
Cauliflower Steak with Gremolata ·············· 83
Cheddar Cheese Wafers ·············· 63
Cheese-Stuffed Blooming Onion ·············· 68
Cheese-Stuffed Jalapeños ·············· 68
Cheese-Stuffed Sausage Balls ·············· 64
Cheese-Topped Low-Carb Lasagna ·············· 41
Cheese-Walnut Stuffed Mushrooms ·············· 78
Cheesy Italian Arancini ·············· 68
Cheesy Mushroom Pastry Tarts ·············· 70
Cheesy Parmesan-Crusted Fries ·············· 71
Cheesy Peanut-Crusted Chicken Strips ·············· 30
Cheesy Spinach Pie Without a Crust ·············· 85
Chermoula-Roasted Beets ·············· 78
Chicken Chimichangas ·············· 35
Chicken Drumsticks with Barbecue-Honey Sauce ·········· 34
Chicken Schnitzel Dogs ·············· 33
Chicken Thighs in Waffles ·············· 37
Chiles Rellenos with Red Chile Sauce ·············· 77
Cinnamon and Raisin Bagels ·············· 12
Cinnamon-Beef Kofta ·············· 48

Cinnamon Sugar Churro Bites	17
Citrus Ginger Skillet Cookie with Anise	92
Classic British Breakfast	9
Classic Fish Sticks with Tartar Sauce	58
Classic Melted Queso	21
Classic Oyster Po'Boy Sandwich	52
Classic Whole Chicken	27
Coconut Brown Rice Porridge with Dates	10
Cod	60
Cod Tacos with Mango Salsa	51
Cod with Avocado	53
Corn on the Cob	74
Crab Burgers with Paprika Seasoning	57
Cranberry Curry Chicken	32
Creamy Leek Noodles with Parmesan Lobster Tails	59
Crispy Artichoke Hearts in Lemon Juice	80
Crispy Battered Shrimp	54
Crispy Coconut Chicken Strips	19
Crispy Cream Cheese-Filled Wontons	64
Crispy Duck with Cherry Sauce	31
Crispy Eggplant and Zucchini Bites	85
Crispy Egg Roll Pizza Sticks	71
Crispy Garlic and Cheese Croutons	67
Crispy Golden Pickles	80
Crispy Kale and Potato Bites	11
Crispy Meringue Cookies	16
Crispy Mexican-Style Tortilla Chips	69
Crispy Roasted Cabbage Steaks	86
Crispy Seasoned Roasted Chickpeas	67
Crunchy Fried Fish Sticks	54
Crunchy Panko Fish Sticks	53
Cube Steak Roll-Ups	43

D

Deconstructed Chicago Dogs	40
Dijon Mustard Lemon Chicken	31
Dukkah-Crusted Halibut	57

E

Easy Cajun Chicken Drumsticks	33
Easy Rosemary Green Beans	80
Egg & Avocado Breakfast Wrap	17
Egg-Free Farina Cake	91
Egg in Toast	11
Eggplant Parmesan	83
Extra Bacon and Meat Combo	43

F

Fajita Chicken Rolls	32
Fajita-Spiced Meatball Wraps	43
Fennel-Roasted Salmon with Carrots	56
Fiery Spicy Chicken Bites	62
Fiesta Chicken Plate	32
Fire-Roasted Tomato Salsa	73
Five-Ingredient Falafel with Garlic-Yogurt Sauce	63
Five-Spice Pork Belly	48
French-Style Beignets	16
French Toast Fingers	11
Fresh and Vibrant Summer Rolls	84
Fresh Broccoli Salad with Dressing	77
Fresh Fig and Chickpea Arugula Salad	75
Fried Cheese Grits	11
Fried Green Tomatoes Slices	25
Fried Green Tomatoes with Horseradish Cream	65
Fried Pastry Elephant Ears	17
Fudgy Brownies with Pecans	90

G

Garlic and Thyme Tomatoes	74
Garlic-Infused Edamame	70
Garlic-Infused Soy Chicken	34
Garlic-Lemon Roasted Mushrooms	76
Garlic Shrimp with Swiss Chard	55
Gluten-Free Granola Cereal	12
Gochujang Chicken Wings	27
Golden Air-Fried Venison	40
Golden Fried Oreo Cookies	89
Golden Lemon Pork Schnitzel	44
Golden Onion Rings	65
Golden Potato Croquettes	77
Golden Salmon Croquettes	22
Graham Cracker Cheesecake	93
Greek Pork with Tzatziki Sauce	41
Green Eggs and Ham	13
Greens Chips with Curried Yogurt Sauce	66
Grilled BBQ Chicken	33
Grilled Cilantro Chicken Kebabs	33
Grilled Fish and Veggie Taco Wraps	15
Grilled Ham and Cheese on Raisin Bread	64
Grilled Peaches	90
Grilled Ribeye with Rosemary	45
Grilled Steak and Veggie Skewers	17

H

Hash Browns with Mushroom & Tomato Filling	7
Herb-Buttermilk Chicken Breast	32
Herb-Drizzled Shishito Peppers	67
Herbed Milanese Pork Cutlets	42
Herbed Parmesan Focaccia	74
Herbed Roast Chicken Breast	27

Herb Pistachio Rack of Lamb··45
Herb-Roasted Parmesan Butternut Squash ················75
Herb-Rolled Chicken Breasts ··31
Herb-Seasoned Air-Fried Veggies ······································87
Hoisin-Glazed Turkey Sliders··35
Hole in One ···10
Homemade Beef Jerky ···18
Homemade Crunchy Croutons··25
Homemade Potato Chips with Lemon Dip ··················21
Honeyed Roasted Apples with Walnuts·························93
Hot Cheese Sandwich ··24
Hot Pepperoni Pizza Cheese Dip ······································63

I

Italian Chicken with Sauce ··34
Italian Sausage and Cheese Meatballs ····························41
Italian-Style Rolled Steaks ···40

J

Jalapeño-Lime Fish Tacos ··51
Juicy Beef Chuck Cheeseburgers ······································39

K

Kentucky Chocolate Nut Pie ···92
Kielbasa Sausage with Pineapple and Bell Peppers ········40
Korean Honey Wings···37

L

Layered Cake··10
Lemon Beet Salad ···21
Lemon & Garlic Asparagus Spears····································24
Lemon Poppy Seed Macaroons ··89
Lemon Shrimp with Garlic Olive Oil ································66
Lemon-Thyme Asparagus ···81
Lime-Infused Cauliflower ··75
Louisiana-Style Crab Cakes ··58

M

Maple Bacon Moonshine Bread Pudding ·····················91
Marinated Swordfish Skewers ···57
Meatball Sub Sandwich ···18
Meatballs with Zucchini Noodles ·····································45
Mediterranean Bagels ·· 9
Mediterranean Style Greek Tacos ····································70
Mexican Egg-Stuffed Pepper Rings ·································· 9
Mexican Street Corn Cups···80
Mini Cinnamon Biscuits with Double Coating ············· 6
Mint and Chile Indian-Style Kebabs ································39
Mixed Berry Cheesecake ···19

Mixed Berry Crisp ··16
Mixed Berry Crumble Dessert ···91
Molten Chocolate Almond Cakes ····································90
Mushroom and Pepper Pizza Squares····························85
Mustard-Breaded Fish Fillets ···58

N

Nigerian Peanut-Crusted Flank Steak ····························44
Nuts Crusted Pork Rack ···46

P

Pecan-Crusted Tilapia ··59
Pepperoni Mushroom Pizza with Marinara Sauce ········79
Pepper Steak···47
Peruvian Herb-Crusted Chicken ·······································28
Phyllo-Wrapped Veggie Triangles····································15
Pickle Brined Fried Chicken ···30
Pizza Eggs ·· 4
Poblano Pepper Cheeseburgers ······································46
Pork Loin Roast ···44
Portobello Eggs Benedict··· 8
Pumpkin Donut Holes·· 7

Q

Quick Cinnamon Sugar Toast ··24

R

Ranch-Flavored Oyster Crackers ······································69
Ranch Parmesan Rice ··· 5
Rhubarb and Strawberry Crumble···································93
Rich and Creamy Spinach ··78
Rich Bourbon-Infused Bread Pudding ···························92
Rich Vanilla Butter Pound Cake··93
Roasted Chickpeas with Orange and Rosemary ·······24
Roasted Grape Tomatoes and Asparagus ····················73
Roasted Mushrooms with Garlic ······································68
Roasted Radishes with Sea Salt··73
Roasted Sweet Potatoes ···76
Rolled White Zucchini with Garlic Flavor ······················84
Rumaki··71
Russet Potato Gratin···86
Rustic Blackberry Cobbler ··89
Rustic Flatbread···81

S

Saucy Beef Fingers ··46
Sausage-Filled Baked Mushrooms···································73
Savory Baked Grits··22
Savory Cheesy Potato Patties ···21

Savory Egg and Mushroom Cups	4
Savory Egg Muffins	5
Savory Egg Rolls with Pork and Cabbage	62
Savory Jalea	52
Savory Onion Omelet	10
Savory Spinach Carrot Balls	23
Sesame Carrots and Sugar Snap Peas	80
Shishito Pepper Roast	79
Shrimp Egg Rolls	69
Shrimp-Filled Cajun Pirogues	66
Shrimp Kebabs	54
Shrimp Pasta with Basil and Mushrooms	59
Shrimp-Stuffed Empanadas	54
Shrimp with Smoky Tomato Dressing	56
Simple Apple Turnovers	90
Simple Greek-Style Ratatouille	73
Skewers	36
Slow-Cooked BBQ Ribs	49
Smoky Shrimp and Chorizo Tapas	55
Southern Fried Okra	23
Southern-style Fried Green Tomatoes	19
South Indian Fried Fish	51
Spaghetti Squash Fritters	7
Spanish Chicken and Mini Sweet Pepper Baguette	28
Spiced Butternut Squash	77
Spiced Nuts	69
Spiced Roasted Cashews	64
Spiced Thai Curry Meatballs	34
Spicy Buffalo Cauliflower Bites	19
Spicy Cajun Chicken Tenders	36
Spicy Sirloin Tip Steak	47
Spicy Tortilla Chips	67
Spinach and Cheese Baked Dish	84
Spinach and Feta Egg Bake	5
Steak Tips with Roasted Potatoes	15
Steamed Cod with Garlic and Swiss Chard	56
Steamed Tuna with Lemongrass	53
Strawberry Toast	5
String Bean Fries	65
Stuffed Bacon-Wrapped Prunes	23
Stuffed Bell Peppers with Sausage	46
Stuffed Figs with Goat Cheese and Honey	67
Stuffed Fried Mushrooms	66
Stuffed Mushroom Caps with Spinach and Artichokes	83
Stuffed Pork Meatballs	18
Stuffed Red Peppers with Herbed Ricotta and Tomatoes	76
Sumptuous Pizza Tortilla Rolls	39
Super Vegetable Burger	84
Sweet and Crispy Roasted Pearl Onions	74
Sweet and Spiced Curried Fruit	79
Sweet and Tangy Glazed Salmon	58
Sweet Apricot Turkey Fillets	35
Sweet Bacon Tater Tots	63
Sweet Pepper Nachos	85
Sweet Potato and Veggie Hash	4
Sweet Potatoes with Glazed Ham	47

T

Tamarind Sweet Potatoes	81
Teriyaki-Glazed Chicken Thighs with Lemon Peas	29
Three-Berry Dutch Pancake	8
Tilapia with Chili Seasoning	53
Tomato and Bacon Chicken Bake	36
Tomato-Braised Snapper with Shallots	55
Tortellini with Spicy Dipping Sauce	64
Tortilla Crusted Chicken Breast	36
Tortilla Shrimp Tacos	57
Traditional Canadian Poutine	22
Traditional Grilled Chicken Chicken with Bacon and Tomato	37
Traditional Potato Latkes	24
Tuna and Veggie Melt Sandwiches	15
Tuna Skewers with Fresh Fruits	60
Turkey and Cranberry Wraps	28
Turkey Sausage and Egg Pizza	8

V

Vanilla and Cardamon Walnuts Tart	91
Veggie Salmon Nachos	62
Vietnamese Shaking Beef	42

W

Western Frittata	10
Whole Roasted Cauliflower with Lemon Drizzle	86
Whole Wheat Blueberry Muffins	5
Wrapped in Bacon	56

Z

Zesty Lime Lobster Tails	55
Zucchini with Seasoned Ground Beef	48